ORGANIZATIONAL DESIGN

The Organizational Audit and Analysis Technology

COMMUNICATION AND INFORMATION SCIENCE

A series of monographs, treatises, and texts
Edited by
MELVIN J. VOIGT
University of California, San Diego

Recent Titles:

Alan Baughcum and Gerald Faulhaber • Telecommunications Access and Public Policy
Mary Cassata and Thomas Skill • Life on Daytime Television
Herbert Dordick, Helen Bradley, & Burt Nanus • The Emerging Network Marketplace
William Dutton & Kenneth Kraemer • Modeling as Negotiating
Glen Fisher • American Communication in a Global Society
Oscar Gandy, Jr., Paul Espinosa, & Janusz Ordover • Proceedings from the Tenth Annual Telecommunications Policy Research Conference
Edmund Glenn • Man and Mankind: Conflict and Communication Between Cultures
Gerald Goldhaber, Harry Dennis III, Gary Richetto, & Osmo Wiio • Information Strategies
Bradley Greenberg, Michael Burgoon, Judee Burgoon, & Felipe Korzenny • Mexican Americans and the Mass Media
Heather Hudson • When Telephones Reach the Village
Robert Landau, James Bair, & Jean Siegman • Emerging Office Systems
James Larson • Television's Window on the World
John Lawrence • The Electronic Scholar
Kenneth Mackenzie • Organizational Design
Armand Mattelart and Hector Schmucler • Communication and Information Technologies
Robert Meadow • Politics as Communication
Vincent Mosco • Broadcasting in the United States
Vincent Mosco • Policy Research in Telecommunications: Proceedings from the Eleventh Annual Telecommunications Policy Research Conference
Vincent Mosco • Pushbutton Fantasies
Kaarle Nordenstreng • The Mass Media Declaration of UNESCO
Kaarle Nordenstreng & Herbert Schiller • National Sovereignty and International Communication
Harry Otway & Malcolm Peltu • New Office Technology
Everett Rogers & Francis Balle • The Media Revolution in America and in Western Europe
Dan Schiller • Telematics and Government
Herbert Schiller • Information and the Crisis Economy
Herbert Schiller • Who Knows: Information in the Age of the Fortune 500
Jorge Schnitman • Film Industries in Latin America
Indu Singh • Telecommunications in the Year 2000
Jennifer Daryl Slack • Communication Technologies and Society
Keith Stamm • Newspaper Use and Community Ties
Robert Taylor • Value-Added Processes in Information Systems
Sari Thomas • Studies in Mass Media and Technology, Volumes 1-3
Barry Truax • Acoustic Communication
Georgette Wang and Wimal Dissanayake • Continuity and Change in Communication Systems

In Preparation:

Sara Douglas • Labor's New Voice: Unions and the Mass Media
Fred Fejes • Imperialism, Media, and the Good Neighbor
Howard Fredericks • Cuban-American Radio Wars
W. J. Howell, Jr. • World Broadcasting in the Age of the Satellite
David Paletz • Political Communication Research
Lea Stewart & Stella Ting-Toomey • Communication, Gender, and Sex Roles in Diverse Interaction Contexts
Tran Van Dinh • Communication and Diplomacy in a Changing World
Tran Van Dinh • Independence, Liberation, Revolution
Frank Webster & Kevin Robins • Information Technology: A Luddite Analysis

ORGANIZATIONAL DESIGN:

The Organizational
Audit and Analysis
Technology

by

KENNETH D. MACKENZIE

University of Kansas
and
Mackenzie And Company, Inc.

ABLEX PUBLISHING CORPORATION
NORWOOD, NEW JERSEY

Library of Congress Cataloging-in-Publication Data

Mackenzie, Kenneth D.
    Organizational design.

    (Communication and information science.)
    Bibliography: p.
    Includes indexes.
    1. Organizational effectiveness.   2. Organizational change.
    3. Management audit.   I. Title.
HD58.9.M34   1985   658.4   85-13454
ISBN 0-89391-348-0

Ablex Publishing Corporation
355 Chestnut Street
Norwood, New Jersey 07648

CONTENTS

This book is dedicated to four unique men, each of whom has his own brand of courage:
John H. Whitaker, Robert S. Goodale, J. Alex McMillan, III, and John L. Burch.

Preface

There is an old piece of advice that used to be given young cavalry officers concerning what they should do in the noise, smoke, and confusion of a battle. The advice: "When in doubt, always advance in the direction of the sound of the cannons." I have always interpreted this to mean that, whenever I am in doubt about how to proceed with my research, I should move towards direct contact with the phenomena under study.

My first serious effort to understand organizational structures came when I was working with the U.S. Forestry Services' Range and Experiment Field Station in Berkeley. After doing a lot of reading and thinking, I decided to study actual structures—the various wood products market structures. This experience then led me into the study of small group structures. I spent 12 straight years, without interruption, attempting to understand the processes of structural change in little laboratory groups. I found that the immersion in the actual phenomena, when combined with persistent attempts to understand, paid off with much new knowledge and a keener respect for what I still did not understand. The apprenticeship of 12 years made me impatient to move closer to the study of real organizations. I could hear the cannons and I wanted to advance in their direction.

So, with the approval of the University of Kansas, I founded a little company in 1976 to do just that. I went galloping toward the noisy cannons of organizations. When I arrived there, I quickly found out that my weapons, so carefully constructed out of the previous laboratory research, were woefully inadequate for the task. I got cut up pretty badly. From 1976 to the present, I have essentially been moving towards and among the guns and improving my tools. This book is an effort to report what I have learned and to describe the Organizational Audit and Analysis technology for organizational design. Some of the real world lessons learned were recently summarized in a paper (Mackenzie, 1983).

This 8-year adventure and any small success it has enjoyed is a result of contacts with many people. The most thanks is owed to those business men who have entrusted me or my lieutenants to work with their own organizations. Included in this group are Jack F. Whitaker, John H. Whitaker, Jack Greenwood, Arly Allen, Bob Goodale, J. Alex McMillan, Bernard Scott, Serge Lashutka, John Burch, the late Jack Posey, Bob Treanor, Charles Staples, Jack Joyce, R.A. Edwards, and many others.

I owe a large debt to my friends and collegues who have acted as a Board of Advisors to provide both moral and intellectual support to these efforts.

These include George Arneson, Jim Brooks, Walter Baker, Ralph Christoffersen, the late Don Clough, Bill Cooper, Cal Downs, Alan Filley, Larry Friedman, Al Gallup, Larry Gordon, Roger Hall, Bob House, Steve Kerr, Ralph Kilmann, Harold Krogh, Arie Lewin, Wiley Mitchell, Ian Mitroff, Franco Nicosia, Jeff Pfeffer, Will Price, Ralph Reed, Jim Taylor, Dan Toole, Doug Tuggle, Po-Lung Yu, and Milan Zeleny. I owe a vote of thanks to several former students, including Mary Lippitt Nichols, Raj Khandekar, Andy Luzi, Mike Milliken, Mary E. Howes (nee Bird), and Doug Beynon for their help and support.

I especially want to thank Mary Bird and Doug Beynon for sticking with this grand adventure for years. The present state of the OA&A technology would be much more primitive if it had not been for their support, personal sacrifices, and direct involvement.

I don't owe any thanks to the U.S. Government. These adventures, these calvary charges out of the academic and into the real world, were made without the receipt of one penny from the U.S. Government. If anything, the government owes me because of taxes paid.

I must acknowledge support from Clarine F. Smissman who was there at the beginning and through the early difficult times. Everyone who has been associated with Organizational Systems, Inc. has invested hopes and energy into the development of this technology. The fact that the old OSI has evolved to a new corporate identity is a tribute to the support of so many for so long a period of time.

Dean John Tollefson of the School of Business at the University of Kansas has been supportive for a long time. A faculty member who shunned committee work, missed faculty meetings, and spent much time off campus attacking unknown problems must have caused him some embarrassment. His forebearance, encouragement, and support are rare in academia and are very much appreciated.

My faithful and courageous wife, Sally, has been a mainstay. She has shared in both the sacrifices and the work. She is cool in a crisis, and her level headed advice has saved me from my enthusiasms many times. The Mackenzie daughters, Carolyn Beta, Susan Gamma, and Nancy Delta, have also pitched in to help out.

Kathy Rothwell, a steady and cheerful companion for the past 6 years, has done the typing, the proofing, the retyping, and all of the support work that usually passes without recognition. She has really been helpful. Cyndi Weigel has proven to be positive and competent in the typing and retyping of the manuscript.

Special thanks are due to Chiekwe B. Anyansi Archibong, Rajendra Khandekar, and Allen L. Perrin who carefully read the entire manuscript for errors, omissions, and content. Their suggestions proved valuable in improving this book. While they are not responsible for any remaining defects, they certainly helped to remove many from an earlier draft.

One thing I have learned over the years is to appreciate the concept of a task process, about which much will be said later. There has been an interesting process leading to the completion of this book. Back in 1981, Doug Beynon and Mary Bird thought that there needed to be a book describing the work we were doing in designing organizations. That idea was placed on a back burner, along with a growing notebook full of carefully typed ideas and methodological developments. Then Cal Downs invited me to speak at the International Communications Association annual meeting in Boston in 1982. I had to prepare a paper to hand out, and I wrote "A Strategy and Its Application for Organizational Design." This paper was much too long for journal publication and much too short to tell the whole story. Melvin J. Voigt, representing Ablex Publishing Company, happened to hear my talk and asked if I had any interest in publishing a book based on the paper. It seemed like a good idea, so I agreed.

It quickly became clear that the paper had to be completely redone. My first effort resulted in a trilogy of papers that were published in *Human Systems Management* (Mackenzie, 1984c, 1985a,b.) These papers were an improvement but were still inadequate. I was, at that time, teaching a graduate seminar in Organizational Design, and as an interim step I organized a collection of papers about this technology for use by the class. I then toyed with the idea of a slender volume accompanied by the set of papers. Reflecting on the marketability of a too-slender volume and a too-fat set of obscure papers, I decided to write a book on the Organizational Audit and Analysis technology which would be self contained.

The earlier conception of this book was to be a case study of an actual organizational design project. I found that it was difficult to simultaneously describe the details of an actual study and to introduce the theory and methods. The writing became simpler and clearer when I could separate three sets of issues. Thus, this book has three parts. Part 1 is a discussion of organizational design and the development of a technology; Part 2 presents the theory underlying this organizational design technology, and Part 3 discusses, in detail, the specifics of how an organizational design was accomplished.

I believe that, having faced the cannons, having ridden among them, and having had my own cannon to fire, that I am now able to understand some of the real world phenomena about which I write. I believe that there will be several benefits of this book. First, I hope that the theories presented here will begin to take root in the broad course of academic research into organizations. Second, I hope to provide more encouragement and support for others who might wish to leave their cozy offices and venture forth towards whatever cannons they hear. Third, I hope to encourage and inform practitioners whose orgnizational design work affects the lives and careers of others, so that they can improve their ability to serve. Fourth, I hope that this effort will act as a stimulus for future improvements of my theories and methods. Finally, I wanted to get this book off my chest.

This book contains many ancedotes that are included to help provide readers with a sense of what awaits them when their horses frantically leap over the first row of cannons. Every ancedote is based directly on an actual experience. This book is written with first person personal pronouns rather than passive subjunctive expressions. I think that this improves exposition and helps the reader to fix responsibility for an idea or a result. In many places I have inserted personal opinions and beliefs, and have identified them as such.

This book is not a compendium of the massive research literatures about organizations. The reader will find few citations to the works of others. I wanted to present a straightforward account of my commitments, my ideas, and my adventures, without the usual clutter. I avoid pointing out possible deficiencies of the work of others. I step around the many mini-controversies in the literature. For the most part, I find that the new paradigm I have been developing since 1964 does not fit very well into the existing literatures. It would take a separate chapter for almost every point I make to insert them into the current literatures. And, if I did that, this book would have to stretch over several volumes and the main thrust of the new approach would be lost.

A diligent scholar who takes the time to unravel the skeins of citations in the papers and books I have written on this new paradigm would find that I have made good use of the wisdom and experience of many other scholars. During the past 20 years of research, I have encountered so many intelligent scholars in so many fields that it is not possible to unravel their influences. For example, although they are nowhere referenced in this book, my old mentors, Fred Balderston, Wes Churchman, and Franco Nicosia probably had as much influence on my thinking as any author. Others have had the effect of steering my research in different directions. I was strongly affected by the early promise of the work of Herb Simon, Jim March, and Dick Cyert. But, in the end, I had to break away, as they have, from the decision making approaches of the Carnegie School. I could not make them work for my research on group structures.

At heart, I am an old fashioned bench scientist who is fascinated by the beauty, brutality, and intricacies of group and organizational behavior. For 12 years I just ran experiments in order to develop a theory of group structures (Mackenzie, 1976a, b; 1978). From 1976 on, I have changed my venue from the laboratory of little organizations to the study of real ones. The intent has always been the induction of improvements to this theory. Always the effort has been to understand *how* groups and organizations operate. Each minor improvement in how they work becomes connected into alterations in the evolving theory. The Organizational Audit and Analysis technology for organizational design is a mixture based on my commitments, the drive to improve theory, and the challenge of actually being able to apply it to improve how organizations work.

Every organization is a complex social mechanism. I believe that we need theory that does them justice. A theory helps us know what to look for and how to piece together what is found. A good theory ought to work. The interplay among one's commitments, theory development, and application is exciting. On the other hand, it is humbling to discern that one has been wrong. But it is the pursuit that is so much fun. I realize that the current state of the theories and methods presented in this book will be changed in the future. Nevertheless, I believe that the approach of this book is a preferred way to come to grip with the reality of organizational life. The ideas, theory, methods, and technology contained in this book represent the testimonial of an approach that has been persistently and enthusiastically pursued. Only time and more research will sort out the crucial residue that will be preserved in the corpus of a science of organizational behavior.

PLAN OF THE BOOK

This book has three parts and thirteen chapters. Part 1 introduces organizational design and the development of a technology. Chapter 1 contains a discussion of the meaning and importance of organizational design. Chapter 2 describes the strategy which I have followed for developing a theory and a technology for organizational design. Chapter 3 is concerned with desirable features of an organizational design process, as well as its desirable properties. Part 1 is built upon the recognition that there is much to be done in developing a working theory of organizations and a technology for applying it to improving organizations.

Part 2 of this book describes the theory underlying the organizational design technology, the Organizational Audit and Analysis, employed in Part 3. Part 2 is divided into five chapters. It begins with an exposition of task processes and their resources characteristics in Chapter 4. Chapter 5 summarizes research ideas and theories about group and organizational structures that have been central to this research and which form the heart of the organizational design technology. Chapters 4 and 5 contain the kernel of the whole approach. These chapters ask *how* the work of an organization is related to *how* it structures itself to perform it. Chapter 6 emphasises the dynamics of organizational changes. It contains many new ideas that are central to the process of organizational design. It is not possible to understand this book without recognizing the need to manage change. Organizational dynamics are both a result and a cause of change and need to be understood in order to comprehend the challenge of organizational design. Chapter 7 is a process description of the concept of an organizational boundary, and some important properties of a boundary. The ideas of Chapter 7 are interwoven with those of Chapter 8, which presents a process theory of organizational interdependencies. I describe task process interdependence, task process resources interdependence, interpositional interdependence, and environmental interdependence. These ideas are extended to define a new general class of organizational forms defined by the stability and regularity of their task processes called Data Base Organizations. The theory and methods described in Part 2 provide the intellectual foundation for Part 3.

Part 3 describes the Organizational Audit and Analysis technology for organizational design. This evolving technology illustrates how a viable field technology has been erected out of the commitments and desiderata made in Part 1 for developing a strategy and the theory presented in Part 2. The Organizational Audit and Analysis (OA&A) technology has nine stages and many steps. The basic and key stages of the OA&A technology are described in Chapter 9. Chapter 10 picks up on two stages that are as yet relatively untested. These are the techniques for organizational playbooks and organizational game plans. The OA&A technology has numerous supplementary analyses in the human resources management area. The more interesting ones for which the OA&A technology offers special advantages over existing methods in the human resources field are described in the context of the supermarket chain in Chapter 11. Chapter 12 contains a fairly detailed summary of the applications of the OA&A technology to the design of a supermarket chain. Chapter 13 contains a summary and conclusion about this research and development program.

Lawrence, Kansas
1984

PART 1

Organizational design
and the
development of a technology

CHAPTER 1

Introduction to organizational design

INTRODUCTION

This is a book about designing organizations to be more productive. This often means realigning the people, the resources, and the work, from the Chairman of the Board of Directors down to the janitor's assistant. Organizational design involves intervening to *design the entire organization*. It must consider the environments in which the organization operates, the goals and strategies, the underlying assumptions, the organization of all the task processes, the assignment of people and task processes to positions, how it actually operates, and the results produced. It must be done while the organization operates and continues to change. The results of an organizational design can determine the success or failure of the organization as well as the impacts on individual careers.

Organizational design is the responsibility of the organization's Chief Executive Officer (CEO). Organizational design must consider the whole of the organization, and not just its parts. It is macro rather than micro in orientation. It involves simultaneously rearranging the interdependencies that exist within the organization and those it shares with its environments. It involves knowledge of economics and of the organization's industry, policy and strategy, organizational behavior, psychology, accounting, finance, human resources, production, marketing and sales, planning, power, and many specialties that arise for specific organizations. It requires common sense and judgment. It demands clarity and tough mindedness. It is both a technical and a political process. There is often a wide separation between a technically desirable solution and the one that will actually work in practice. It involves every part of the organization and all of the many interdependencies. The person with the vantage point to see the whole of the organization and its relationships to others is the CEO.

Many writers from Plato to Mintzberg (1979) have written about organizational design. Organizational design is the natural study of princes, commanders, and leaders. It is concerned with the age-old issues of who governs the organization and for whose benefit does the organization exist to serve. Consequently, the process of designing an organization is not politically

3

neutral to its many stakeholders. In most cases, organizational design rearranges the bases of power within an organization. It is no wonder that, since the dawn of man, there has been an interest in organizational design. What is surprising is the extent to which, despite the antiquity of concern and experience, organizations today remain poorly designed. Peters and Waterman (1983) provide a lively and fascinating description of how a select group of large successful corporations are organized. This popular book has many trenchant critiques of current organizational designs. It is only recently that scholars have undertaken to develop a science and a technology for designing organizations. Collectively, the many theories and studies about organizational behavior are cumulating to an evolving literature on organizational design. There is a long way to go.

It is useful to consider each organization as an invented social mechanism to convert goals into results. Few, if any, operate as initially planned by the founders. In many ways, each organization is an unplanned experiment in organizational design. Each organization has its own unique characteristics which evolve over time. Somehow an idea, some implicit theory of organizing, the available resources, a strategy, and learning combine into the evolution of each organization. These and other forces combine to produce uniqueness. The variety is immense, even within a specific industry. Scholars who study organizations and their processes try to extract theories to explain why some work better than others. The immediate object of these efforts is to construct better theory and methodologies for analyzing organizations. The long term purpose is to be able someday to improve organizations. Thus the field of experimental design hopes to move from these unplanned experiments to the development of a science whose purpose is to improve how organizations operate.

Each of us has a vital stake in organizational design. All of us are affected by organizations, and most of us try to affect those of which we are a part. And, given that we spend almost all of our lives in organizations, it is natural and right that we have such systematic development of theories to explain them. We share a common interest and motivation to improve organizations. The mere fact that each of us belongs to many organizations, are affected by them, and wish to use them to achieve our own purposes has led to a growing body of research and practice whose purpose is to improve our knowledge of how they work. In short, organizations are important to each of us. The complexity, variety, and social importance of organizations has led to many efforts to develop systematic theories about how they work.

We seek to understand why some organizations succeed for a while, why others fail, and why some are more successful than others. Curiosity and self interest make each of us a student of organizations. We vary primarily in how deeply we are involved with this search for understanding, our responsibility for organizational design, and how we think we should do it. Organizations can be studied and analyzed as phenomena. The ultimate purpose of this research and reflection about organizations is to improve them. Each of us seeks significance and dignity. For most of us, this search for personal dignity and meaning involves collective organizational behavior. When the organizations of which we are a part succeed, it enhances us. And, when we are part of an unsuccessful organization, our lives and our sense of worth suffer. We want to be part of successful organizations, and we are frustrated and confused when they flounder.

We realize that every organization has the problem of continually organizing itself to achieve its goals in the face of change, much of which it does not control. No organization is immune from the necessity to adapt to change. And no organization, no matter how large and currently powerful, has full control over its own destiny. Every organization has the continuing problem of successfully adapting itself to change. Consequently, all organizations must redesign themselves as changes occur.

Just as there are many varieties of organizations, there are many responses and methods employed to design organizations. Some rely on tradition and conventional wisdom, and these methods can be very effective when the changes are mostly under the control of the organization. But, increasingly, organizations are forced to adapt to changes that lie beyond their control. The loss of control is forcing many organizations to rethink how they intend to employ resources, people, and the organization of work. These changes have created demands for new ways to design organizations. Thus, the whole area of how to design organizations to be more effective has become important, especially as traditional methods fail.

It is useful to think of organizations as social mechanisms embedded within a larger environment. Any change to this environment has potential impact on the organization. New technology, new regulations, deregulations, inflation, and macroeconomic change, new competition or new forms of competition, and growing global interdependence have created an environment in which traditional and habitual learned responses are increasingly irrelevant. The research by P.L. Yu (1981) presents a fascinating synthesis of ideas about the issue of habitual thinking.

The deregulation of U.S. airlines and the rapid price changes in fuel have caused old airlines to fail, have created new opportunities for others, and have changed the prices of airfares and even those of competing forms of transportation such as railroads, trucking, and bus companies. The rise of foreign competition in many heretofore stable and secure industries such as primary metals, energy, and textiles has forced changes in almost every major industry. U.S. Steel has had to cut back, retrench, and diversify in order to survive. Changes in banking regulations and technology have blurred the distinctions between banks, savings and loans, and brokerage firms. Now, for example, Sears Roebuck may become a major force in the financial industry. Osborne Computer went from zero revenues to $100,000,000 to zero in two years. The changes in electronics and computers have created havoc for unadaptive organizations and great opportunities for others. All of these changes force organizational change. No organization is immune. They differ primarily in how they adjust.

Most organizations are, frankly, a mess. They certainly do not operate the way they have been set up on paper. Figure 1.1 shows the actual organization of a savings and loan company which had the closest correspondence between the actual organization and the official organization that I have seen in 8 years. The degree of correspondence was 63%. Most real organizations operate with less than 50% correspondence. This widespread discrepancy between what is and what is supposed to be brings into question every study relying on the assumption of no such discrepancies. It calls into question the efficacy of management information and control systems, management by objectives systems, all human resources programs such as incentives, compensation, training, development, affirmative action, etc. These widespread and persuasive gaps mock attempts to correlate overly aggregated and crude data about organizations by elaborate statistical manipulations. They are more than just a gap between formal and informal systems. They are not just based on personal whims and friendships. They are often systematic and always pervasive. We need to develop theory and methods to capture the reality and complexity of the dynamics of real organizations. We can't do this if we persist in adapting our perception of organizations to fit our theoretical models without accurate and validating information. Rather, it's time to improve our models to capture the reality. Figure 1.1 represents one reality I have seen in every organization that I have ever had the privilege to study. I think that the reader will recognize features of his own organization in this figure. All the reader has to do is to draw up an organizational chart with the official titles, and then superimpose onto it the lines representing how the interactions actually occur.

Organizational design is the generic label attached to how an organization adapts itself to change. This book explains how to do this systematically, and then applies these techniques to the design of a regional supermarket chain. Its purpose is to help organizations learn to think about how to renew themselves organizationally and to convert problems into opportunities. As one can see from Figure 1.1, there is lots of room for improvement.

THE VALUE OF AN ORGANIZATION

For years, management scientists have been studying problem solving. We realize that a problem is an unwanted discrepancy between an actual and a desired state. For example, if costs are rising, then increases in costs are the problem. If revenues are rising, the increases are not a problem. It is the

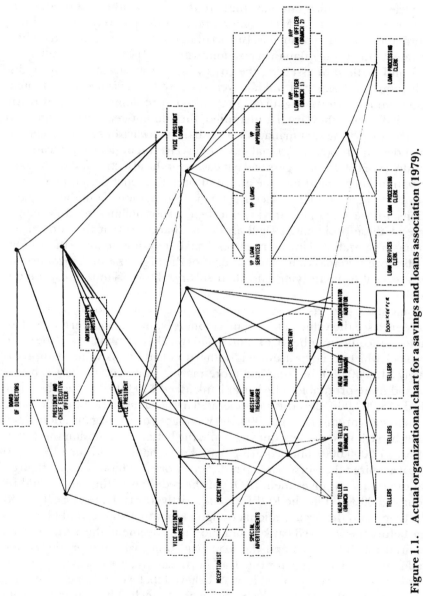

Figure 1.1.   Actual organizational chart for a savings and loans association (1979).

presence of a negative discrepancy between what we have and what we want that creates problems. Problem solving is a procedure to detect, eliminate, and remove such discrepancies. These ideas are useful because, unless there are measures by which one can compare the actual and the desired, problems are not recognized. Most companies, for example, rely on accounting information to define problems. But accountants have never agreed on how to evaluate the value of an organization. Kilmann (1983) presents a framework and method of assessing the costs which promises to help make this evaluation, but I expect it will take years before his ideas become adopted. Hence, most serious organizational design problems are not directly identified. When they are not identified, they do not get solved. Thus, it is not at all surprising that managers are usually unaware of serious organizational design problems. An inability to perceive them does not mean that they do not exist. If managers had a measure of the effectiveness of their organization, they would become aware of organizational design problems.

Even though most CEOs lack systematic information about their organizations, I believe that, in carrying out their responsibilities, most develop a sense of these problems. I shall argue in Chapter 6 that they do this by sensing organizational incongruencies. I shall show how to make these judgments more systematically. The patterns of the organizational incongruencies are vital to identifying and then solving these organizational design problems.

Sometimes, one has to rise above the internal organizational information in order to see the value of an organization. A bank in a Southern U.S. state wanted to acquire another bank, and it had two alternative banks in the same city block which could be acquired. Both banks had a book value of approximately $15,000,000, but one had more market value because it was better run and more profitable. The better bank asked $30,000,000 and the other asked $18,000,000. Because both operated in the same market with the same technology, a premium of $12,000,000 was placed on the organization of the better bank. Thus, to the acquiring bank, the better organization was worth at least $12,000,000. The acquiring bank knew that it could spend $50,000 after it acquired the worse bank to redesign its organization. Thus, it figured that the return on investment (ROI) of the redesign of the bank would be about 24,000%. While the ROI figure is strictly incorrect, because it would take time to do the organizational design (3 months) and it would be some time before the acquired bank would show improvement, the bank could be acquired for 40% down and the loan paid back from the profits, which would give good leverage for the deal. Furthermore, because the acquiring bank had recently reorganized itself, it believed that it could transfer its new organization to the other bank and run it as a branch. Thus, from the viewpoint of the acquiring bank, there were tremendous returns to having the capacity and opportunity to conduct an organizational design.

Actually, one's organization is one's best competitive weapon. Military history is replete with examples of how a better military organization could accomplish great deeds even when outnumbered by an enemy with a poor organization. Examples include Charles V of Sweden, Julius Caeser, King David, Alfred the Great, Genghis Khan, General Robert E. Lee, George Patton, Irwin Rommel, Moshe Dayan, and Alexander the Great. Essentially, a battle is a competitive struggle between two rival organizations and, ceteris paribus, the better organization usually prevails.

As Weick (1979) points out, there is danger in using military metaphors in discussing organizations, because they conjure up images and rhetoric that can confuse cooperative and synergistic relationships that must exist among organizations. On the other hand, a careful study of military history and military organizations (cf. Thucydides (1952) or B.H. Liddell Hart's (1954) *Strategy* and others) point out the needs and advantages of alliances and organizational forms that are far more sophisticated than the overly simplified notions of our Hollywood or parade-ground ROTC images. I think that Weick is correct when he rejects the mechanistic language used to conjure up images of military organizations. However, Weick fails to note how decisive organizational forms can be for competing successfully.

The History of the Peloponnesian War describes the first 20 years of the war between two ancient Greek alliances. It was written by a failed Athenian admiral. It contains details of how alliances were formed and used, how strategies changed, how overconfidence led to disaster, and how the ancients reasoned about strategy and the costs and benefits of loyalty and treachery. I was rereading this classic while working with Supermarket Systems, Inc. I was very impressed with how, with a little imagination, this 2,400-year-old book could be applied to chain store competition. In fact I found Thucydides to be a more timely book for how to think through a strategy than any text I could find in marketing. It gives one a longer time perspective. It allowed us to see the weaknesses of competing chains, and it provided a framework for thinking through the dynamics of technical problems.

The study of history, and especially military history, provides a useful background for organizational design. The events leading up to war, the conduct of a war, and its aftermath provide perspective. The conflicting analysis of what happened and why it happened yields insight into the effects of the environments, goals, strategies, assumptions, and the organizational design on the results. Military history provides rich detail about the organization, training, and deployment of resources, and the results of direct conflict between two organizations. I fail to see how rivalries between economic competitors are unable to demonstrate the decisive advantages of better organizational designs.

There is probably too much emphasis on financial and accounting considerations and not enough on organizational design in most U.S. corporations.

It takes an excellent organization, implementing a viable strategy, to success-fully compete. An excellent strategy without the proper organizational design to implement it is of little use.

The design of an organization is valuable because the organization is important. But one must bear in mind that an excellent design is worthless unless it is implemented. It takes leadership, courage, persistence, and commitment to make an organizational design effective. Thus, the development of an effective organizational design is a necessary but not sufficient condition for organizational success. Every organization must maintain a positive flow of resources in order to sustain operations. An organization without the capacity to attract such resources cannot be effective for very long. In my view, any organization that cannot attract the necessary resources is not well designed for its specific environments, no matter how good it may look on paper. And, in almost every case in which I have been involved, improved organizational design leads to increases in sales and return on investment.

ORGANIZATIONAL DESIGN

The discussion so far has emphasized the importance and value of an organization. The value of an organization depends upon how well organizational design is able to implement an effective organizational strategy. The prevalence of change to which an organization must adapt in the face of the larger environments in which it operates means that organizational design is more of a process of redesigning to adapt to changes than it is a pure exercise in logical application of static principles. March has been quoted by Peters and Waterman (1983, p. 109) as suggesting that "organizational design is more like locating a snow fence to deflect the drifting snow than like building a snowman." This quote emphasizes the fluid nature of organizations and how they are influenced by their environments. With the technology introduced in this book, we can do a lot better, and one can improve this process.

Figure 1.2 illustrates the essential means-end linkages in the organizational design process. This figure illustrates the ABCE model. Let the square A designate the goals and strategies of an organization, the rectangle B designate the organizational technology, the square C represent the results produced by the organization as it operates, and the surrounding space E represent the environments in which the organization resides.

Figure 1.2 is interpreted simply by following the arrows. Goals and Strategies in square A depict the selection of environment and the path to be taken by the organization within it. Rectangle B, which shall be opened up in more detail in Chapters 4, 5, 6 and 8, depicts the Organizational Technology which is seen as derivative of the selection of the goals and strategies. The Organizational Technology represents the means by which goals and strate-

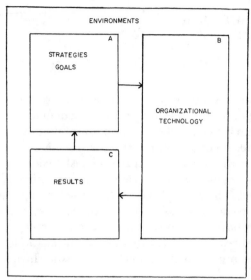

Figure 1.2. The ABCE Model.

gies are converted into results. Results in square C are seen as outputs of the operations of the Organizational Technology. Results, in turn, are inputs to the selection of goals and strategies. The organizational design process is a continual clockwise flow around these elements.

Organizational design, then, is defined as *the continuing cycle of adapting goals and strategies, arranging and maintaining the Organizational Technology to implement them, and producing desired results in the face of changing environments while the organization continues to function.* This last phrase, "while the organization continues to function," is especially important to this concept and to the whole approach taken in this book. The organizational design is dynamic and "online." The organization cannot be seen as dormant while the organizational design is being done. Organizational design, in other words, is analogous is repairing a truck while it continues to travel at top speed down an interstate highway. It is more akin to surgery than to automobile repair. It is more like maintenance than architectural design. It is more similar to trench warfare than grand strategy. It is carried out amidst the buzz and confusion of uncertainty and change. It is really never completed. It has phases or stages, but they cycle continually. One of the challenges facing an organizational designer is to help the organization adapt in his absence. It is more of a process of thinking and planning than a recipe. It is an intensive process that never ends. The art is to develop organizational designs that produce good results which are relatively stable. There are stages to the organizational design process, described in Chapter 9. Stages are completed, but, as the cycles through the ABCE Model occur, refinements and adjustments are required.

AN EXAMPLE

This book contains new theory and concepts that are probably unfamiliar to most. Chapters 11 and 12 present an actual and detailed example of the design of a supermarket chain. This section is a preliminary and abbreviated example of the design of a community bank. It shows the official organizational chart, along with how it organized the task processes of the organization. It presents the actual organization, along with how the work was actually organized. The example zeros in on the loan operations side of the bank to illustrate some of the issues in designing an organization. The example demonstrates how changes in strategy and technology leads to changes in both the structures and the task processes. The example is placed here so that the reader can get a better "feel" of the issues involved in designing organizations.

Some of the terminology, such as "a module of task processes" (which is a relatively low level of aggregation of a firm's activities), or the notion of a "control module" to direct, control, and coordinate activities, will be explained in detail in Chapters 4 and 8. This may make the example difficult to follow. However, if one tries to get the basic ideas and is willing to wait until later chapters for the details, this example will help gain an appreciation for some of the issues addressed in later chapters.

A $100,000,000 community bank recently opened up branch offices in order to attract more deposits, expand its markets for loans, and to beat its competitors to choice locations. It had a major problem in organizing the loan functions between the main bank and its new suburban branches. This bank was organized around its traditional functions of operations, loans, trust and trust services, and administration. The main bank had each of these functions, but the branches were chiefly engaged in operations and consumer loans. The branch managers reported to a Vice President (VP) of Loans rather than to the VP cashier. The VP of Loans reported to a Senior Vice President (SVP) of Loans, as did an Assistant Vice President (AVP) for Debit and Credit Cards. Because each branch was involved with operations and because the task processes of the AVP for Credit and Debit Cards were involved with both operations (by means of automatic teller machines) and loans (via the credit cards), there were organizational confusions among these officers which were seen as creating serious problems.

Figure 1.3 shows the official organizational chart for this portion of the bank. Note the dotted lines from the VP cashier and the branch managers and the AVP for Credit and Debit cards. Figure 1.4 shows the portion of the Organizational Logic (cf. Chapter 4) describing the organization of the task processes involved with loans. The control modules are task processes for directing, controlling, and coordinating loan processes. Note that the network of task processes extends from the Board of Directors to the personnel in the loan department, the branches, and the credit and debit card department. Figures 1.3 and 1.4 provide a snap shot of how an organization and its task processes for loans were integrated.

This bank had many other problems besides this one. After conducting a strategic assessment and an organizational audit (cf. Chapter 9 for details for doing this), an analysis was made of the bank's strategic options. These were studied during the later phases of the organizational audit and during the early parts of the organizational design. These strategic options were analyzed for financial implications such as market share, capital adequacy ratio, return on assets, return on equity, and percentage 5-year compound growth. The strategic options were also analyzed for their impact on the selection of organizational design. After a considerable amount of iterating

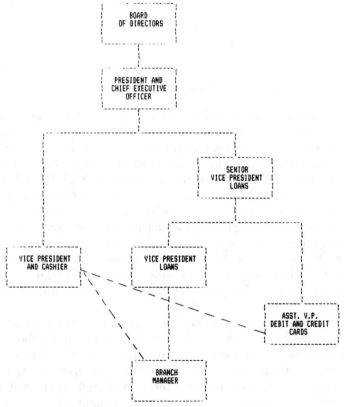

Figure 1.3. Organizational chart for loans.

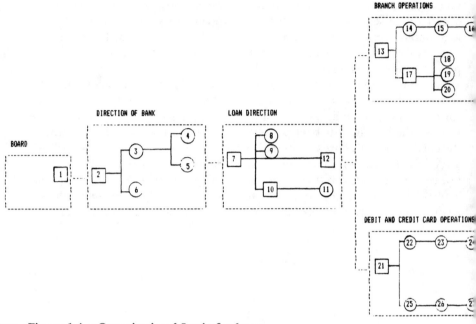

Figure 1.4.   Organizational Logic for loans.

among the strategic options and choices, a new overall strategy was chosen. The new organizational strategy was to expand its business with its commercial customers. This meant rearranging its task processes to serve its consumer customers and its commercial customers as profit centers. This reorganization to serve its primary market segments made the old functional organization obsolete. It was decided to center all commercial operations in the main bank. Branches were to specialize in consumer operations.

Figure 1.5 shows the organizational chart for the new strategy. Note that there are two new positions: SVP commercial and SVP consumer. The old VP cashier position is gone. The branch managers and a new VP for Credit and Debit card now report to the SVP consumer. On the surface it would appear that only a few changes were made in the organizational chart positions.

There were, of course, many changes necessary in the bank's task processes that lay behind the new organizational chart. Figure 1.6 shows the Organizational Logic behind the new organizational chart of Figure 1.5. The numbers on the task processes in Figure 1.4 are preserved in Figure 1.6 in order to allow comparison. Note that there were many changes in the Organizational Logic necessary to implement the organizational design. The changes are summarized in Table 1.1.

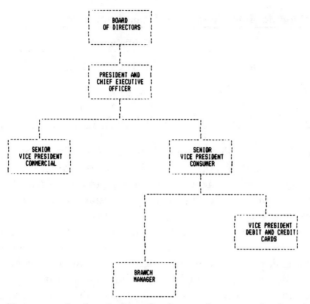

Figure 1.5.   New organizational chart for loans after organizational design.

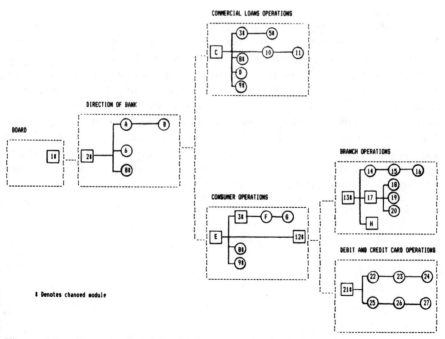

Figure 1.6.   Organizational Logic for new organizational design.

Table 1.1.   Module shifts due to new organizational design

	Module number	Total
Modules remaining unchanged	6, 11, 14-20, 20, 23-27	15
Modules changed and/or at new location	1-3, 5, 8-10	7
Modules dropped	4, 7	2
Modules added	A, B, C, D, E, F, G, H	8

There are 27 + 8 = 35 modules in both the Organizational Logics in Figures 1.4 and 1.6. Of these, only 15, or 43%, remain unchanged. A full 57% of the task processes were altered in the change in the organizational chart of Figure 1.3 to the new one in Figure 1.5. This magnitude of change is not at all uncommon. It illustrates the need to adjust both the organizational positions and the task processes jointly. Crude organizational designs that only relabel organizational positions without addressing the underlying organization of the task processes usually backfire as soon as they become implemented. One needs to consider how the changes in strategy will affect both the organization of positions and the organization of the work. It must also be recognized that this example only includes a fraction of the whole organization. The changes shown in Figure 1.6 also caused changes elsewhere, especially in the planning and in the direction, control, and coordination of the task processes of the bank.

It is clear that organizational design is more than merely rearranging boxes on an organizational chart. It involves a broad scope of the entire organization, improved theories about organizations, the dynamics of organizational change, continual maintenance in the presence of change, and a willingness to roll up one's sleeves and get down to the arduous process of understanding how the organization operates. It is hardly an arm chair exercise. It also involves many personal and intellectual commitments. Chapter 2 describes the strategy I have been following in developing a theory and the Organizational Audit and Analysis technology for organizational design. Part Three of this book illustrates the real-world, hands-on application to a specific organization.

CHAPTER 2

A strategy for developing a theory and
a technology for organizational design

UNDERSTANDING THE ISSUES

Organizational design involves understanding the environments in which an organization operates, the goals and strategies for coping with this understanding of the environments, the selection of an Organizational Technology for implementing the strategies, and producing results in the presence of continual and (usually) only partially controlled changes. Organizational design is the responsibility of the Chief Executive Officer because it involves the entire organization and its place within the selected environments. Organizational design must consider the whole of the organization as well as its constituent parts. And it must consider the position or niche that the organization occupies within the surrounding environments. It cannot be delegated to any subordinate staff, because of inevitable conflicts of interests.

Organizational design, as does any management consulting (Moore, 1984), always involves organizational political processes. An organizational design usually results in a redistribution of power and authority. The new design rearranges "turfs" and, hence, the bases for the effective exercise of power and authority. Pfeffer's (1978) questions of "who benefits" and "in whose interests are the recommendations made" are always present. The assumption that there is a single entrepreneur holding 100% of the stock in a firm is rarely met in practice. Members of the organization have a stake in the process of redesigning an organization. They can be expected to exert influence in the behalf of what they believe are their interests or the interests of the groups or coalitions they presumably represent. Because politics is the word attached to the process of exerting influence to affect the outcome of a decision, it is inevitably true that organizational design is a political process.

Every change benefits someone, and most changes have some perceived adverse consequences to others. Those who perceive benefit will generally favor the changes, and those who sense a real or potential loss can be expected to resist the changes. Experience has taught me to be very cautious about underestimating anyone or minimizing the importance of any issue, no matter how insignificant it may appear on the surface. For example, it is usually easier to rearrange the task processes and reporting relationships among the Vice Presidents than it is among their supporting clerical staffs. Every effort should be made to accomplish the purposes of the organizational design with the least number of changes. My experience is that most organizations can be radically redesigned by initially changing less than five percent of the jobs. Heavy handed methods and "meat cleaver" approaches usually backfire and reduce the effectiveness of the organizational design. The art and the science of organizational design is to make the necessary changes with the greatest likelihood of implementation. Care, completeness, and accuracy are essential to successful implementation.

Wisdom and good judgment reside widely in most organizations. The members of the organization are usually competent in what they have been doing. They are experienced, and they have strong vested interests in doing what they think is necessary. An experienced organizational designer learns to listen carefully in order to understand the many task processes involved. Senior management is usually not as competent as those they supervise in carrying out most of the task processes in the organization. For example, it may have been a long time and several technologies ago when the Senior Vice President of Manufacturing had direct experience in manufacturing products. Those on the firing line, especially those in management information systems, are usually much more competent in their areas of expertise than the Chief Executive Officer or members of the Executive Committee (cf. Chapter 11). Thus, a "broad brush" approach taken with disregard to the specifics of how the work is done, and the relationships among the task processes, is no more than a starting point. The organizational designer can expect to be surprised and informed by listening to those who do the actual work.

The processes of designing an organization are dynamic, because changes occur while the design is being done. In addition to the usual internal changes due to turnover, temporary rearrangements, and every conceivable problem in scheduling and equipment, there are the external events that occur which impinge on the organizational design process. In 1979, I was working with a Savings and Loan Assocation when the Chairman of the U.S. Federal Reserve announced a sudden increase in interest rates. The interest rates that the S. and L. had to pay for deposits rose above the state usury limit on what interest rates could be charged for mortgages. The result was negative incentives to continue making home loans. In another case, the Chairman of the Board of Directors of a telephone interconnect company made a power play through his position on the Board of Directors of a bank to seize control of the corporation for his personal benefit. On one occasion, the Chief Executive Officer of a statewide lobbying group had a bad accident in which he almost cut off his arm. This accident derailed the organizational design process until he could get well. Unhappy mistresses, unexpected law suits, a surprise assault by heavy handed regulators, unanticipated union problems, and many other events have occured during the years I have been designing corporations. New competitors can suddenly enter the scene, and their arrival can affect the organizational design. In one case, the President suddenly resigned and his successor (an old rival) stopped the organizational design process altogether.

Organizational design, consequently, is hardly an arm chair, coldly rational and objective process. Because of the changes and the political efforts taking place, and because the organization must continue to operate during changes, the process of designing organizations is dynamic and requires both intuition and flexibility. The processes included in organizational design are played more like soccer than football. They are fluid, and offense can suddenly change to defense and vice versa. The dynamics and changes create challenges to one's theory. Having a viable theory and a working technology helps the designer cope with the surprises. Given the present state of knowledge about organizational behavior and organizational design, organizational designers need to continually review and improve their methods and assumptions. That is one of the main reasons there needs to be a strategy for developing a theory and a technology for organizational design. Designing organizations is an excellent supplement to arm chair, laboratory, and survey research.

The organizational and personal impacts of an organizational design can be significant. The design process itself causes changes, each of which sets off subsequent and interlocking chains of events and effects. The design and its implementation can set into motion many changes. The health of the organization, the concerns of its members, and the well being of all of the stakeholders is affected. Events concatenate into flows of events, each of which is influenced by and exerts influence on the organization. The pattern and importance of the effects of the design process, and the resulting organizational design, place heavy ethical and professional burdens on the organizational designer and the organization that is being designed. These effects are magnified more during a "cutback" than in an expansion (cf. Hirschorn and Associates 1983). Expansions are relatively easy to manage. Cutting back forces very difficult choices with attendant ethical conflicts for all concerned. This awareness of responsibility creates strong pressure to improve one's methods. There is always room for improvement and efforts to do so should be made. Unless one is callous or irredeemably arrogant, one accepts the obligation and the need to learn more to improve procedures. Needed is a strategy for combining organizational design and research directed towards improvements.

This strategy is on the right track for three reasons. First, client organizations have always implemented our organizational designs. Second, no employee has ever been fired as a result of our organizational design. Third, the clients have always reported that the designs helped them.

The second reason may surprise some because of the way they see the issue of productivity. Productivity is usually measured by the ratio of some output measure divided by some measure of inputs. Because most organizations have more control over their costs than they do of their revenues, some implicitly assume that the safest way to improve productivity is to reduce inputs while maintaining the same measure of outputs. This translates into cutting costs and terminating employees. My view is more positive. I prefer to improve productivity by increasing the measure of output rather than decreasing the level of inputs. In short, I try to get more accomplished by the same people. The challenge is to determine how to make better use of the talent and experience of the members of the organization. This often means removing organizational impediments that block initiative and constrain leaders from acting decisively.

The third reason, reported improved operating results, is much more problematical in the attribution of cause and effect. The organizational designer realizes that he or she can do much to remove impediments, help resolve some old political disputes, and to redirect the organization onto more positive paths. But he or she is not the the one who runs the organization and controls external events. For example, in one case both sales and profits went up because of the collapse of a competitor. In another, sales and profits went down because of a sudden change in the economy. This firm, a manufacturer, had signed contracts for $75,000,000, but only $25,000,000 materialized because of a long recession which forced the firm's customers to curtail production. This company provided original equipment manufacturer (OEM) equipment to other manufacturers. When its customers sharply reduced production, they reduced their orders and, hence, our client's revenues plummeted. The organizational design, however, helped them adapt quickly and effectively to these changes which were outside their control. Revenues, profits, and return on investments rose rapidly the first year after the new design was implemented, but the later economic events had their effects too. So, despite the fact that the manufacturer client wanted more services, and was pleased with the results, I remain unconvinced that I was more than a catalyst. One always faces the problem of events that lie outside the organization which affect it in unplanned ways. Simplistic statistical analyses comparing "before" and "after" always bump into the issues of which "effect," which "after," and the complex processes changing linkages among multiple cause and effect relationships. These basic issues are why the Organizational Audit and Analysis technology is constantly seeking to improve its effectiveness.

A STRATEGY FOR DEVELOPING THE ART AND TECHNOLOGY FOR ORGANIZATIONAL DESIGN

Let us begin the discussion of strategy for development with some realistic admissions of inadequacy. First, there is no acceptable paradigm for organizational behavior. Second, there is no theory that is generally and universally valid in all contexts. Third, we lack the ability to measure many of the variables we think we need. Fourth, it is usually unclear how to convert a theory into a practice. Fifth, most of our theories are too simplistic to match the actual detail and richness of real organizations. Sixth, there have been few systematic organizational design efforts. (Kilmann (1977) is a notable exception.) Seventh, the canons of research propriety usually conflict with those for professional propriety. We have to start somewhere and build the art and science. Knowledge about organizations is as yet inadequate. (cf. Kilmann et al., 1983). Consequently, attempts to apply this knowledge to organizational design should be viewed as part of the world wide effort to improve usable knowledge about organizations. Common sense, and concern for those whom we affect, demand a strategy for developing a technology for organizational design which coordinates the simultaneous evolution of theory, methods, and analysis of feedback. Clients deserve the commitment to systematically improve theories and methods.

The strategy for developing the art and technology for organizational design presented in this section is essentially a strategy for developing a better scientific paradigm. I have been following it since my dissertation (Mackenzie, 1964), the first field studies of market structures (Mackenzie and Frazier, 1966; Mackenzie, 1969), the early work on decision making (Mackenzie and Barron, 1970), the intensive series of laboratory studies to develop a theory of group structures (Mackenzie, 1976a, b) and early attempts to extend these laboratory studies into a text on organizational structures (Mackenzie, 1978a).

The proposed strategy of the development of a theory and a technology of organizational design is based on the more general strategy of improving a theory of group structures. The chief reason for my work in organizational design is to develop this theory. The underlying beliefs guiding this work are these: (1) the capacity to effectively perform organizational designs is dependent upon the underlying theories of group structures and their task processes, (2) direct experience would intersect with the theoretical development to foster such improvements, and (3) it is my responsibility to do this work in order to repay society for its many investments in me and my research.

The basic strategy for developing a science and a technology for organizational design is a mixture of science, engineering, and technology. Following

Anna Harrison (1984), science is a process of investigation of phenomena. "Process is used in a collective sense, encompassing everything the investigator does from the selection of the phenomena to be investigated to the assessment of the validity of the results, and includes the selection of methodology, the selection of instrumentation, the delineation of protocol, the execution of protocol, the reduction of data, the development of constructs, and the assessment of the certainty associated with the results . . . Engineering is the process of investigation of how to solve problems. Technology is the process of production and the delivery of goods and services, and technological innovation is the process of investigating how to produce and deliver more effectively goods and services, modify significantly their characteristics, or create and deliver new goods or sevices." In the strategy for development, I use science to drive engineering and technology, and then use the engineering and technology to produce science. These elements are continually adjusting themselves to each other as each organizational design unfolds. The basic strategy is to consider each organizational design project as part of a larger process of investigating the development of a theory of group structures. The strategy has five parts:

1. Development of the theoretical framework which is an unending process;
2. Development of methods and technologies to apply this knowledge which is also a never ending process of search;
3. Application of these methods to the organizational design of real organizations, which is a constant challenge to (1) and (2);
4. Analysis of the results of each application and the processes used in each application, in order to
5. Identify needs for improving both the theory and the technologies.

This research strategy can never end. Figure 2.1 illustrates this general research strategy and the main linkages among its five components.

This strategy is similar to most programs in serious theoretical development, except that field investigations have replaced laboratory experiments. The applications to real world organizations have forced the loss of control over known and unknown assumptions (cf. Mackenzie, 1983), the abandonment of classical statistical before—after methods of data analysis, the need to "scramble" in order to solve the clients' problems even if they are theoretically inconvenient, and the loss of the sweet satisfactions of desk top cynicism and pedantry. The sideline's criticism and second guessing of the fan is inappropriate for a player who has entered the fray. The priorities shift from publishing to service. There is a loss of objectivity as one does one's best to help an organization design itself. Its needs become paramount. The application of this strategy never ceases. In between engagements, and even during them, the strategy is applied. The never ending confrontation

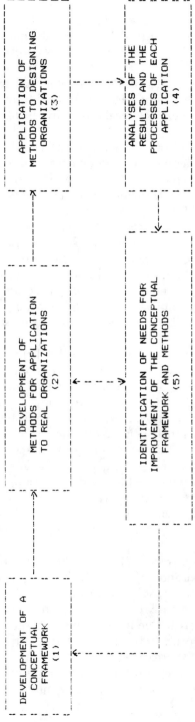

Figure 2.1. A strategy for development of useful knowledge for organizations.

23

between the conflicting roles of a scientist, a consultant, and an entrepreneur is a continual source of energy to the persistent application of this strategy. The application of this strategy since 1976 has proven rewarding and liberating.

It is very clear that this strategy of development does not differ, in kind, from the practice of normal science. However, the different arena in which the work is done raises numerous ethical problems which are magnified in a field setting.

First, there is the problem of confidentiality which, while also existing in laboratory settings, becomes more important because the economic well being of the organization and the lives of its members are affected. One cannot publicly report much of the information that one obtains. Such disclosures, even if authorized, could ruin careers and marriages and reveal trade secrets.

Second, the freedom to manipulate the selective use of knowledge is sharply restricted. One can experiment in the laboratory with control groups, but how can one do this in organizational design? No two organizations are alike or have the same precise problems. To withhold knowledge and treatment in order to improve theory while harming the interests of a client is ethically reprehensible. The client's interests must supersede those of the researcher.

Third, there is the ethical problem of who is the client. What benefits, say to the Chief Executive Officer, may harm the Sales Manager or the stockholders? The old question of "Who benefits?" is front and center as an ethical concern. This is partially resolved by insisting at the outset of any engagement that the organizational designer's client is the organization itself, rather than any individual, including the person who signs the checks. This problem of the identity of the client never goes away in practice.

Fourth, the issue of informed consent causes anguish because, as the engagement unfolds, so do the methods and conclusions. It is fairly easy to explain to an experimental subject just what one intends to do and what will happen along the way. But, in the course of an organizational design, no matter how carefully one explains the process, events beyond the control of any person occur.

Fifth, the comfortable distinctions between theory and practice have little utility, because, in organizational design, each depends intimately on the other. The intellectual standards for quality must be at least as high in actual practice as they are for scholarly publication, because of the high personal stakes of the client. This creates genuine problems as one learns about deficiencies of one's own theories and methods. One does the best one can despite knowledge of these shortcomings.

The strategy becomes a means for development. I think that the application of this strategy is the best assurance of remaining ethical. The development of improvements is important to improving the ability to assist an organization in solving its organizational design problems. The members of an organization are normally as smart as the organizational designer, and their experience and concerns must be considered even if they are inconvenient to the application of the theory. The organization must never be used as a "subject" who is either unwilling or uninformed. Those in the organization should have access to all scientific data or theory that is being applied. Usually, however, they do not seem to really care much for the details of one's theory. They are more concerned with how the results will affect them personally. This raises the most troubling question of all: How can one be assured that the results will work? This concern is undoubtedly the number one source of energy leading to application of this strategy.

Fortunately, one does not have to bear these burdens in isolation. Over the years, a sort of "common law" has evolved for ethical professional conduct. The Institute of Management Consultants, Inc. has evolved a Code of Professional Conduct for its members, who are all Certified Management Consultants. As a C.M.C., I am sworn to uphold this code. Greiner and Metzger (1983) devote a chapter to these ethical issues, and present the ACME's Standards of Professional Conduct and Practice (Chapter 17). Kubr (1978, pp. 49-51) also discusses some of these issues.

The strategy for developing a theory and a technology for organizational design is, of course, by itself, not very helpful to organizational design. One needs a theory, a technology, and the opportunity to apply it. A sense of what is desirable in the technology, and a few rules of thumb for selecting an organizational design from viable alternatives, are very helpful. Chapter 3 contains a discussion of 13 desiderata that I believe are well worth using.

CHAPTER 3

Desiderata for organizational design

INTRODUCTION

There is an extensive literature about organizational design. This literature consists of books such as those by Burack and Negandhi (1977), Galbraith (1977), Khandwalla (1977), Kilmann (1977), Kilmann, Pondy, and Slevin (1976), Magnusen (1979), Nystrom and Starbuck (1981), Ouchi (1981), and Pfeffer (1978). Recent management texts tend to have a chapter, or at least a section of a chapter, devoted to it. There are numerous journals— *Management Science, Administrative Science Quarterly, Human Systems Management, Academy of Management Review, Harvard Business Review,* and many others—which published research papers about organizational design issues. There are many books such as those by Child (1977), Mintzberg (1979), Mackenzie (1978a), Williamson (1975) and others about organizational theory, whose application would lead to organizational design. There are even review papers such as the one I wrote for the American Productivity Center (Mackenzie, 1981a) on the subject. Just about every social science discipline—social psychology, anthropology, political science, economics, sociology, ergonomics, management, organizational behavior, and organizational communications—all have an interest in organizational design related research.

Despite this outpouring of writing about the subject, there is little being done by these authors to actually design organizations. The growing recognition and acceptance of this new category of research is building pressure to develop technologies for applying these theories and ideas. Now, however, there seems to be little awareness of what such applications might entail. For example, the author was involved with efforts by the College on Organizations of The Institute of Management Science on two occasions (1981 and 1983) to conduct an international prize competition for original research on organizational design. None of the submitted papers in either competition described an instance of designing an organizations. I serve on the editorial boards of two international journals, review for others, and referee research proposals, and I never see reports on designing an organization. What I do see is an effort to extend some work done in one field by describing its possible applications in another. Implicitly, the authors assume that it is up to someone else to apply the ideas. These partial prescriptions, speculations, and limited theories are not very useful to a practitioner.

One of my fantasies is to ask randomly selected author from this literature, one who is full of advice for others, to design his or her own organization. I would expect to hear more excuses than the number of fleas on a junkyard dog for why he or she could not do it. I am convinced that most would fail if they tried. I know the troubles I had when I began and I, at least, had a comprehensive theory of group structures to rely upon. The shock is immediate and overwhelming. Suddenly one becomes aware of the limitations of one's work (Mackenzie, 1983). A secondary fanatasy is to also require that one could be sued in a court of law for damages caused by one's organizational design. This would force the consideration of the responsibility one must bear when offering advice.

Organizational design means designing an organization. Unless this simple truth is accepted, the bulk of this book is incomprehensible. For 5 years, I have been teaching a graduate seminar on organizational design in the School of Business at the University of Kansas, and I have found it far easier to explain the mathematics of hierarchy than to get the students to accept the idea that we are talking about designing organizations. Even in a professional school, the graduate students are surprised (and sometimes upset) by the thought of being professionals. They enjoy the idea of helping others and they are well trained to critique theory. Few, however, are ready, emotionally and mentally, to seriously contemplate actually designing a real live organization. The very though of being sued for malpractice because of their work does not seem to enter their minds. It should.

As the idea that organizational design means designing an organization penetrates their defenses, I find that my students begin to examine theory in a whole new light, and they begin to consider what are desirable features of an organizational design technology, which is the subject of this chapter. But before I get into these desiderata, I would like to ask each reader to try a thought experiment.

Select an organization about which you are intimately familiar. This could be a university, a manufacturer, a church, a branch of government, a foundation, or even an army. Now imagine yourself as its Chief Executive Officer. Suppose further that you actually have a complete grasp of the organization, its personnel, its place in its environments, its problems, its opportunities, and a sure sense of future events. Of course, it is very rare for a real CEO to have such thorough knowledge. But, since we are conducting a thought experiment, let's ignore these uncertainties. Finally, let's go one step further and assume that you could actually implement any organizational design you devised, quickly without conflict. What would you do?

Would you, for example, try to do it by the "pigeon hole" method in which you develop a typology of environment, technology, technological change, structure, and then look for the "treatment"? Do you, as the CEO, really believe that such crude methods actually describe the circumstances of your organization? Probably not. Now examine the recommended "treatment" or organizational design. Are any of these sufficiently clear that you *could* apply the "treatment"? For example, suppose the indicated treatment is to change from a mechanistic organization to one that is organic. What exactly does this mean? How would you convert the choice of solution to the realities of your organization? Would you accept the uncertainties of such fuzzy suggestions? Of course not.

Or would you, having decided on the "solution," be unconcerned with the procedure to convert your organization into the recommended solution? Not if it's your neck that's at risk. But even if you "knew" the solution and "knew" exactly how to proceed, would you be unmindful of the probable consequences of the implementation? That is, would you be sufficiently confident of the "theory," "solution," and results to go ahead and apply the solution without having to worry about what might happen if you actually implemented your solution? It is hard to conceive of a successful CEO who would be so foolish and survive.

Now if you actually perform this thought experiment, your sense of responsibility and concern for your personnel, your grasp of the complex realities, and your sense that you must lead in the face of uncertainty and possible opposition, would cool your ardor for the ready-made "solution." Being sensible, you would seek more information and, as you proceeded, questions would surface. Among these would be: (1) Does the classification of technology make sense? (2) Do you have more than one technology? (3) Can you believe the classification of environment? Or (4) Do you face multiple environments? (5) Will the environmental description match your perception? (6) Do you understand the linkages between your strategies and your structures? (7) Do you really believe that you understand the many structures in your organization? (8) Do you really believe that there would be unquestioned acceptance and that (9) you are immune from political processes? (10) Do you acknowledge that some of the information you might gather could be tainted by the self-interest of the persons providing it? (11) How good are the studies and data behind the pigeon in the pigeon hole? (12) Finally, what would happen the day after you implemented the new organizational design?

Acknowledging your lack of information and knowledge, your partial control of events, the diverse goals of your personnel, your dependence on others, and the weaknesses of your "pigeon hole" model would sober you quickly. Once the responsibility of the task of redesigning your organization settled onto your shoulders, you would change and become serious. Yours is not a pure exercise of logic. Careers, reputations, commitments, money, fear, hope, loathing, and uncertainty all play their part and are affected by the methods you use, the conclusions you reach, and the way in which you follow through. You begin to realize, deep down, that doing organizational design has little in common with most research about issues relating to organizational design. And the more you know the literature, the less certain you will be of the "solution."

For the most part, the extant literature on organizational design is based upon simplistic concepts of structures, technology, task processes, environments, strategies, change, and results. Chapters 4–8 and the elaboration in Chapters 9–12 present more useful ideas. But even if you accepted and learned every syllable, you still could not design organizations. These ideas, while useful and relevant, do not provide the rudder by which you guide your design process. That is why I have provided 13 desirable features, called desiderata. These desiderata provide benchmarks against which you can steer the organizational design process.

DESIDERATA FOR ORGANIZATIONAL DESIGN

Please recall that organizational design is defined as "the continuing cycle of adapting goals and strategies, arranging and maintaining the Organizational Technology to implement them, and producing desired results in the face of changing environments while the organization continues to function." Organizational design takes time, and changes occur to the organization and within the organization while you work. Please remember too that it is very likely that there are many organizational incongruencies (cf. Chapter 6), and, consequently, much of the information you start with may prove incorrect and misleading. The most difficult issue in most cases is defining the problem to be solved. I have never received an initial diagnosis of the organizational design problem that turned out to be the one that emerged during the design process. The hard thing about defining the problem is separating reality from data, beliefs, guilt, and many, many hidden assumptions. One does not really know the outcome of the organizational design process until one has gone through it. Even then, it continues to evolve as the ABCE Model (cf. Figure 1.2) cycles in response to change. Many times, I have begun with a flash of intuition that pointed the way to the solution, only to discover later that I was only partially correct. Sometimes, just walking in the door and meeting a few people is enough to spark instant diagnoses. Previous experience, common sense, knowledge of the industry or of the firm, come to play in these early judgments. One must learn to consider these as mere hypotheses whose probability of being correct should be considered small. These hypotheses need testing, because of the importance of the work. More information usually produces confusion, and reconciling the conflicting points of view has been, for me, a detective game which often leads to new hypotheses. And, even if these early intuitive judgments prove on target, it is still a problem to act on them. Incidentally, these early institutions are generally closer to the mark than are results of intermediate analysis. However, it takes years of experience to build this capability. And one must always act as if these intuitions are incorrect.

In this section, I propose 13 desiderata which fall into three broad categories: (1) Desiderata about the design process itself, (2) Desiderata for the resulting design, and (3) Desiderata for the following up processes. These desiderata are from the viewpoint of the organizational designer and the definition of organizational design. They are seen as benchmarks by which the organizational design process can be evaluated. They have proven useful, but should not be considered as the ultimate and final list.

Desiderata about the design process
The first desideratum is:

D_1: Reach agreement on the process to be followed rather than the expected result. The introduction to this section gave reasons why one should be wary of working to achieve a solution to the organizational design problems before one is sure of the exact nature of the problem. In most cases, the client organization is unclear or has conflicting opinions about what should be the resulting organizational changes. The intuition of the organizational designer is often faulty, especially when he or she does not know the organization well. Many times, there are problems of semantics and linguistics. For example, one CEO told me at the outset of a study that he did not want divisions. After about 2 months, he reversed himself. It turned out that he had a concept of a division that allowed for no corporate direction. In another case, the CEO wanted control by lower levels in the organization, but was against delegation. In another, the CEO thought he wanted a matrix organization when what he really wanted was to organize for acquisitions. Sometimes, the issues lie deep in the traditions of a long-departed organizational hero. One simply does not know for certain what the outcome will be before beginning the process of developing an organizational design. So, rather that starting with a solution, one should seek to reach agreement on the steps to be taken, and to make sure that, to the greatest extent possible, each party understands and accepts the process to be followed. This agreement includes the scope of the engagement, description of the stages, agreement on administrative and logistical effort, agreement on review and creation of progress reports, agreement on whom the designer is to work with, agreement on implementation procedures, and agreement on costs and the estimated time schedule. Full information and agreement on the process to be followed helps gain commitment and cooperation. The organizational design process is viewed as a means by which to identify, solve, and implement

solutions to the design problems. Agreement on the design process avoids surprises and conflicts. "Pulling rabbits out of a hat" is dramatic, but usually harms the prospects of successful implementation. Predetermined solutions never fit, and attempts to make the organizational design conform to them engenders a loss of trust.

The second desideratum is:

D_2: The analysis of the problem should be as complete as possible. The full ABCE Model has 11 elements (cf. Chapter 6). An organizational design process that is derived out of the consideration of A, B, C, and E and their transitions is said to be *complete*. Complete analysis, ceteris paribus, is preferred, because it considers the organization as a whole and in the context of the environments and the goals. It is more orderly and more likely to uncover hidden assumptions. For example, in one study, the problem became less a matter of how to organize than of how to arrange for the orderly succession for a gifted CEO.

The problem of completeness is that one can always be more complete. This takes more time and increases the costs. Consequently, desideratum D_2 involves a trade-off with D_3.

D_3: The organizational design process should be cost effective. Any organizational design process involves the costs of the organizational designer and the costs of the time of the personnel in the organization. Care must be taken to continually strive to keep the ratio of benefits to costs high. One way of doing this is to divide the organizational design process into stages, and then to proceed to the next stage if and only if there is agreement. Desideratum D_3 is consistent with the Code of Professional Conduct of the Institute of Management Consultants. It helps if the organizational designer can place the client's interests before his or her own, and determine whether or not he or she would recommend more analysis if he or she were the CEO. If the organizational designer cannot be assured of the benefits, he or she should so advise the client organization. Another way to reduce costs is to first take on parts of the organization whose problems are judged to be most critical. This was what was done in the case study of this book described in Chapter 12. In one example, there was a community bank with very serious organizational problems, but after the initial Organizational Assessment it was decided to terminate the project because the real problems of the bank were location and size. There had been a flood 27 years earlier, and the surrounding community had been replaced by manufacturing and warehousing facilities. The average depositor was near retirement age, and so the bank could be expected to wind down as, one by one, the old depositors died or retired. In another case, that of a paper manufacturer, there was an ongoing, decade-old conflict among the family for control of the firm. Any solu-

tion was seen to be unstable as long as the control of the firm was in doubt. The Chairman of the Board, the President, and the Senior Vice-President were embattled in entangling litigation. They were engaged in an all-channel lawsuit, and each party had staffed his part of the organization with "loyal" family members whose alliances were shifting. If a client organization will not implement the organizational design, it is, by definition, a violation of D_3. This is the main reason why I personally refuse to work for any branch of the U.S. Government. Desideratum D_3 is slippery, because one never really knows the benefits. However, it does provide a guideline which can be very helpful. For one thing, it forces the organizational designers to think about the practicality of their work. This is very beneficial, because most persons starting out in organizational design have no experience as CEOs, and trying to place themselves in the shoes of the CEOs improves judgment.

Anyone who has ever studied perception or who has had experience with data has long since been disabused of the myth of perfect objectivity. Nevertheless, the organizational designer should try to be objective.

D_4: The Organizational Design process should be objective.   It takes discipline to approach objectivity. Current organizational members are rarely objective because of vested interests, prior conclusions about what should be done, habitual thinking, political alignments, and because of their organizational positions, which usually involve only a subset of the organization's task process. Furthermore, the organizational designers can have personal biases and preferences which blind them. One should expect each member to be vigorously pursuing his or her own interests, despite public avowals of innocence. Most people will stay with an organization so long as it serves their interests. Some are even loyal to the last dollar. In principle, the design process should be conducted by someone who does not have vested interests in the outcome. An outsider who is independent of the organization can afford to be more objective and can be seen as capable of designing the organization in the best interests of the organization. Internal staff, no matter what their intentions, are inherently politically tainted and, consequently, should not be used to do major design work where they are seen as beneficiaries of the outcome. Their proper role should be limited to minor adjustments and implementation where they are seen as being neutral about the final results.

This issue of objectivity is thorny. One rule of thumb is to consider the whole organization as the client. In some cases, for example, the main organizational design problem is the CEO. It helps to reach an agreement about whose interests the designer is working. Take the high road and be an advocate of the organization. It helps maintain objectivity, and engenders trust which, in the end, aids in implementation. The organizational designer can be and should be prepared to be fired.

The objectivity of the outsider comes with costs and benefits. It takes a while to understand the organization, and the designer is being paid while learning. An insider knows more about the organization, and so he might be less expensive. But the outsider is a variable cost and the insider becomes a fixed cost which tends to increase. Consider the following:

A manufacturer's Human Resources Department decides it needs a specialist in organizational design. It hires one for $36,000 per year, plus $10,000 in fringe benefits, plus $10,000 in various overheads. The designer needs an assistant, who is hired at $15,000 with fringe benefits of $3,000, plus an overhead of $4,000. The total cost the first year is then $78,000. In the second year, he wants a raise and another assistant, and so the costs rise to $100,000. But, by the second year, the designer has become part of the problem. The outsider is more costly per month, but he or she only takes a few months and can spread fixed costs over several clients. Thus, usually, the outsider is both more objective and more cost effective than the internal staff. Furthermore, the outsider can serve the important social role of scapegoat if there are problems. We call this the corporate "fire hydrant" effect. The inside staff member, being no dummy, learns quickly that he or she has a vested interest in being involved in organizational design. Otherwise, why should he or she be kept on the payroll? Thus, the inside staff member would like to prolong and extend the scope of his or her work. It is difficult to see how the insider could remain objective. A later desideratum (D_{13}) will address the isue of the consultant who acts as if he or she is a lamprey fish who permanently attaches himself or herself to an organization.

The fifth desideratum for the organizational design process is:

D_5: *The Organizational Design process should be swift.* Any problem analysis process takes time. Problem analysis includes identifying the problem and formulating, solving, and implementing a solution. Any problem can change over time. Designate by T_A the time taken to analyze the problem and by T_C the time taken for the problem to change. A desideratum for the problem analysis is that T_A should be less than T_C. If T_A is less than T_C, the analysis is swift relative to the problem change. If T_A is greater than T_C, then the analysis produces solutions to obsolete problems. This desideratum is very important in judging processes for organizational design for two reasons: (1) most methods do not meet it, and (2) it implies a different strategy for conducting the intervention.

It takes time to design a dynamic and complex social institution. It takes time for the designer to understand the organization. Learning occurs while the designer proceeds. There is a simple and important implication of the desideratum that $T_A < T_C$. It implies that one should conduct the design process in the order of stability and leverage. Stable elements have greater values of T_C, ceteris paribus. That makes it more likely that $T_A < T_C$. But some problems, when solved, speed up solution of other problems and even eliminate others. This tends to decrease T_A and increase T_C. Consequently, the desideratum that T_A be less than T_C leads to a design intervention process that begins with the work, proceeds to the positions, and then on to the selection of the position holders. Thus, the strategy for the intervention stresses the work and then proceeds to the individuals. Many writers on organizational design seem to focus on resolving interpersonal problems first. Such a strategy may be indicated if the symptoms of interpersonal problems are the same as the causes. But, in practice, one cannot know this beforehand.

The second implication that T_A be less than T_C is the need to develop a working technology for rapidly adapting the organization to changes, both internal and external. Thus, there are relentless demands on the designers to improve their technology, so that, with their help, minor design changes can be made rapidly and consistently. It also speeds up the T_A for the main design, and thus increases the likelihood that T_A will be less than T_C at every stage. Recalling the definition of organizational design, there must be a concern for the maintenance of the organizational design in the face of continual change.

Desiderata for selecting the organizational design

Usually there is more than one possible feasible organizational design. It is natural to consider how to select one from among these alternatives. This issue of selection yields six additional desiderata which are roughly parallel with those used to select a preferred theory from its competition. It also involves the need to consider the implementability of the organizational design.

The first of the selection desiderata is:

D_6: *Given any two alternative organizational designs, the one involving fewer position changes is preferred.* Desideratum D_6 is that of parsimony. All organizational designs involve changes, and D_6 states that an organizational design with fewer changes is preferred to one with more changes. Of course, both must be acceptable alternative designs. A design is acceptable if it allows the organization to become organizationally congruent (cf. Chapter 6 for a discussion of organizational congruency). The reasons for D_6 are: (1) Ceteris paribus, the fewer the position changes, the easier the implementation and the less the political problems associated with the new design; (2) It means less disruptions during the changeover; and (3) It limits the "ripple" effects. Any organizational change involves the initial change plus the subsequent adjustments that are consequences. These ripple effects cascade through the organization, and their cumulative effect can easily outweigh the initial changes. Containing these ripple effects is always a problem. Desideratum D_6 is a guideline for reducing both the scope and the time for these ripple effects.

Desideratum D_7 is an organizational analogue to the old Occam's razor in the philosopy of science, and states:

D_7: Given any two alternative designs, the simpler one is preferred. Usually, if D_6 is used, D_7 becomes a corollary. However, it is useful to consider the desideratum of simplicity (D_7) in its own right, because of a tendancy to create extra complexity by avoiding making clear choices. Complexities can cause confusion and conflict. The policy of KISS (Keep It Simple and Straightforward) improves the ability of the members of the organization to understand their new organizational design. Simplicity is easier to implement, is more likely to be stable, and is easier to adapt as further change becomes necessary. Speaking personally, D_7 is the most difficult desideratum, because of the scholar's "itch to innovate" and his training to seek ideal solutions. The temptation is to complicate an organizational design in order to handle all of the many task processes, resources, and interpersonal and environmental interdependencies (cf. Chapter 8 for a discussion of organizational interdependencies). Adhering to D_7 usually means replacing the search for the optimum organizational design with a feasible organizational design. However, D_7 guides the analysis towards ever more sophisticated and hence simpler designs. It takes a great deal of thought to achieve a simple design. The art is to make the organizational design as simple as possible while preserving the necessary interdependencies. A simple design has fewer interdependencies than one that is less simple. However, if the design goes too far in achieving simplicity, it backfires and becomes more complex, because it won't work and its inability to work will set off "ripple" effects. This desideratum only applies when comparing alternative designs. Another consideration is the specificity of an organizational design.

D_8: Given any two alternative designs, the one that is more specific about the details and assumptions is preferred. Any organizational design involves some rearrangement of power and task relationships. The creation of uncertainty by being vague and imprecise tends to set ripple effects into motion. The members of the organization will seek clarification. The lack of specificity will retard implementation and complicate maintenance. A lack of specificity can create conflict and uncertainty. Because of the high stakes and because careers are involved, a lack of specificity can create the conditions for prolonged organizational conflict. Specificity and simplicity go together in improving the implementability of an organizational design. It should be pointed out, on the other hand, that, because interpersonal power can be based on the control over uncertainty of the task processes, some organizational members really do not desire clarity, because it can erode their base of power. When the CEO enjoys manipulation or when he or she has powerful staff members whose ability to create and control uncertainty is high, the achievement of D_6, D_7, and D_8 is most difficult. To achieve parsimonious, simple, and specific designs requires that the CEO be decisive. In the case of high-technology firms, the CEO who was originally an inventor may have lost contact with the newer technologies and no longer feels confident of his or her knowledge. This insecurity, based on reality, may result in "playing games" in order to maintain power and to feel good about himself or herself. This is self-defeating and can be corrected by understanding the CEO's strengths and weaknesses and deciding how to organize to take advantage of strengths rather than to cover up weaknesses.

The next desideratum is more subtle, because it looks into the future and recognizes the lack of full control by the organization. This desideratum is that of robustness.

D_9: **Given any two organizational designs, the more robust is preferred.** The robustness of the organizational design is a key consideration for developing more stable designs. A *strategic option* is defined as a combination of environment, goals, and strategies (E, G, S). There are normally more than two feasible strategic options. Each strategic option implies a different Organizational Technology (Rectangle B in th ABCE model of Figure 1.2). The elements of the Organizational Technology are defined in Chapters 4 through 6. Each Organizational Technology has its own Organizational Logic (describing how the work of the organization fits together) based on the design premises. The design premises are the key assumptions about the environment, the strategies, and the rationale for the Organizational Logic. As the organization does not control all of these assumptions, changes in the environment, for example, can occur that are beyond the control of the organization. This means that the organization must adapt itself to these changes.

Fortunately, in most cases, because of the stability of the work itself, most of the selected stategic options have many similarities in their respective Organizational Logics. The task process components common to the set of strategic options is called the *core set* of task processes. Once the core set has been identified, the differences in the Organizational Logics can be identified. Adjustments can be made to increase the core set. The percentage of task processes in the core set is the *organizational robustness*. Increasing organizational robustness improves the adaptablility of the organizational design to environmental change. Desideratum D_9 could be restated as the preference for a more adaptable organizational design.

Finally, in comparing any alternative organizational designs, there is the desirability of implementation. D_{10} states this desideratum.

D_{10}: *Given any two alternative organizational designs, the one that is expected to be easier to implement is preferred.* Normally, if the alternative is parsimonious, simple, specific, and robust, it will also be easier to implement. But in the imperfect world of organizations, it is very helpful for the organizational designer to keep the issue of implementability foremost in his or her analysis. The technical problem of deriving a technically superior organizational design is only a part of the problem. The other part is whether it can be implemented, given the strengths, weaknesses, and resources of the members of the organization. An organizational design that will not be implemented, no matter how ideal in concept, is not considered adequate. The purpose of doing an organizational design in the first place is to develop an implementable organizational design that improves the operations of the organization. If an organizational design will not or can not be implemented, it is not a good solution. Thus, the issue of implementability forces compromises between the theoretical ideal and the reality of the organization.

All organizations that have existed for more than a few years have made commitments that must be honored. There are the realities of political issues involving the control of the organization that cannot be ignored. These can include family relationships, leverage by prominent stockholders, union problems, creditors, vendor relationships, personnel having both great strengths and limitations, and many others. These real world considerations always act to constrain the implementability of an organizational design.

CEOs who are owners and who have a secure power base are less likely to be immobilized by these constraints than are those whose positions are less secure. Many times, it is necessary to perform "worst case" analyses of the CEO's worries in order to sort them out. Often, the process of the organizational design gives a mandate to the CEO to make changes. Thus, the process itself can create confidence, and, hence, more courage to make decisions and then see them through to implementation. The first five desiderata for the organizational design process itself do much to enhance implementability.

The issue of implementation is *not* one that should be left to analysis after the organizational design has been reached. Implementation processes begin at the start of the design project and are considered at each stage. Implementation is comparable to adopting an innovation. The more radical and the greater the amount of change associated with the innovation, the more likely adoption will be difficult (Bernhardt and Mackenzie, 1969, 1972). However, if, at every stage of the organizational design process, care is taken to meet the major desiderata, by the time "cut over" to the new design begins, the new organizational design is no longer an innovation. It is understood that there is consensus, and that there is excitement to begin. The designer must consider the impacts of the new design on individuals. They will want to know about the overall design, exactly how they fit in with others, and changes in title and/or compensation, training issues, office layout, etc. One of the critical issues is the assignment of clerical help. These issues are part of the implementation planning process that occurs between the time the new organizational design is reached and the day of "cut over." After "cut over," many little problems will arise, and it is necessary to actively monitor the implementation process. Consquently, D_{10} is complex, subtle, and ongoing.

The desideratum of implementability, D_{10}, is the prime desideratum. The desiderata of parsimony (D_6), simplicity (D_7), specificity (D_8), and robustness (D_9) are viewed as contributors to the achievement of implementability. One may trade off D_6-D_9 against one another, but never D_{10}. Desideratum D_{10} is supreme.

Desiderata for the following up processes

Change does not stop during the organizational design process, nor does it cease after the new organizational design has been implemented. The organizational design will help the organization simplify itself, become organizationally congruent, and usually far more productive. However, provision should also be made for organizational maintenance in order to assist the organization in remaining flexible and adaptable to future changes. There are many supplementary services that are a direct follow through of the organizational design. The results of the organizational design should allow these to be developed at little additional cost and effort to the organization. There is also the need to reduce the organization's dependency on the outside consultant. Care should be taken during the organizational design process to ensure that the organization can continue to renew its organization without excessive reliance on an outsider.

D_{11}: The organizational design should leave provisions for maintenance and updating. Changes will occur, and the new organizational design will require maintenance and updating. The organizational design will be more manageable if provision is made to assist the organization in ensuring that this is done. Experience has demonstrated that this maintenance process is one of management. It should not be delegated to the personnel and human resources staffs, because they rarely understand the task processes of the entire organization and have many other important and often conflicting duties. The Chief Executive Officer has responsibility for organizational maintenance, and the CEO can use his or her staffs to assist. The designer can work with the CEO and staff to design a system for organizational maintenance. This may include installation of computer software and reporting and review procedures. It helps to write these duties into the positions before the organizational design is announced.

It does no good to present a lengthy report on the new organizational design if those in the organization, including the CEO, do not understand why and how the conclusions were reached. Thus, the organizational designer is a teacher, and the success of the teaching effort has much to do with the ability of the organization to analyze, change, and develop solutions for maintaining and updating the old organizational design. Ideally, when the organizational design process has been completed, the CEO should "own" the solution personally. It should be his or her solution, and his or her lieutenants should also share in this sense of "ownership." I personally believe that, after the design has been completed, the organization should be *their* design, because they are the ones who must make it work. Ideally, the organizational designer should be viewed as a catalyst whose efforts helped make it possible to improve the organizational design.

D_{12}: *The results of the organizational design should provide the basis for numerous follow-up services.*   A good organizational design process not only develops an implementable design, it should also provide the basis for follow-up analysis. This is called *leverage*.

The results of organizational design lead to the development of position descriptions, wage and salary systems, job descriptions, training, EEO compliance, manpower planning, management succession, management development, career planning, performance incentive systems, organizational playbooks, organizational game plans, executive counselling, crisis intervention, stategic planning and other supplementary services. A desideratum for an organizational design is to provide for such supplementary services as a natural follow-up that can be accomplished at low marginal cost to the organization.

D_{13}: *Reduce Dependency.*   The organizational designer is analogous to the architect, where the client organization is owner and occupant. The occupant must live in the new building. Similarly, in designing an organization, the designer must bear in mind that it is not his or her organization. The designer's role is more humble: he or she assists in the design. Those in the organization must make it work, and they should be able to do so in his or her absence. Consequently, care must be taken during the organizational design process to explain the reasoning, so that the occupants understand how to think through the issues that inevitably arise. Reducing the dependence of the client on the organizational designer is seen as beneficial. One of the main objects of an organizational design is to strengthen the capacity of the organization to control its own destiny. To achieve this, the organizational designer must ensure that dependency is reduced.

These 13 desiderata for the process of organizational design should not be considered exhaustive and complete. One could include desiderata for employee job satisfaction, improved organizational climate, improvements in the quality of work life, and others. These are not mentioned here because I see them as by-products of the other 13 desiderata. These 13 desiderata point out the types of concerns I have come to believe are important. The achievement of these desiderata drives the application of the research strategy for the development of a science and technology for organizational design described in Chapter 2. While one hopes to achieve a working compromise that satisfies all 13, sometimes one can only be reached at the expense of another. Desiderata D_5 (swiftness), D_{10} (implementability), and D_{11} (manageability) are the three which should not ever be compromised for another desideratum. Implied in these desiderata is the necessity for the organizational designers to place the interests of the client organizations before their own. Also implied is the need for organizational designers to continually strive to improve their technology.

The next five chapters, Part 2, of this book describe the theoretical foundation for the organizational design technology called the Organizational Audit and Analysis technology. The Organizational Audit and Analysis technology is designed to ensure that the 13 desiderata are met in practice. The ethical and intellectual commitments of Chapter 2, the concepts of organizational design used throughout this book, the 13 desiderata, and the Organizational Audit and Analysis technology are interwoven with each other, and should be considered as a whole system for organizational design.

PART 2

Theory underlying
this organizational design technology

CHAPTER 4

Task processes and task process resources characteristics

INTRODUCTION

Organizations have many different types of resources, such as capital, equipment, supplies, market position, information, knowledge, and people. All of these resources must be renewed for the organization to remain viable. Microeconomic theory has looked at the flows through an organization (inputs and outputs) and has remained unconcerned about *how* inputs are converted into outputs, except for the abstract development of something called a "technological production function" which describes how the inputs are expected to be related to the outputs by means of a mathematical formula. Such formulae are too vague to be of much use for organizational design, because what is assumed to be given by an economist is really the focus of the problem for organizational designers. They face a complex, subtle social mechanism that acts oftimes in mysterious ways. In a real sense, the organizational design involves the specification of the production function of the organization. Designers cannot assume a priori that an organization is efficient and it is operating at some optimum. If it were, they would not be needed. Their task is to identify design problems, analyze the organization to reach a solution to them, and then to implement the new organizational design. And they must do this while the organization continues to operate and change. Individuals are not important to the economic theory of the firm except to the extent to which they act in accordance to the theory. Individuals are vital to achieving improvements in the design of an organization. Somehow, organizational designers need to describe *how* all of these inputs are transformed into outputs. They need to understand the *work* of the organization.

On the other hand, organizational psychologists are trained to examine motives, attitudes, expectations, and values of the personnel. While organizational psychologists are rightly concerned with the individual, they are not, in most cases, really concerned about the economic and competitive forces that surround the firm. They see the individual as the producing unit, and believe that proper leadership and motivation will help the individual to be more productive. There is the notion that somehow the productivity of the organization is an aggregate of the productivity of every individual. Many organizational psychologists and industrial psychologists realize that the productivity of the individual is influenced by a host of other variables. such as the structure of the primary group, the cohesiveness of each unit, and the climate of the organization. But, for the most part, one cannot find any concern for the structure of *work*. The description of how all of the task processes involved with the work of the organization are done, how they are organized, is, for the organizational psychologist, one of the givens. It is a background or the setting upon which psychological forces operate. However, the direct analysis of work itself is rarely attempted for its own sake. Notable exceptions are J.D. Thompson (1967) and the Tavistock sociotechnical school (cf. Rice, 1958; Emery and Trist 1965; Miller and Rice, 1967). Thus, at either extreme both the organizational psychologist and the microeconomist systematically ignore or avoid the issue of describing and organizing work. Most organization theorists employ research methods and theoretical constructs which allow them to overlook the details of how an organization's work is accomplished.

The neglect of the structure and nature of work is reflected in the usual handling of the concept of structure. One comes across loose descriptions of properties of structure, such as formal, informal, organic, mechanistic, bureaucratic, participative, centralized, decentralized, rigid, and (actually!) loose, flat, and tall. The very methods of survey research and statistical analysis force the avoidance of examining either structure or the task processes of work in the detail they merit. Monge et al. (1984) describe improved methods of such analyses for tracking processes, but they cannot capture the logic of the work or the structures of the organization with such methods. These models cannot incorporate the structure of phenomena. And, until these methods are abandoned, people using them can only gain a shadow of the rich texture of the fabric of organizational work and its structures. Correlational models, Likert scales for questionnaire items, and questionnaires cannot trap causal relationships, the structures of the variables and observables, and the logical relationships that are so prevalent.

This situation reminds one of the problem for selecting a lens through which one peers at a phenomena. The lenses of the economic theorist and the organizational psychologist allow each to see interesting phenomena and prevent them from seeing the richness of group and organizational structures, and especially how they are joined with the task processes or work of the organization. Just as it is very difficult to see X-rays with an optical lens, so it is also difficult to see structures and task processes through the lenses of either mathematical economists or the industrial psychologists, determined to use statistical or quasi-quantitative models. Of course, there are economists and industrial psychologists, who have risen above the deficiencies of their formal training, who have a good feel for organizational pheonomena.

The real question of lenses is whether it is unthinkable to construct a new one in order to perceive new phenomena. While the phenomena do not officially exist until they are perceived, the phenomena may remain unnoticed until the new lenses are fabricated which allow them to be "seen." For example, magnetism, electricity, gravity, and nuclear radiation existed long before the science of physics was able to "see" them. I believe that the phenomena of task processes and the group and organizational structures resemble electricity and nuclear radiation in this regard. They are ignored because the conventional wisdom is thus far not prepared to "see" them.

However, they cannot be ignored in organizational design because they reflect that which is being designed. The old adage in biology that "Form Follows Function" is replaced by a new adage that "Structure Follows Work." Of course, organizations are subtle, in that persons can change both work and structures and are a part of both. It is helpful to consider the organization of work and the organization of people simultaneously rather than as a cause and effect. There are task processes governing the mutual adjustment of one to the other in a never-ending process as long as the organization survives.

This chapter contains a rigorous development of the concept of a process, and then a task process. This is then developed into a consideration of task resources characteristics. The development of task processes and their interdependencies yields a structure of task processes called the Organizational Logic. In Chapter 8, I shall bring together these and other ideas into a discussion of organizational interdependence.

The most noticeable feature of the following discussion of task processes is the relentless emphasis on *how* they are done. This analysis and discussion does not concern itself with motivations and other such theological analyses. This "neglect" is pointed out at the onset, in order that the reader not waste time looking for it. This emphasis on how work is performed is essential and necessary. Process descriptions of work are easily refutable and verifiable by those performing the tasks. The reader who has been training to think cause-effect, independent-dependent variables, and stimulus-response will find this discussion mostly incomprehensible. These older lenses are not appropriate, and the determination to use them here is understandable but very inefficient for grasping the ideas and concepts of task processes. I can only urge a serious effort to try to fit the new lens after taking off the friendly old lens for a while. This is very hard to do. Try it anyway.

PROCESSES

A *process* is a time dependent sequence of elements governed by a rule called a process law. Every process has five components. These are:

(a)   The entities involved in performing the process
(b)   The elements used to describe the steps in a process
(c)   The relationships between every pair of these elements
(d)   The links to other processes, and
(e)   The resource characteristics of the elements

A *process law* specifies the structure of the elements, the relationships between pairs of elements, and the links to other processes. Thus, a process law assumes both the entities and the elements of the task process resource characteristics of a task process. The steps in a process can be described by a state that is attributable to the process. More precisely, the *state of a process* is an ordered pair of the attributes representing the outcome of the state and the value representing the degree to which the process state has been completed. For example, if a small group has a process for sharing data, the steps could be (a) initial exchange of data, (b) compilation of data, (c) dissemination of compiled set of data, and (d) the reaching of agreement about the compilation and lists of the data. In this case, the state of each process can be described by four ordered pairs in which the first element is the step number, and the second element is a binary number whose value is unity if the step has been completed, and zero if not.

All process laws can be represented symbolically by the following function:

$$Y = F(X),$$

where **X** is the set of elements, **F** is the graph of the relationships among the elements in **X**, and **Y** is the state of the process. Different processes have different **X**s, **F**s and **Y**s. Processes can be combined by forming new process laws. An organization may have 10,000 processes. The ability to combine them is essential if one is to maintain the capacity to describe how work is done in an organization.

This discussion about processes has two fundamental axioms:

A1.   A process is always linked to another, and
A2.   A process law is activated by an event.

Axiom A1 is an assertion that no process exists in isolation. All behavior can be seen in terms of processes, and any given process never stands alone. While one may, for the purpose of analysis, isolate a specific process, in reality every process has predecessor and successor processes surrounding it. The analysis of organizational processes looks for the processes and how they are linked together to form the whole. But, given Axiom A1, there needs to be some mechanism to move from one process to another. This mechanism is called an event. An *event* is a process that signals or sets off the transition from one process to another. Organizational behavior is seen as an unfolding sequence of a pair of process laws. They signal the transition between process laws and any change in the elements of a process. There are multiple events, chains of events, parallel events, exogenous events, and chains of process laws. In fact, an event is itself a special process. Furthermore, there exist hierarchies of events and process laws. There are sequences of events and process laws. The situation is not unlike the problem of having a Chinese puzzle of Chinese puzzles, in which opening one leads to the opening of others. We shall need these ideas when the concept of an Organizational Logic is introduced to describe the structure of work.

Let me give a fairly humorous example. In one company I helped redesign, I was assisted by a female consultant. In my relationship with the male president, he always minded business, but when he was with the female, the president kept making little "advances" (an event!). These events caused us to wonder if he was not doing the same with his employees. He was! His paramour was a woman in the sales force. The President and his girlfriend made a lot of sales calls together, and the saleswoman would use her close relationship with the President to get special favors from manufacturing. The Director of Manufacturing, frustrated by her demands and requests for special favors complained to the Vice President of Operations. The Director of Manufacturing was concerned about his own future in an organization headed by a married Romeo. The Vice President discussed the problem with his wife who, in turn, discussed it with the President's wife, who brought the matter up with her husband. This sequence of events and processes took abut 2 months before they set into motion new events to separate the President from the saleswoman. Amazingly, the Romeo processes were stopped by hiring the woman's father as an accountant, which, of course, led to even more processes. The President's wife was alerted to the problem and began spending more time at the company. This in turn led to new processes. It would take a gifted novelist to fully describe these unfolding processes. Contrast the natural description of these processes with that of an earnest technocrat bent on explaining behavior in terms of an independent variable (degree of successful lusting) and a dependent variable (Return on Investment). The chaining and sequence of events in this larger process would have been lost, and, undoubtedly, not even considered. By the way, some firms control such processes by promptly terminating both parties. Others develop sexual harassment policies which are not very effective unless one of the parties is unwilling. Some are sued, and the lawsuit sets off a long chain of events and processes.

TASK PROCESSES

Task processes are a type of process used to describe the work of an organization. Each task process is a part of two hierarchies of task processes. There is a task process law hierarchy and a task process hierarchy of aggregation. I employ three levels in a task process law hierarchy. There are, at the lowest level, execution process laws. These are embedded in directing, controlling, and coordinating task process laws (DCC process laws), and DCC task process laws are embedded in a higher level of planning or change in proces s process laws.

An *execution* process law has fixed elements, **X,** and fixed functions, **F,** and is characterized by

$$e = E(X)$$

where the elements **X** are activities or sets of activities, **E** describes the sequential and parallel interdependencies between the activities, and **e** is the state of the execution process law. In an execution task process, the entities are those who perform the activites. The state, *e*, of an execution task process law is given by

$$e = (A, v)$$

where

$$A = \begin{cases} 1 \text{ if DCC processes are required} \\ 0 \text{ if not.} \end{cases}$$

and

$$v = \begin{cases} 1 \text{ if the process is in progress} \\ 0 \text{ if not.} \end{cases}$$

The attributes of the state of an execution task process law describes whether or not the execution task process requires any integrating help from another source and whether or not the process is ongoing. Most routine task processes in an organization are execution task processes. Execution task process laws are the most common type in mature organizations which must remain competitive in order to survive.

A directing, controlling, and coordinating (DCC) task process law may have variable **X**s and **F**s and is described by:

$$d = D(X_d)$$

where the elements of the DCC task process include the states of subordinate execution process laws in addition to special activities to accomplish the directing, controlling, and coordinating. The state, **d**, of a DCC task process law is an ordered pair of its attributes:

$$\mathbf{d} = (A_d, v_d)$$

where

$$A_d = \begin{cases} 1 \text{ if planning task processes are required} \\ 0 \text{ if not} \quad \text{and} \end{cases}$$

$$v_d = \begin{cases} 1 \text{ if the DCC process is in progress} \\ 0 \text{ if not.} \end{cases}$$

DCC task process laws represent the integrating processes believed necessary in order to integrate execution task processes by directing, controlling, or coordinating them. Most supervisory and leadership processes are DCC task processes. The entities range from decision makers, committees, and policies to even central processors in a computer program. DCC task processes need not be performed only by individuals, but usually in practice they are.

The third task process law level is the planning or change in process-process. A *planning or change in process-process law* is a task process law whose **X**s and **F**s are variables, and is described by:

$$\delta = \mathbf{C}(\mathbf{X}_\delta)$$

where the elements of a planning task process law include the states of subordinate DCC task process laws in addition to special activities to accomplish the planning, which usually results in a change in task processes of either DCC or execution types. The state δ of a planning task process law is an ordered pair of its attributes.

$$\delta = (A_\delta, V_\delta)$$

where

$$A_\delta = \begin{cases} 1 \text{ if more changes in task processes are required} \\ 0 \text{ if a transition to a DCC task process law is required.} \end{cases}$$

and

$$V_\delta = \begin{cases} 1 \text{ if planning process is in progress} \\ 0 \text{ if planning process is not in progress.} \end{cases}$$

These three levels of task process laws form a hierarchy, with the lowest being the execution task process laws which are governed by DCC task process laws which, in turn, are changed by planning task process laws. Most lower level employees perform execution processes. Most supervisors perform a mixture of both execution and DCC task processes, and most senior management perform a mixture of all three levels. Some organizational staff members perform execution portions of a planning task process.

The distribution of the three levels of task processes depends upon the stability of the existence and performance of the task processes of the organization. I shall delve more deeply into dynamics in Chapter 6. For example, an established firm such as a public utility will tend to have relatively more lower level task processes than a high-tech, entrepreneurial organization. Futhermore, some parts of an organization are more stable than others, and so different units in an organization can vary widely in their distribution of play levels. Consider these data in Table 4.1, from a start-up, innovative information company where the task processes have been placed into five general areas.

As this firm matures, the distribution of task process laws will shift downward, with a lower percentage of planning processes and greater percentages of DCC and execution task processes. The distribution of task process levels in Area 4 (Research and Development) used to be different. Currently, it is mostly an execution task process area of the firm. But, in the beginning, before they had solved how to do the R&D, the distribution of task processes was more at the planning and DCC levels. Having learned how to do the R&D, this area of the firm has moved from having the main task processes supervised by the CEO to one that is in general support of Division 1 of Area 2 and of the new division being created in Area 5. The distribution of work by level of task processes can be used to monitor the evolution of a firm as it shifts its strategies.

Table 4.1.   Distribution of play levels within a high-tech start up firm (percentage)

Task process area	Process law levels		
	Planning	DCC	Execution
Area one. Direction of company	42%	36%	22%
Area two. Operations of division 1	37%	50%	13%
Area three. Operations of division 2	14%	21%	65%
Area four. Research and development	15%	15%	70%
Area five. New division being formed	77%	18%	5%
For all areas combined	42%	28%	30%

Table 4.2. Hierarchy of task process laws

Task process law level	Task process level		
	Execution	DCC	Planning
Execution	✔	✔	✔
Directing, controlling, and coordinating	—	✔	✔
Planning or change in process-process	—	—	✔

NOTE: Check marks designate that the task process law level of the row can be part of a task process law level of the column.

The hierarchy of levels among the three task process law levels is summarized in Table 4.2.

Task processes can be combined into compound task processes. There are events that signal the transition to other task processes. Those which are signalled by internal events are called *closed compound task processes,* and those signalled by an external event are called *open compound task processes.* An organization which is very stable and has strong control over its market has relatively fewer open compound task processes than does one with lower stability and a low degree of control over its markets. One of the advantages in having a stable organization with good control over its environment is that relatively more of its task processes are closed compound task processes. This issue will be discussed in more detail in the section on data base organizations in Chapter 8.

Task Process Aggregation Levels

The second aspect of the hierarchy of task processes is the level of aggregation of the description of the task process. The idea here is that one can include more and more detail of each task process as one proceeds from broad concepts (e.g., Sales) to the specific of how it is done (e.g., Customer Order Data Entry). The level of aggregation provides the structure of the task processes, and the hierarchy of task process levels are combined later into a concept called an organizational play (cf. Chapter 10). These two aspects of hierarchy of task processes are very helpful in describing the organization of work and the position descriptions of each member. This analysis of task process levels is also used to define a chain of command among both the positions and the task processes. This result is very valuable for organizational design, because it allows the derivation of the structures of the organization and the capacity to understand how to change the organizational structures as there are changes in the task process.

There is no fixed limit to how much detail can be supplied to the description of any task process. Consequently, the number of levels used is selected arbitrarily. Generally, the greater the detail, the more time and the greater the expense for obtaining this information. And in firms with relatively unstable task processes, the higher the level of aggregation, the more stable the task processes. So, keeping the actual situation in mind, a balance must be struck between the trade-offs of precision, stability, time, and costs. Typically, I find it useful to block out the task processes at the organizational level and then proceed to expand and elaborate the details as time permits, and if there is a need to be more precise.

Let us begin at the bottom of the hierarchy of aggregation with an activity. An *activity* is a task process for which there are no nonempty subsets of task processes at the level of analysis selected. An activity is the lowest level of aggregation of task processes. Later on in the course of the development of a firm, activities may be subdivided, and the older activities become aggregates of newer, more detailed, activities. The level chosen will depend upon the balance among the purposes of the analysis and the factors of stability, time and costs.

The next level of aggregation of task processes above the activity is the module. A *module* is a set of activities having a common predecessor activity. There is a hierarchy of structure connecting the activities within a module. The highest activity in the module is called the common predecessor activity. The following example will illustrate a task process and its module.

Example.   A supermarket chain operates a warehouse and some of the grocery items arrive by rail. An activity, "Inspect for damaged or bad product," is part of a module called Rail Receiving. The rail receiving module has eight indentified activities.

Module-06. Rail Receiving
Activity-01   Ensure receiver has freight bill, packing list and stickers with slot numbers, date received and tie and height
Activity-02   Unload freight cars, pile product properly on pallets
Activity-03   Inspect for damaged or bad product
Activity-04   Count product received and verify against freight bill
Activity-05   Approve receipt if undamaged, correct count, and proper quality
Activity-06   Refuse receipt if damaged product
Activity-07   Document any pallet exchange
Activity-08   Place slot tag on pallets

Module-06   (Rail Receiving) has a structure or logic among its eight elements as shown in Figure 4.1.

Note that A1 is the common predecessor activity to the set of eight in this module. In the language of task process laws, this module is at the execution level, the elements $\mathbf{X}$ are A1, A2, . . ., A8, the function $\mathbf{E}$ is shown by the graph of Figure 4.1, and the state is (1, 1) when rail cars arrive at the loading dock and (0, 0) after the products have all been unloaded, stacked, inspected, and approved. Incidentally, if A6 occurs and the product is refused, there are special task processes to bring in an inspector or negotiate a

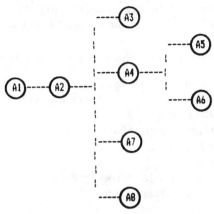

Figure 4.1. The logic for the activities in module − 06.

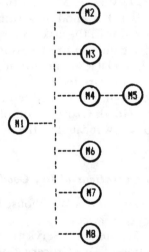

Figure 4.2. The logic of the modules for bundle − 05 (grocery receiving).

settlement. Also, once the paper work begins, there are many task processes within the Supermarket System which set into motion other task processes, such as those involving data processing, accounting, billing, and store coordination.

The next level of aggregation of the task processes is the bundle. A *bundle* is a set of modules having a common predecessor module. The predecessor module acts like the predecessor activity in a module in the functions or graph of the task processes. However, the predecessor module has two other properties: (1) It represents a DCC or planning module for the bundle, and,

(2) it brings the required task process resources together. Let us now examine the bundle which includes Module-06, Rail Receiving.

Example. Bundle -05 (Grocery Receiving) has eight modules. These are:

Module-01. Direction of Grocery Receiving
Module-02. Coordination of Grocery Receiving with Other Units
Module-03. Truck Receiving
Module-04. Determining Slotting System
Module-05. Slotting Product
Module-06. Rail Receiving
Module-07. Clerical Support for Grocery Receiving
Module-08. Salvage Dock Operations

Note that M1 is the common predecessor module for Bundle-05. Figure 4.2 shows the logic of Bundle-05 (Grocery Receiving).

In the language of task process laws, this bundle is an execution bundle. Its elements X_d = (M1, M2, . . . M8). Its function E is the graph of Figure 4.2. Note that M1 is a DCC module within the execution bundle.

The next level of aggregation of the task processes is the group. A *group* is a set of bundles having a common predecessor bundle. This common predecessor bundle is either a DCC or a planning bundle, and serves the same purposes as the common predecessor module in a bundle.

Bundle-05, Grocery Receiving, is embedded in a group called Direction and Operations of Dry Goods Grocery Complex. This is Group 02. So Module -06 in Bundle-05 is now located by the notation 02-05-06. Group 02 has eleven bundles.

Group 02. Direction of Operations of Dry Goods Warehouse Complex

Bundle 02-01. Directing Dry Goods Warehouse Complex
Bundle 02-02. Maintenance Services
Bundle 02-03. Fork Lift Maintenance Services
Bundle 02-04. Coordination of Dry Grocery Operations
Bundle 02-05. Grocery Receiving Operations
Bundle 02-06. Restocking Operations
Bundle 02-07. Repack Operations
Bundle 02-08. Grocery Selection Operations
Bundle 02-09. Grocery Loading Operations
Bundle 02-10. Overfill Warehouse Storage Operations
Bundle 02-11. Buildings and Grounds Services

Figure 4.3 illustrates the logic of Group 02. Group 02 is a DCC task process group. Its elements X_d are the 11 bundles, each of which is at the execu-

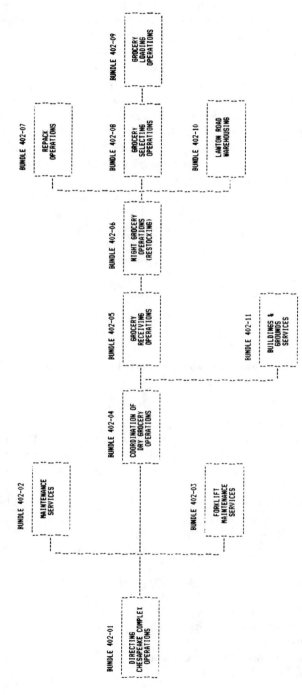

Figure 4.3. Logic for the direction of operations of dry goods grocery complex.

BUNDLE 402-07
REPACK OPERATIONS

BUNDLE 402-09
GROCERY LOADING OPERATIONS

BUNDLE 402-08
GROCERY SELECTING OPERATIONS

BUNDLE 402-10
LAWTON ROAD WAREHOUSING

BUNDLE 402-06
NIGHT GROCERY OPERATIONS (RESTOCKING)

BUNDLE 402-05
GROCERY RECEIVING OPERATIONS

BUNDLE 402-11
BUILDINGS & GROUNDS SERVICES

BUNDLE 402-04
COORDINATION OF DRY GROCERY OPERATIONS

BUNDLE 402-02
MAINTENANCE SERVICES

BUNDLE 402-03
FORKLIFT MAINTENANCE SERVICES

BUNDLE 402-01
DIRECTING CHESAPEAKE COMPLEX OPERATIONS

55

tion task process level. Bundle 02-01 is the common predecessor to the whole group, Direction of Operations of Dry Goods Warehouse Complex. Note that Bundles 02-01, 02-02, and 02-03 could be used to form a Group called Dry Goods Warehouse Operations. They are all placed in the same group because Bundle 02-01 is the common predecessor to both. Bundles 02-04 to 02-10 are assigned to the Dry Goods Warehouse Superintendant, and Bundles 02-01 to 02-10 are under the direction of the Director of Dry Goods Grocery Complex Distribution. The Director is the immediate superior of the Superintendant. All but Bundles 402-01 and 402-04 are managed by Superintendants or Foremen of the bundle of activities. For example, there is a Foreman of Maintenance Services (Bundle 402-02) and a Night Grocery Supervisor (Bundle 402-06).

The next level of aggregation of task processes is the area. An *area* is a set of groups having a common predecessor group. The common predecessor group is usually at the planning task process level but often at the DCC task process level. For the same supermarket chain Area 4 is called Distribution and Transportation. There are five groups in Area 4. These are:

Area 4. Distribution and Transportation

Group 401.   Direction of Distribution and Transportation
Group 402.   Direction and Operations of Dry Goods Grocery Warehouse
              Complex
Group 403.   Direction and Operations of Perishable Warehouse
Group 404.   Transportation
Group 405.   Fleet Maintenance

The logic of Area 4 is shown in Figure 4.4.

The first bundle of Group 401 is called Planning for Distribution and Transportation. This is a planning level task process. But Area 4 is overall an execution task process level of operations. Group 401 is a DCC level task process.

The supermarket chain has seven areas of task processes. The next and highest level of task process aggregation is called the Macro-Logic of the organization. A *macro-logic* is a set of areas having a common predecessor area. The supermarket chain's macro-logic is given below.

Macro-Logic. Supermarket Chain Operations

Area 1.   Corporate Direction
Area 2.   Sales and Merchandising
Area 3.   Store Support
Area 4.   Distribution and Transportation
Area 5.   Employee Relations

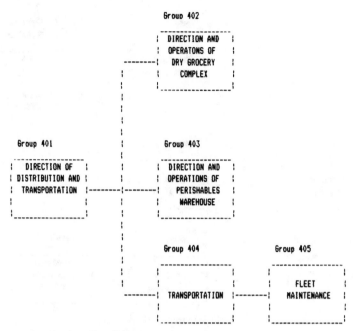

Figure 4.4. Logic for distribution and transportation.

Area 6.   Finance and Accounting
Area 7.   Management Information Systems

Figure 4.5 depicts the macro-logic for the entire supermarket chain.

Figure 4.5 is the macro-logic for Supermarket Systems, Inc. whose design is described in Chapter 12. Figure 4.5 represents the macro-logic after the organizational design.

The hierarchy of the aggregation of the task processes is:
Macro-Logic—Supermarket Chain Operations
   Area 4—Distribution and Transportation
      Group 402—Directions and Operations of Dry Goods Grocery
         Complex
        Bundle 402-05—Grocery Receiving
           Module 402-05-06—Rail Receiving
              Activity 402-05-06-03—Inspect for Damaged or Bad
                        Products

Figure 4.6 illustrates the procedure and the relationships for constructing modules, bundles, and groups out of activities. If one considers

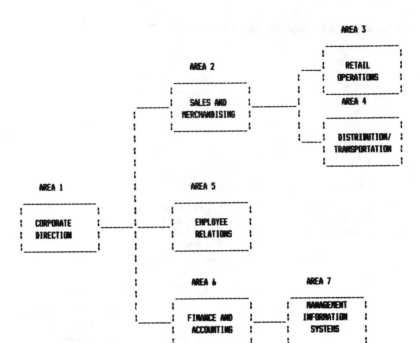

Figure 4.5. Macro-logic for Supermarket Systems, Inc.

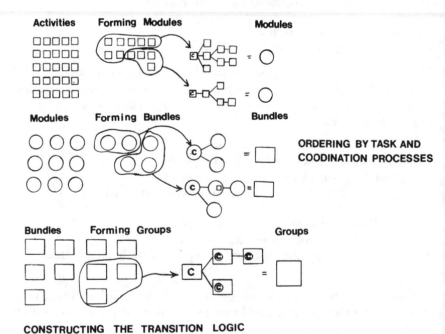

CONSTRUCTING THE TRANSITION LOGIC

Figure 4.6. Constructing modules, bundles, and groups.

each activity as being written on a 3 x 5 card, then this process is one of organizing these cards into module stacks, and the bundle stacks are organized into group stacks. Note the existence of activities, modules, and bundles with a "C" in them to the left of any level of aggregation. These "C" boxes represent DCC or planning task processes that serve to integrate the constituent task processes. More will be given on the idea of integration in Chapter 8.

Figure 4.7 extends the construction of groups from Figure 4.6, and extends them to formation of areas and the macro-logic. Please note that the elements in Figure 4.6 are arranged by the logical transitions, and those of Figure 4.7 are ordered by vulnerability and postponability. These distinctions will be discussed further in the next section.

ORGANIZATIONAL LOGIC

The *Organizational Logic* is a full listing of the task processes, along with their logics, of every level of aggregation. The organization of the work is represented by the Organizational Logic. The Organizational Logic describes how the organization functions. It is the primary data for the analysis and design of an organization. It shows how the organization has organized its

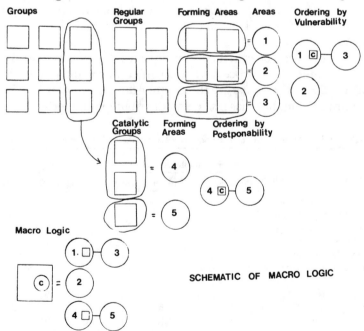

Figure 4.7. Constructing areas and macro logic based upon type of task processes.

work, from the Board of Directors to the part-time janitor. The Organizational Logic has, for the supermarket chain, in Area 4 (Distribution and Transportation), 38 bundles and 192 modules. The distribution of the bundles and modules by level of their task process law is summarized in Table 4.3. Note that the majority of bundles and modules are at the execution task process law level, and that there are relatively fewer (56% vs. 71%) execution modules than bundles. One reason for this is that every execution bundle has at least one DCC module serving as the common predecessor to the modules in the bundle. Also note that Group 401 has the only planning bundles and modules. Groups 402 and 403 are more complex operations than Groups 404 and 405, and have relatively more DCC bundles and modules. Distribution and Transportation operations run nonstop for 132 straight hours every week. They are stable operations, but there is a proportionately greater number of DCC bundles and modules necessary because of the issues of coordinating among shifts and across a four-state store operation and with the other areas of the company. Even a distribution and transportation area of a company is experiencing technological changes, such as increasing use of computers and scanning devices for repack operations. There are many bundles and modules for personnel because of the existence of a hostile union in this area of the company. The problems with the union have created strong needs to plan, direct, control, and coordinate all relationships with the workers, in order to prevent grievances, OSHA, and NLRB cases.

Task processes can be classified usefully in two other ways: (a) By Type, and (b) by Timing. Task processes are classified into two types: (i) line, and (ii) catalytic. *Line task processes* are those either directly or indirectly involved with the production, purchase, sale and distribution of goods and services.

Table 4.3. Distribution of task processes by process law levels

Group number and description	Number of bundles at level				Number of modules at level			
	Planning	DCC	Execution	Total	Planning	DDC	Execution	Total
401. Direction of distribution and transportation	3	2	2	7	5	11	10	26
402. Direction and operations of dry grocery warehouse complex	0	2	9	11	0	32	44	76
403. Direction and operations of perishables warehouse	0	2	7	9	0	16	18	34
404. Transportation	0	1	6	7	0	13	25	38
405. Fleet maintenance	0	1	3	4	0	9	9	18
Total	3	8	27	38	5	81	106	192
Percentage distribution by level	8%	21%	71%		2%	42%	56%	

Catalytic task processes are any task processes not classified as line task processes. Many staff functions are catalytic. The word "catalytic" is used because these processes are primarily services that can act to speed up or slow down processes. Area 4, Distribution and Transportation, is considered a line area. But Area 5, Employee Relations, is considered a catalytic area.

The classification by type is important to determining the main features of an Organizational Logic. The classification by the timing of the task processes includes (i) regular, (ii) infrequent, (iii) calendar, and (iv) future task processes. *Regular task processes* are those task processes performed on a regular basis as part of ongoing operations. *Infrequent task processes* are special task processes called into being on an exceptional and ad hoc basis. *Calendar task processes* are a special form of task process that is activated according to preset schedule. Monthly payroll, quarterly budgeting, and annual strategic planning are examples of calendar task processes. *Future task processes* are ones not yet executed but which are anticipated for the future as the plans for them come due. New entrepreneurial organizations will have future task processes. So will firms that plan to change technologies or launch the production of new goods and services. The classifications of task processes by (1) task process law level, (2) level of aggregation, (3) type, and (4) timing will be used again and again this text.

In practice, one develops an Organizational Logic as one proceeds through an Organizational design project. The Organizational Logic will change as the organizational designer progresses through his or her analysis. Chapter 9 describes the Organizational Audit and Analysis technology, and Chapter 12 provides an example of the application of this organizational design. Tables 12.2 and 12.4 describe the changes of an Organizational Logic.

The best way to develop an Organizational Logic is first to define the Macro-Logic, and then to break each area in the macro-logic into its groups. Some of the groups of activities are well enough understood to subdivide them into the constituent bundles, modules, and activities. In less-well-understood task processes, one often constructs modules out of activities, and bundles out of modules. Generally, the execution task processes are easier to specify than DCC or planning task processes. Usually, the grouping of modules and bundles requires the creation of DCC and planning modules and bundles in order to tie them together. These ideas are illustrated in Figures 4.6 and 4.7.

Writing modules, bundles, and groups is an art. One should proceed at first by very carefully constructing the task process laws. But, after a while, experienced organizational designers can literally write them as they are interviewing individuals about their work. Many execution modules and bundles are applicable across different organizations in the same industry.

Consequently, one develops a dictionary of execution task processes which can be maintained and expanded as one gains more experience.

The numbering of the parts of an Organizational Logic follows two sets of rules. For the macro-logic and area levels, the key consideration for regular task processes is the probable importance of these task processes in containing or handling major recurring vulnerabilities facing the organization.

Area 1 is usually reserved for the task processes of the CEO and called Direction of the Organization. But Area 2 is the task process that involves a major recurring vulnerability. For example, Area 2 in a bank could be Asset/Liability management. For the supermarket chain, Area 2 is Sales and Merchandising. In cases where production of product is the most vulnerable area, it would be Area 2. Ordering the regular areas by impact on vulnerability recognizes that the CEO will always want direct access to handling major recurring vulnerabilities. Some areas are predecessor or successor areas of others. For example, in Figure 4.5, the areas of Store Support and Distribution and Transportation are successors to Area 2. They are called Areas 3 and 4, respectively.

Catalytic task processes (usually staff task processes) area and group are ordered according to their postponability. For example, in Figure 4.5, Employee Relations is not postponable at Supermarket Systems, Inc. (SSI) because of the union problems which it is charged to contain. Note that Finance and Accounting is the immediate predecessor of Management Information Systems, as most of the MIS function involves data about purchases and sales. Fussing with MIS programs is postponable in a supermarket chain. The reader should recognize that just because something is postponable does not imply that it is unimportant.

Vulnerability and logical dependency is a key to numbering regular areas and groups. Postponability and logical dependency are keys to numbering catalytic areas and groups. But, as one delves deeper into the bundles and modules and activities, the elements are always ordered by their logical dependencies.

Environmental changes, or changes in either goals or strategies, can reorder the macro-logic and the area logics of an organization. The lower level execution bundles and modules are usually unaffected, unless the bundle or module is radically altered. Thus, much of the detail of an Organizational Logic is relatively immune from major change.

Infrequent and future task processes are ordered after the regular and catalytic task processes. For example, Area 5 of Table 4.1 (New Division Being Formed) is a future task process. It is the last of the set in the macro-logic. In the early stages of this company, Area 4 (R&D) was Area 2. But as this company regularized its R&D, it was positioned lower in the macro-logic. In case after case, whole departments and divisions of a firm will rise and fall as they involve the direct interactions by the CEO. Those large movements in the Organizational Logic are like tides in the flow of influence within an organization.

The numbering system illustrated in this chapter has evolved over an 8-year period. It is robust and allows expansion and rearrangements of the Organizational Logic. A clear system for numbering task processes and their levels is vital for efficient data processing.

An Organizational Logic is always a hierarchy of task processes. It is meant to show how the task processes are logically ordered. It is not a decision tree, and it is not concerned with the issues of feedback. The specifics and interactions are provided in the description of the modules, bundles, groups, and areas rather than by a confusing set of extra lines. Nonhierarchal Organizational Logics create excess interdependencies and structural maladaptions, as we shall see in Chapter 8. Figure 4.8 presents a schematic diagram of the geometry of an Organizational Logic.

A more thorough analysis of task process interdependency and other types of interdependencies is the subject of Chapter 8. The next section is devoted to another feature of task processes: the task process resources characteristics.

TASK PROCESS RESOURCES CHARACTERISTICS

Every task process uses resources. Many of the planning and DCC task processes exist to help allocate and regulate the flows of these resources. When the Organizational Logic is incompatible with the types and levels of resources to perform the task processes, the struggle for control affects the or-

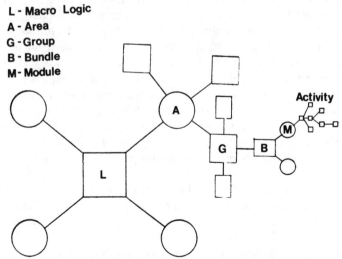

Figure 4.8.   Schematic of an organizational logic illustrating a single string.

ganization. Generally, the allocation of task process resource characteristics should be, as much as possible, parallel to the Organizational Logic. Failure to achieve this sets into motion new task processes to ensure the allocation. These new task processes can change the Organizational Logic, and the working of the Organizational Logics can affect psaure allocation.

There are many ways of classifying the types of resources used in the performance of an organization's task processes. The list of eight used in this chapter (cf. Table 4.4) should not be considered either final or exhaustive. These have arisen from problems encountered in designing organizations having a wide variety of interesting and special interdependencies. The early organizational design work did not recognize the differentiation of task processes by levels of task process laws, levels of task process aggregation, by type, by timing, and did not consider task process resources characteristics. The early ideas about task processes came out of laboratory studies in which the set of task processes was known. However, as I became aware of the nuances of classifying task processes, I and my associates found ourselves ordering them and breaking modules and bundles rather spontaneously. As we thought about what we were doing, I began to see an underlying pattern to our choices and breaks. Once I knew what we were doing, it was a relatively simple matter to recognize different types of rules. These rules were based upon the types of task process resource characteristics. For example, we might have broken a module into two modules because different activities were done in different locations, with different personnel using different equipment. The task process resources characteristics described in this section came out of these "natural" breaking rules.

Typically, organizations require many different types of resources in order to operate. These include capital, budgets, physical plant and equipment, personnel, management, inventory, supplies, technology, energy, information, market position, government regulation, legal and patent rights, and many more. *Task process resource characteristics* are a classification of resources in use as they impact directly on the performance of a task process or on the coordination among interdependent task processes. That is, they are characteristics of the resources when applied to the organization and functioning of the many task processes. Monetary and capital resources are considered a given because they lie behind the decision to perform or not to perform a task process. They are not part of the task process itself. In some cases, they are used to judge the efficiency of the task processes, are the raison d'etre for performing it, and must be made for many task processes to even occur. The decision to perform or not perform a task process is governed by the anticipated effects on the health of the organization, one of which is the flow of monetary resources. Execution task processes describe how various task processes are to be performed. The performance requires resources, but the decision to perform is not the same as the performance.

Directing, controlling, and coordinating task processes are those to direct, control, and coordinate execution task processes. The performance of DCC task processes is more directly linked to the flow of resources than to the application of resources already committed. Planning task processes are those made to select and organize the task processes. Planning task processes clearly move towards a greater concern for the resource flows expected under different choices. However, many planning task processes are not directly connected to an economic analysis of the choices. Thus, resources and the task process resources charactertistics are not the same when it comes to operating an organization. We have the greatest knowledge about how to allocate monetary resources, but the bulk of the task processes in an organization have no direct bearing on financial events, which usually take place on the organizational boundaries or by the artificial means of a system of transfer prices. Despite the emphasis on money by doctrinaire economists, accountants, and financial scholars, only a tiny fraction of what goes on in any organization ever has any direct trace on the events that trigger exchanges of money. Most task processes work in parallel to those task processes of the accountants. Money is important. Without a positive net flow of it, organizations cease to be effective. But money is only a measure attached to the task processes and their interdependencies. Most task processes neither stand alone nor have a directly measurable market value. Thus, in most cases they are difficult to evaluate by the normal financial yardsticks, and yet, despite this, the personnel in an organization do work without the direct guidance and discipline of prices and budgets. Ideally, organizations are more than the sum of their parts. Tracing the economic consequences of every task process and then combining them to fit into an overall picture is conceptually too complex, as well as being, in the last analysis, arbitrary. Most task processes exist in conjunction with others, and separate evaluation makes no practical sense. Task processes are interdependent, not independent, and this interdependence is shown by the Organizational Logic. And the interdependence among the task processes involves the interdependence of the resources.

The foregoing discussion may seem to the reader to be a long-winded argument for avoiding economic analyses. That is not the case. The very existence of the organization is dependent upon being able to attract at least as many resources as are employed. The task processes of economic analysis of other task processes is a subclass of those performed by the organization. Most task processes take place with little or no concern for these monetary flows; and most remain uncontrolled and unenlightened by the organization's financial task processes. For example, a professor who avoids administration can live out his entire career without having to consider the economic consequences of his teaching or research. An accountant's value to the firm may be the opportunity cost of what would happen if he did not do his job. A merchandiser never really knows whether or not his merchandising ideas produce the results he intended, because there are so many other factors involved in store sales. The decision to introduce kiwi fruit into a store chain may be taken as part of a grand strategy to attract higher-income shoppers. The kiwi decision is, by itself, difficult to evaluate. Most task processes, even those directly involving exchanges of money, are difficult to measure in monetary terms.

The following list of task process resources characteristics (TPRC) has evolved in the examination of management problems in designing organizations created by resources interdependence. The *location* at which the task processes are performed is the first TPRC. Whenever task processes performed in one physical location overlap those in another, interdependencies are created. The *personnel* performing the task processes are the second TPRC. When personnel performing a task process are not in the same organizational unit, extra interdependencies are created.

Technology embodied in the *capital equipment* used to perform a task process is a third TPRC. The same task process peformed by different technologies creates extra task processes to obtain consistency. For example at SSI, there are several generations of cash registers. These range from electrical to electronic to computer scanners. These different technologies vastly complicate the work of the Management Information System department. They also hinder the evaluation of the effectiveness of various promotions. It is simpler to use the same technology for a given task process than it is to manage a mixture of different technologies.

Knowledge of these task processes is another TPRC. Many times, the supervisors or managers expected to perform DCC task processes for execution task processes requiring a specified technology are not competent with it. In a bank, for example, the technology for tellers doing paying and receiving task processes is not the same as for tellers handling loan payments. A supervisor, or head teller, who knows one of the technologies but not the other would have difficulty managing the tellers. A supervisor having execution task processes requiring different technologies should have the knowledge to coordinate them with the personnel.

Another TPRC of task processes is their *timing* in relation to other task processes. Unequal production rates and different paces of operation create many problems of direction, control, and coordination. For example, in the organizational design project for SSI (cf. Chapter 12), one of the major issues in the organization was separating interdependencies according to the time lags of the interdependencies. Many staff functions were clearly interdependent with sales and merchandising operations, but linking purchasing, advertising, merchandising, store operations, and the distribution and transportation task processes required daily and often minute by minute interdependencies to occur. The real estate and store construction processes also have interdependencies, but their timing has much more allowable delays. In another example, the paying of benefits on life insurance is logically part of the long task process of selling and servicing customer accounts. But the timing is (hopefully) much less close. Thus, the department handling benefits on life insurance claims can be organizationally separate. This may change as insurance companies broaden their near bank task processes. As these services emerge, one can expect organizational changes to occur which take into account the task resource characteristic called "timing."

Knowledge and the *information used* are key task process resources characteristics. A technology for knowledge and information used is presented in Chapter 11. Personnel, ideally, should have the necessary knowledge and the appropriate information to perform their jobs. Ensuring that this is the case is a continual problem for supervisors and managers, especially when there are rapid changes.

Task processes have predecessor and successor task processes. Many interdependencies occur when these links are being activated. Those other persons whose task processes are interdependent with one's task processes are called *contingent others*. Contingent others are a TPRC. For example, the VP of Industrial Relations has task processes that are to be implemented by a representative of a manufacturing facility. The contingent others to the plant's Industrial Relations person can be the Director of Manufacturing as well as the VP on the corporate staff a thousand miles away.

Some organizations function for 40-hour weeks. Others operate "round the clock." Those organizations with a cycle exceeding human capacity create special task processes to provide *continuity of DCC task processes*. The availability of systems and procedures to ensure continuity of direction, control, and coordination are a critical TPRC for many firms. These task process resources characteristics are listed in Table 4.4.

Two task processes have the same task process resources characteristics if they are the same on all eight of those listed. Most task processes do *not* have the same TPRC. Hence, an important function of task processes management is to provide the linkage so that, as an organiztional unit, there is a superset of TPRC including the TPRC of each constituent task process. Just as the task processes and the personnel form hierarchies, so do the TPRC of the directing, controlling and coordinating task processes. When the task processes, personnel, and TPRC are mutually consistent, the magnitude of excess interdependencies and process maladaptations are minimized. The visible hierarchy of organizational positions should be built upon a less-visible hierarchy of task processes. The hierarchy of task processes is supported by parallel hierarchies of task process resources characteristics. In Chapter 8, following a more precise description of task processes and after

Table 4.4. Tests for determining if two task processes share a resource characteristic

Resource characteristics	Test for sharing
(a) Location	Processes are performed in the same location
(b) Personnel	Personnel performing the task processes are in the same organizational unit
(c) Technology	Task processes require the same capital equipment
(d) Timing	Task processes have same general pace and cycle duration in completion
(e) Knowledge	Task processes require the same technical background
(f) Information	Task processes use the same sets of information
(g) Contingent others	Those providing inputs or requiring output from the task processes are in the same classification
(h) Continuity of DCC	There is provision for directing, controlling, and coordinating the task processes throughout the entire length of time of the operation of the organizational units involved.

introducing concepts of structures in Chapter 5, organizational dynamics in Chapter 6, and organizational boundaries in Chapter 7, I shall explore the concept of interdependency and its meaning for organizational design.

CHAPTER 5

Group and organizational structures

INTRODUCTION

Organizational design always involves some changes in the structures of an organization. An organizational designer needs to be especially careful in the use of the concept of a structure. The purpose of this chapter is to explain precisely what I mean by the word "structure." I recognize that structure is usually a vague term having different meanings to different persons for different purposes. Nevertheless, if one hopes to meet the desiderata of specificity (D_8 in Chapter 3), it is necessary to be very clear about this idea.

This chapter is a short tutorial on the concept of group structure, structures and task processes, Organizational Responsibility Grouping charts, organizational position levels, and Organizational Architecture. All of this is important to organizational design in general and to the Organizational Audit and Analysis technology. Table 5.1 contrasts what I term the "traditional view" with the view for the theory of group structures (Mackenzie, 1976 a, b, 1978 a, 1979). Table 5.1 provides a quick overview of how I intend to use the concept of an organizational structure.

Twenty years of research into group structures, and 8 of designing them for firms, has led to the views that:

1. Structures can and will change
2. An organization has many structures
3. Each structure is a result of behavior
4. Structures represent need satisfying interaction patterns
5. Structures are determined by the task processes involved
6. Structures represent the actual relationship
7. A structure includes those who are involved in its task processes
8. Departures from the organizational chart are natural
9. The structures are interdependent
10. Structural change needs to be explained.

The contrast between these summary conclusions against the "traditional" in Table 5.1 provides a useful basis for comparing one's own use of the word "structure" with that used throughout this book.

Table 5.1.   Views of organizational structure

Traditional	Theory of Group Structures
1. A structure is stable	Structures can and will change
2. An organization has one structure	An organization has many structures
3. A structure causes behavior	Each structure is a result of behavior
4. The structure represents reporting relationships	Structures represent need-satisfying interaction patterns
5. Structures are determined by those in authority	Structures are determined by the task processes involved
6. Structures represent the official relationships	Structures represent the actual relationship
7. The structure includes all members of the organization	A structure includes those who are involved in its task process
8. Departures from the organization chart are anomalies	Departures from the organizational chart are natural
9. Not an issue	The structures are interdependent
10. There is no need to explain structural change	Structural change needs to be explained

When one runs a laboratory communications network experiment and records who sends messages to whom about what, one will see major shifts in these communication patterns over time. They change, and the processes for how they change are reasonably well defined and have been used to erect a theory of group structures. Even small laboratory organizations have multiple and shifting group structures. I have never observed a group whose structures did not change during an experiment. Nor have I ever had the experience of studying an organization with static structures.

There are, of course, many differences between, for example, five-person groups of undergraduate subjects and the larger organizations one encounters in organizational design. Nevertheless, the conclusions listed in Table 5.1 hold. Structural changes are the norm rather than the exception. Organizational designers who seek to hold to the traditional view are fighting a losing battle. More important, the traditional view is dangerous because it warps reality. It is an inappropriate lens through which to study organizational structures. This in turn leads the designer to work on the wrong problems and neglect some of the important ones.

GROUP STRUCTURES

Let us begin with a five-person group. The individuals are designated by x_1, x_2, x_3, x_4, and x_5. These individuals can interact with each other on half-channels. If x_1 sends a memo to x_2, he uses the half-channel from x_1 to x_2. The *existence* of a potential half-channel is not the same as the *usage* of it. One can describe the usage of any half-channel by a measure of the use. Let r_{ij}

designate the measure of the relationship between x_i and x_j implied by the usage of the half-channel from x_i to x_j. The value of r_{ij} will depend upon the purposes of analysis. For example, the value could be binary to indicate usage or nonusage for a specified time interval. It could be a count of the number of messages sent from x_i to x_j, etc. Generally, the relationship described by the measure r_{ij} for the half-channel x_i to x_j is not the same as that measured by r_{ji} for the half-channel from x_j to x_i.

Individual x_1 controls the usage of four half-channels which are $x_1 \rightarrow x_2$, $x_1 \rightarrow x_3, \rightarrow x_1 \rightarrow x_4$, and $x_1 \rightarrow x_5$. Individual x_2 controls the usage of the four half-channels, $x_2 \rightarrow x_1$, $x_2 \rightarrow x_3$, $x_2 \rightarrow x_4$, and $x_2 \rightarrow x_5$. In fact, each of the five individuals controls those half-channels that originate from him. Thus there are 5 x 4 = 20 half-channels available to the group of five in a structure. Each of the 20 half-channels has a measure of itself, r_{ij}, which can be summarized in a square matrix or table in which the rows designate the origins of the half-channels and the columns represent the destination of the half-channels. The diagonal elements are usually considered to be zero, because they represent the interactions with oneself and are customarily not considered to be half-channels.

Thus, the structure, S_n, of a group of n individuals, $x_n = (x_1, x_2, \ldots, x_n)$ having a matrix of relationships R_n whose elements are the measure r_{ij} for the half-channel $x_i \rightarrow x_j$, is given simply by

$$S_n = (X_n; R_n).$$

In the example of the five-person group, let us suppose that we use a binary relationship in which

$$r_{ij} = \begin{cases} 1 \text{ if } x_i \text{ uses } x_i \rightarrow x_j \text{ to communicate with } x_j \\ 0 \text{ if not.} \end{cases}$$

Then,

$$
R_5 = \begin{array}{c|ccccc}
 & x_1 & x_2 & x_3 & x_4 & x_5 \\
\hline
x_1 & 0 & r_{12} & r_{13} & r_{14} & r_{15} \\
x_2 & r_{21} & 0 & r_{23} & r_{24} & r_{25} \\
x_3 & r_{31} & r_{32} & 0 & r_{34} & r_{35} \\
x_4 & r_{41} & r_{42} & r_{43} & 0 & r_{45} \\
x_5 & r_{51} & r_{52} & r_{53} & r_{54} & 0 \\
\end{array}
$$

becomes

$$R_5 = \begin{bmatrix} 0 & 1 & 1 & 1 & 1 \\ 1 & 0 & 0 & 0 & 0 \\ 1 & 0 & 0 & 0 & 0 \\ 1 & 0 & 0 & 0 & 0 \\ 1 & 0 & 0 & 0 & 0 \end{bmatrix}$$

if the communication pattern is given by Figure 5.1.

And if, as in Figure 5.2 there is an all-channel communication structure, then every off diagonal entry in R_5 is unity.

There are, of course, many different combinations of entries in R and, hence, a large variety of possible group structures. The choice of which half-

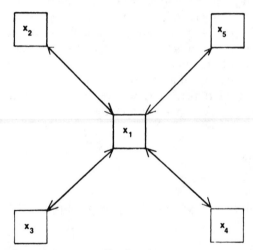

Figure 5.1.   An elementary centralized group structure.

$$R_5 = \begin{bmatrix} 0 & 1 & 1 & 1 & 1 \\ 1 & 0 & 1 & 1 & 1 \\ 1 & 1 & 0 & 1 & 1 \\ 1 & 1 & 1 & 0 & 1 \\ 1 & 1 & 1 & 1 & 0 \end{bmatrix}$$

Figure 5.2.   An elementary decentralized group structure.

channels to use is ultimately up to each of the persons controlling them. There will be many attempts to influence these choices, and this sets off a micro-political process to effect these choices and, hence, the resulting structure. Any change in the value of an entry, r_{ij} in R_n, is a structural change. Any change in the set of members changes X_n and, hence, R_n.

For any group to arrive at a stable set of entries in R, each of the controllers must agree to the pattern of half-channel usage. Thus, a stable structure represents consensus. This consensus is stable only if each of the individuals, after considering the costs of changing the structure and the pressures placed on him or her not to change, believes that he or she will not benefit from making a change. *A structure represents a need-satisfying interaction pattern* which is maintained as long as each member does not perceive opportunity costs to it. But when, for a host of reasons, there are perceived advantages to changing the structure, the members will exercise their control of their half-channels and act to change the usage. Hence, in most circumstances, structures can and will change. In fact, the analysis of who actually works with whom on what task process will almost always depart from those presupposed by the organizational chart. An example was provided in Figure 1.1, and others will occur later in Chapters 6 and 12. The pattern of departures from those sanctioned by the official organizational chart provide major clues about organizational design problems.

The fluidity of group structures, and the implications of the conclusions that each structure represents a need satisfying interaction pattern, has been exhaustively demonstrated in a long series of laboratory studies by this author. In fact, the core problem of any theory of group structures is to explain these changes. The interested reader might want to study the algebras developed for how these structural changes influence attempts to determine structural change (Mackenzie, 1976a). Models for the rate of change using diffusion of innovation models can be found in Mackenzie (1976a, 1978a).

STRUCTURES AND TASK PROCESSES

The individuals in a group are assumed to be purposive in that they act in order to accomplish some purpose. There can be many purposes, such as exchanging information, reaching a decision, selecting a structure, correcting errors, improving procedures, achieving dignity, reducing anxiety, or making social engagements. Each of these is a task process. There can be a different pattern of interaction for different task processes.

This leads to the idea of multiple structures, one for each actual task process. Even small laboratory groups maintain as many as nine structures during an experiment. The matrix of the relationships in a structure, R_n,

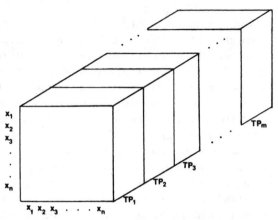

Figure 5.3.   The loaf model of group structures and task processes.

becomes a rectangular solid as shown in Figure 5.3. I call this the "loaf model."

The structure of each task process is a slice of this rectangular solid. If a task process is not done by a group, then the entries in the slice are all zero. And if a task process is done by a group, its structure will be represented by the entries in the slice.

It is possible to arrange the rectangular solid of Figure 5.3 into a very large rectangular matrix where the rows represent the individuals and the columns occur in sets, with a set of columns for every task process. For example, suppose there is a group having two task processes, TP_1 and TP_2, in which the structure for TP_1 is given by Figure 5.1 and the structure for TP_2 is given by Figure 5.2. Then, the new rectangular matrix illustrating the structures for each task process is given by:

| | Task Process 1 | | | | | Task Process 2 | | | | |
	x_1	x_2	x_3	x_4	x_5	x_1	x_2	x_3	x_4	x_5
x_1	0	1	1	1	1	0	1	1	1	1
x_2	1	0	0	0	0	1	0	1	1	1
x_3	1	0	0	0	0	1	1	0	1	1
x_4	1	0	0	0	0	1	1	1	0	1
x_5	1	0	0	0	0	1	1	1	1	0

This example illustrates how the same set of individuals can have different structures for different task processes. I have never observed the structures in a corporation to be all the same. They differ because of the division of labor and the interdependencies among task processes, task process resources charcteristics, and the environments. In the language of Chapter 4, TP_1 is the immediate predecessor of TP_2 and can be shown as

$TP_1 \rightarrow TP_2$.

Most task processes involve people communicating or working together. A sequence of task processes is really a sequence of group structures. Or, a sequence of task processes is actually a structure of structures in which one progresses from one immediate predessor to successor task processes.

By now, it should be clear that organizations have a complex of structures tied to their task processes. And it should be evident that the reality is not simple. Suppose that an organization has 1001 members performing 1000 different task processes. Then there are 1001 x 1000 = 1,001,000 possible half-channels for each task process, and 1,001,000,000 possible half-channels for the set of 1000 task processes. There are over one billion cells in the rectangular array of the type shown in Figure 5.3. The number of possible combinations and permutations of these one billion cells taken one at a time, two at a time, three at a time, etc. is:

$$_2 1,001,000,000$$

which is truly an astronomically large number. This number is much larger than the estimated number of energy levels in all atoms of the universe. And, given all of the changes that occur, a straightforward combinational analysis, uninformed by theory, would be totally impractical. A theory is needed to reduce the potential size of the problem down to a manageable size.

The first simplification is that the task processes are organized into an Organizational Logic. The interdependencies of the task processes means that most mathematically possible combinations of task processes do not exist. A hierarchy such as the Organizational Logic minimizes the number of combinations among the task processes. The second simplification is to realize that most persons have jobs defined by the performance of a small subset of the task processes. This reduces the combinations of people and processes. The third simplification is that most members of an organization only work in fairly small groups. The fourth simplification is that the assignment of task processes to individuals who work in relatively small groups reduces the combinations even further. Thus, almost all of the cells in the rectangular array of structures are zero. This allows one to squash the rectangular array into much smaller pieces. Organizational design, in principle, means arranging the Organizational Logic of the task processes and assigning persons to task processes. Consequently, one organizes the work in order to organize the persons who are to perform the work. These conclusions follow both from the need to reduce the inherent complexity and from the idea that structures are task dependent.

In laboratory studies, one can control the problem given to a small group to solve. Experience leads to precise descriptions of the task processes and to complete analyses of structural change processes. But, as was argued in every preceding chapter, organizations are continually changing. Thus, an organizational designer will not have the time, resources, or information to do a complete analysis of the structures. The organization will change as it is being analyzed, and it must continue to function while it is being changed. Thus, the arm chair theorist is in for many surprises as he or she ventures forth to design a real organization.

Fortunately, most organizations are generally stable, and the greatest stabilizing influence is the Organizational Logic. For example, since 1979, banks and savings and loan organizations have undergone enormous changes created by deregulation and the decisions by the U.S. Federal Reserve. But, despite these changes and other technological advances, many of their task processes have remained relatively unchanged. They still accept deposits (although there are now more types of deposit accounts), they still cash checks (even with Automatic Teller machines and electronic funds transfer), they still prepare monthly statements, make loans, handle trust accounts, do bookkeeping, operate facilities, engage in marketing and public relations, and foreclose on defaulted loans. The positions of a typical bank have changed in response to the demands to effectively manage the task processes. The task processes, while changing, are more stable than the positions of the organization to perform them. The position incumbents are also changing, and are less stable than the positions themselves. Most banks have had changes in the identity of the person called President, etc.

Organizational designers must take advantage of the stabilities in order to have a hope of effectively reorganizing an organization. But, to do their job well, they need a system that indicates what they should look for, and then a technology for how to put this information together before announcing results. Organizational designers must also take shortcuts in defining the group structures. One very useful tool is the Organizational Responsibility Grouping chart, or ORG chart.

THE ORGANIZATIONAL RESPONSIBILITY GROUPING CHART

A *role matrix* is a rectangular matrix whose rows are individuals and whose columns are task processes. A role matrix can always be derived by compacting the rectangular array of all of the structures for each process. Usually, the entries of a role matrix are either unity, if the person on the row performs the activity, or zero otherwise. Role matrices are very useful for analyzing laboratory groups, because the individuals and the activities do not change. But, in real organizations, these simplifications are rarely present. Furthermore, there are usually more levels as one proceeds from the Chairman of the Board of Directors to the new teller. The relationships are more complex than perform/not perform, because of DCC and planning task process level processes (cf. Chapter 4). The Organizational Responsibility Grouping chart (ORG chart) is a type of role matrix. It is used in order to trace the vertical linkage or chain of command for any task process. It combines structural and task process interdependence in one easy to use chart. Data in an ORG chart is used directly to derive organizational design.

An *Organizational Responsibility Grouping chart* is a rectangular matrix whose rows are organizational positions, whose columns represent task processes at the same level of aggregation, and whose entries represent the task process involvement. There are varying degrees of task process involvement, as shown in Table 5.2.

Example. Suppose that positions x_1, x_2, x_3, x_4, x_5, x_6, and x_7 are involved with task processes 1, 2, 3, . . ., 10 respectively. The combined organizational structure is given by Figure 5.4.

Suppose further that the ORG chart is given by Table 5.3.

Table 5.2 Symbols used in ORG charts

Symbol used in ORG chart entry	Meaning of ORG chart entry
O	Position is not involved in the task process
P	Position directly performs the task process
S_1	Position supervises the person(s) having a P only
S_1/P	Position both performs and supervises the task process
S_2	Position supervises the person(s) having an S_1 entry
"	
"	
"	
S_K	Position supervises the person(s) having an S_{K1} entry
X	Position is consultant in the performance of the task process

Table 5.3 An ORG chart

	Task processes									
Position 1	2	3	4	5	6	7	8	9	10
X_1 P	S_1	S_2	S_1	S_1	S_2	S_1	S_2	S_2	S_2
X_2 O	P	S_1	P	O	O	O	O	O	O
X_3 O	O	O	O	P	S_1	P	O	O	O
X_4 O	O	O	O	O	O	O	P	S_1	S_1
X_5 O	O	P	O	O	O	O	O	O	O
X_6 O	O	O	O	O	P	O	O	O	O
X_7 O	O	O	O	O	O	O	O	P	P

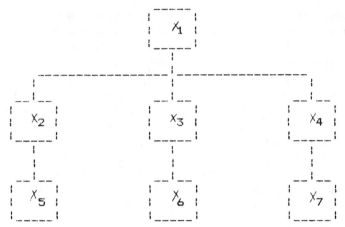

Figure 5.4.   Example of organizational chart.

In this small organization of seven members and 10 task processes, the persons on level three (x_5, x_6, and x_7) perform directly TPs 3, 6, 9, and 10. The immediate supervisor of x_5 is x_2, who performs TPs 2 and 4 and acts as S_1 for TP 3, performed by x_5. Similarly, x_3, the immediate supervisor to x_6, supervises TP 6 and performs TPs 5 and 7. And x_4, the immediate supervisor to x_7, supervises TPs 9 and 10 and performs TP 8. Note that x_1 performs TP 1, is S_1 for 2, 4, 5, 7, and 8, and is S_2 for TPs 3, 6, 9, and 10. The ORG chart shows the chain of command for each task process and allows one to study, at a glance, the relationships among the seven members.

Figure 5.4 can be redrawn to show the supervisory chain, as is done in Figure 5.5. The numbers to the left of a vertical line are those task processes that are supervised, and the numbers to the right are those directly performed by the position.

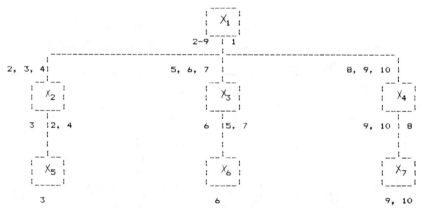

Figure 5.5.   Organizational chart showing supervisory responsibilities.

Of course, one cannot define an ORG chart until one has an Organizational Logic which allows definitions of the task processes depicted by the columns in the ORG chart. The identity of the positions may include individual positions, such as VP Manufacturing, Sales Manager, Plant Manager, etc., as well as composite positions such as standing committees (e.g., Executive Committee) and task forces (e.g., DP task force). The positions in large companies may be the titles of leaders of the many divisions and thus represent subordinate sets of positions. Refining the details of the task processes leads to a detailed breakout of subordinate positions. Every entry with a S_1, S_2, . . ., S_k represents a DCC or a planning task process law level. Note that the entries which are nonzero for a subordinate are always a subset of those of his or her superior, at all levels, if the organizational structures are hierarchical. Task Process 1, which is done by the top level person x_1, could be a planning task process level process.

Of course, in most cases, the ORG chart that emerges from the study of an organization is not as simple as this one. Process maladaptations can be spotted immediately by examining the ORG chart. For example, suppose that in the preceding example, the following changes were made: Add P to x_3 for TP 9, add P for x_4 for TP 7, add P for x_6 for TP 9, and add P for x_7 for TP 7. Then the new ORG chart will be as shown in Table 5.4. But these changes confuse the relationships among x_3, x_4, x_6 and x_7. In fact, the added Ps become S_1/Ps for x_3, and x_4 for TP 7 and TP 9. These changes create process maladaptations shown by the dotted lines in Figure 5.6.

The added Ps are circled, and the changes in type of supervisor are shown by the boxes with the P or S_1/P entry circled. Thus far, changes in assignments of performance resulted in seven changes in the ORG chart.

The horizontal dotted lines represent cousin relationships between x_3 and x_4 for TP 7, and between x_6 and x_7 for TP 9. This illustrates the point that task process maladaptations usually create structural maladaptations. Note that the two cousin relationships on level 2 for TPs 7 and 9 create two uncle–nephew relationships on level 3, and one cousin relationship on level 3. The precise definitions of "cousin" and "uncle-nephew relationships" and

Table 5.4. The revised ORG chart due to changes

	Task processes									
Position	**1**	**2**	**3**	**4**	**5**	**6**	**7**	**8**	**9**	**10**
X_1	P	S_1	S_2	S_1	S_1	S_2	S_2	S_1	S_2	S_2
X_2	O	P	S_1	P	O	O	O	O	O	O
X_3	O	O	O	O	P	S_1/P	S_1/P	O	S_1/P	O
X_4	O	O	O	O	O	O	S_1/P	P	S_1/P	S_1
X_5	O	O	P	O	O	O	O	O	O	O
X_6	O	O	O	O	O	P	O	O	P	O
X_7	O	O	O	O	O	O	P	O	P	P

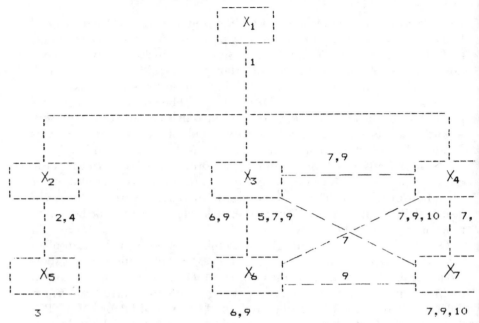

Figure 5.6. Organizational chart showing cousin and uncle–nephew structural maladaptations.

the task process measure of the degree of hierarchy, can be found in Mackenzie (1974, 1976a, 1978a, b, c, d).

These process maladaptations might lead to a new organizational design, as shown in the ORG chart of Table 5.5 and the organizational chart of Figure 5.7. This new design removes the process and structural maladaptations by reassigning the responsibilities for TP performance and responsibility for supervision. The common relationship between x_3 and x_4 in Figure 5.5 has been resolved by changing the job of x_3 and placing x_4 on level 3. This also cleans up the uncle-nephew relationships and the cousin relationship on level 3.

Table 5.5. Revised ORG chart after organizational design

	Task processes									
Position 1		2	3	4	5	6	7	8	9	10
X_1	P	S_1	S_2	S_1	S_1	S_1	S_2	S_2	S_2	S_2
X_2	O	P	S_1	P	O	O	O	O	O	O
X_3	O	O	O	O	P	P	S_1	S_1	S_1	S_1
X_4	O	O	O	O	O	O	P	P	O	O
X_5	O	O	P	O	O	O	O	O	O	O
X_6	O	O	O	O	O	O	O	O	P	O
X_7	O	O	O	O	O	O	O	O	O	P

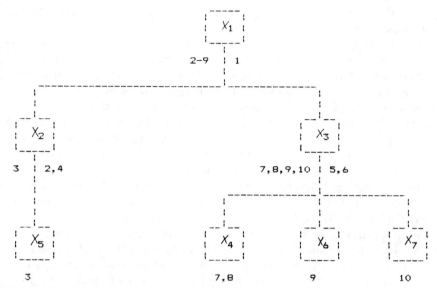

Figure 5.7.   New organizational design.

ORGANIZATIONAL POSITION LEVELS

Given that the organization rarely operates as it is supposed to, as illustrated in the organizational chart or summarized in the set of position descriptions, an analyst needs to be careful about assuming that the oganizational positions are properly ordered to reflect how the organization actually operates. An independent analysis of who does what with whom yields many surprises in the assumption of levels. One can use the ORG chart to define actual organizational levels. An algebra for determining levels can be found in Mackenzie (1976a, 1978a).

Let x_i and x_j belong to the set X_n. Position x_i is said to be the *immediate supervisor* of the immediate subordinate x_j, designated by $x_i \gtrsim x_j$, if the level of task process involvement of x_i is exactly one level higher than the task process involvement of x_j for every entry in the row of x_j in the ORG chart. For example, if x_4 has a P for TPs 7 and 8, and x_3 has an S_1 for TPs 7 and 8, as in Table 5.5, then x_3 is the immediate supervisor of x_4. Similarly, since x_1 has an S_2 for TPs 7 and 8, x_1 is the immediate supervisor of x_3. Position x_1 has no immediate supervisor, and serves in that capacity for both x_2 and x_3.

If $x_i \gtrsim x_j$, then for every P in the ORG chart for x_j there is either an S_1 or an S_1/P for x_i. And, given that there is a P in the ORG chart for x_i, the entry for x_j is either 0 or an X. This same rule moves up the line for the immediate supervisor of x_i. And because of the Organizational Logic, if $x_i \gtrsim x_j$, the common predecessor of the task processes of x_j is in the role of x_i. Thus, the hierarchy of the Organizational Logic becomes reconciled, in principle, with the hierarchy of the positions. This reconciliation reduces organizational interdependencies (cf. Chapter 8).

The ORG chart can be used to scan for all immediate supervisors–subordinate pairs and all process and structural maladaptations. Care must be taken to understand the relationships among the task processes, because some seemingly process maladaptations can be created by improper specification of the task processes. It should be pointed out here that, while consistent hierarchies of the aggregation of task processes and the organizational positions leads to great efficiency (if maintained in operations), after 8 years of designing organizations, I have never yet designed such a "perfect" one. There are always other considerations, such as costs, prior commitments, creating checks and balances, controls, training and development of back up personnel and future strategies. I have come close. The new design is always closer than what was revealed in the initial Organizational Audit of the actual organization.

Many positions, such as teller, store manager, industrial engineer and bookkeeper, have more than one incumbent. These persons all perform the same task processes. Such positions are called *multiple positions*, and are usually shown by an organizational chart position with a title followed by a list of all of the position holders:

Paying/Receiving Teller
x_1 x_2 x_3 x_4 x_5

A *normal position* has one incumbent, and is designated by:

VP Loans
x_1

The concepts of normal and multiple position will be used in Chapters 10 and 11.

Given an ORG chart, the existence of more than one P, more than one S_1 or S_2, etc. entry in any column represents one of three possibilities: (a) multiple positions, (b) improper descriptions of the task processes, and (c) a process and a structural maladaptation. Thus, the ORG chart allows the analyst to spot the location of many organizational design questions.

Now, let x_i and x_j be any two positions; then x_i and x_j are *disjoint positions* whenever the P, S_1, S_2, . . . row entries of each are everywhere different. Furthermore, x_i and x_j are *parallel positions* if they have exactly the same entries everywhere. Parallel positions are like multiple positions, but are as yet uncombined into a multiple position in the ORG chart. Two positions, x_i and x_j, are said to be *separable* if (a) they are disjoint or (b) they are in a different chain of immediate supervisor-subordinate pairs. For example, two bank tellers at two different locations are separable positions. Two tellers at the same location with the same head teller are in a multiple position if they do exactly the same task processes.

ORGANIZATIONAL ARCHITECTURE

The *Organizational Architecture* is given by the set of organizational positions along with the assignment of task processes to each position. The Organizational Architecture can be inferred directly from the ORG chart. Whenever the ORG chart describes the official responsibilities, the Organizational Architecture is said to be the *formal organizational structure*. But, in many instances, especially during an organizational design, the ORG chart represents the actual distribution of task processes. Hence, in only the rare and special case where the ORG chart is the official assignment will Organizational Architecture be the same as the formal organizational structure. This distinction roughly parallels the distinction between the formal and the actual organizational structure. During the process of organizational design, one evolves the Organizational Architecture. Only at the moment of the cut over to the new design is the Organizational Architecture the same as the formal organizational structure.

The admonitions in the introduction to this chapter concerning the importance of a useful concept of organizational structure is very important. There are many organizational structures. These are linked to the Organizational Logic, they change, and have different properties. The Organizational Responsibility Grouping chart is a simple way of combining positions and task processes, and is the starting point for many analyses of organizational design problems. As we shall see in Part 2, often the result of the organizational design is a changed set of task processes, a changed distribution of task process involvements, and a changed set of organizational positions. The ORG chart, while useful, is only one starting point. Its real value is that it highlights many of the potential issues. Resolving them, however, may result in changes in the rows and columns as well as the entries in the ORG chart.

CHAPTER 6

Dynamics of organizational changes

INTRODUCTION

The dominant theme of this book is change and how organizations respond. Organizational design is a change process which takes place amidst other changes. The reality of incessant change has had much to do with the evolving strategy for developing a theory and a technology for organizational design. The necessity of working with and managing change has led to dynamic concepts of task processes and organizational structures. Conceptual tools for thinking about and integrating task processes and structures are necessary to be able to design organizations.

There may be some who are uncomfortable with the theme of change and the need for conceptual tools that can handle it. It means that there is a need to reconsider how we think about organization. Some may wish to deny that there is any problem, because they believe that all of these changes and their management really only require strong leadership and energy. There even might be some who believe that these changes are a result of poor management and incompetence. There are many reasons to believe that we need better theories about organizations, that exceptional leaders can make a big difference, and that there are many organizations that are poorly managed. Nevertheless, there are compelling reasons to believe that many of these changes and problems are a permanent part of organizational life and cannot be traced directly to any single cause or person.

Managers in a free society are able to control only a subset of the forces to which they must adapt their organizations. The relationships between an organization and its environments are not static. Managers are forced to adapt in order to survive. Just as there are interdependencies among task processes, task process resources characteristics, and organizational positions within a firm, so too do interdependencies exist between an organization and its environments. Wise and capable managers acknowledge this freely. Insecure and foolish managers try to deny it. The better manager, while accepting the inevitable need to adjust, wants to do something about it. Those who hope that the problems will go away are often correct in the short run, and even lucky in the near future, but wrong in the long run. One of the most interesting phenomena I have observed is that organizations seeking my services to help them design their organizations usually have three characteristics: (a) a capable and confident Chief Executive Officer, surrounded by a team of capable subordinates, (b) a track record of success, and (c) a sense that, somehow, it is becoming increasingly difficult to change the organization to implement new strategies. They are all bullish about their opportunities. Firms in trouble may get that way for many reasons that lie outside their control. Some firms seem to be "snakebit" in that they go from disaster to disaster. I have come to believe, however, that most firms get into trouble and stay in trouble because they lack the capacity to identify and solve problems, and they lack the will to implement solutions. One of the reasons that they lack this capacity is that they act as if they have stopped searching for new ways of taking advantage of these changes. Usually they also seem to refuse to act on their knowledge of their partial control of change. In most cases, these changes should not be used as an opportunity to wallow in guilt or doubt, but rather as a challenge to be brave. Fortune favors the brave and is cruel to the tentative and indecisive.

The main differences between the brave and the foolish are that the brave recognize reality and still act. The reality of organizational change, and the dynamics producing process and structural maladaptations, are inevitable for any organization residing in larger dynamic environments in which it exercises only partial control. Process and structural maladaptations exist as necessary consequence of these changes. It is neither "bad luck" nor incompetence that causes most of these maladaptations. They are a logical and natural consequence of the changes themselves. The brave seek to understand these forces, and the foolish try to ignore them.

Perhaps, in this chapter, the reader will gain a better appreciation of these forces of change. That way, perhaps, the timid and the foolish may become braver. It is easier and more fun to be brave. I shall begin by explaining the concepts of authority-task gaps, authority-task problems, and the relative pace by which competing organizational systems change. This leads to a further articulation of the ABCE Model introduced in Chapter 1 and the concept of design premises. The maladaptations lead to a new concept called a "virtual position," and to defining the issues and arenas for the exercise of power. Finally, we come to the general concept of organizational congruity, and thence to an analysis of the different types of incongruities.

AUTHORITY-TASK GAPS AND PROBLEMS

Another lens through which to examine organizations is to consider each as having three systems (cf. Lippitt and Mackenzie, 1976, 1979). The first is the official-role system, which describes who is supposed to be doing what with whom. The *official-role system* is that of the formal organizational structure. It comes complete with organizational charts, position descriptions, and manuals of policies and procedures. The official-role system describes how the organization has been planned to operate. The official-role system, by its very nature and interdependencies, is slow to change in recognition of changes in the organization's task processes and the environment. It is usually conservative and recognizes changes after they have been identified and rationalized. Changes in the official-role system are often painful and upset existing coalitions, and, hence, can be hazardous. They often ratify and legitimate actual changes that have already begun to emerge. Official-role system changes are usually announced formally.

In contrast to the offical-role system, there is the *task-role system* that describes who actually does what and with whom one actually works on what task process. The task-role system describes how the organization actually operates. The task-role system is highly responsive to change. It changes all the time as a response by responsible personnel to get their jobs done in spite of how they are supposed to work. For example, if a supervisor is incapable of handling problems, those around and below him begin structural change processes to remedy the situation. If the official-role system is organized around market contingencies that are no longer relevant, the personnel of the organization will begin to work out new arrangements of task processes and structures. Changes in the task-role system are rarely announced formally. They just seem to happen. Changes in the task-role system occur more rapidly and with more precision to the actual work and personalities than do changes in the official-role systems. Changes in the task-role system are, by their nature, illegitimate in terms of the official-role system, and need to be ratified as they accumulate into large differences with the official-role system. The fact that most organizations do not operate in strict accordance with the official-role system is just another way of recognizing the existence of changes in the task-role system.

There is a third system called the authority-role system. The *authority-role system* is similar to the official-role system in that it specifies who has the legal authority to make what types of decisions about what task processes and resources. In a world without conflicting government regulations and fuzzy laws whose meaning is interpreted and applied as a result of "chance" legal and legislation processes, there would be little need to differentiate the authority-role system and the official-role system. But that world does not exist anymore. One example is the treatment of human resources, which places constraints or priorities on selection, hiring, training, promoting, rewarding, and punishing employees. An official-role position might have the responsibility of making decisions and yet lack the legal authority to act. The authority-role system can change whenever there are new laws and regulations, whenever ownership changes, by decisions made by the Board of Directors, and by changes in the official-role system.

While the task-role system is the most responsive to change, its changes are capable of affecting and being affected by changes in both the official-role system and the authority-role system. These three systems are interdependent, and all three change. But they do not always change at the same rate or in the same direction. Consequently, inconsistencies creep into the operation of the three systems, and these inconsistencies are called *authority-task gaps* (ATG).

Most organizations have substantial authority-task gaps, and most of these ATGs are either unrecognized or tolerated. Some authority-task gaps are deliberately created in order to effect a system of checks and balances or a system of control. Accountants, for example, set about separating task processes of obtaining, handling, and recording of monetary flows in order to prevent theft and waste. The Constitution of the United States of America permanently enshrined authority-task gaps in the system of executive, legislative, and judicial branches of government. Ombudsmen, inspectors general, and protection of "whistle blowers" are all attempts to control and organize by the deliberate creation of ATGs.

Any ATG represents either a process or a structural maladaptation. That there can be reasons for deliberately creating some ATGs should not obscure the fact that most are unplanned and uncontrolled. Unplanned and uncontrolled ATGs abound in organizations. They flourish when there are excess resources in an organization and when there are many changes taking place. Larger, more mature oganizations tend to have more than lean, hungry entrepreneurial firms, because it takes longer for them to effect changes and the senior administrators operate in comparative isolation from the daily forces of the larger environment. One joke that illustrates the greater insulation of some organizations is that the University of X could suddenly lose all of its students and most of the administrative task processes would not change for a year. The system of overlapping task processes, committees, task forces, commissions, etc. would keep on operating. But a firm in direct competition with formidable competitors would notice immediately the defection of its customers. It would be forced to act.

Some, but not all, ATGs become recognized and dealt with by organizations. ATGs are ignored most of the time because it is in no one's interest to resolve them. But when the personal stakes in them become high, an ATG becomes an *authority-task problem* (ATP). Lippitt (1975) and Lippit and Mackenzie (1976, 1979) have studied the processes of ATGs becoming ATPs, and the strategies for solving them. It takes a position holder whose position in the ORG chart makes him or her the lowest supervisor whose task processes are common predecessors to the protagonists to recognize an ATP. This position is called the *lowest common ancestor*, or LCA. In studying how an LCA solves ATPs, Lippitt uncovered only seven strategies: do nothing, solve the problem, appoint a committee, assign it to a standing committee, appoint a task force, pass the buck upwards, or hire a consultant. A model was developed to explain and predict which of the seven choices of strategy to solve an ATP would be selected. The model is based on a theory of group structures, and on the belief that experienced administrators approach ATPs with two main questions: (a) What would be a solution? and (b) Would the solution be politically acceptable? An improper handling of an ATP by an LCA creates more ATPs.

Organizations with lots of committees, standing committees, task forces, and meetings have many authority-task gaps and authority-task problems. These are telling clues that the design of the organization needs to be rethought. And if one has a list of the committees, the members, their charges, and the frequency of meetings, along with the length of the meetings, one has very strong indications of the nature of the organizational design problems. This census of committees is a reliable and key part of the Organizational Audit which will be described in Part 2 of this book. The basic premise is that, if the task processes and the organizational structures were aligned with one another, there would not be as much need to direct, control, and coordinate by organizationally artificial means such as committees.

Authority-task gaps cannot be avoided. They can, however, be identified and resolved before becoming crises. In many ways, organizational design is a process of identifying and resolving authority-task gaps in order to improve an organization's productivity. ATGs, and especially ATPs, waste enormous amounts of talent. Instead of acting to increase sales, improve services, or take initiatives, the overlapping and interlocking ATPs misdirect efforts which, by their nature, are mostly political struggles for power and authority and are directed internally, instead of towards the environment. This waste of resources not only increases costs and leads to the proliferation of staff positions in terms of excess resources, but it also has large opportunity costs on the asset side of the balance sheets through lost opportunities and sluggish response to change.

Managers who have spent their careers in organizations with endemic ATGs learn to cope and even expect that this is how organizations operate. They learn to adjust their initiative and energy downward to meet the slow pace of coping with change. Managers who work in organizations where committees are rare are more sincere when they gripe about meetings. Probably, this difference in acceptance of ATGs leads to different speeds of operations. These learned expectations, plus a bias for action, are behind much of the reluctance of some corporations to hire personnel who have worked for the government for more than 3 years, unless there is a position requiring meticulous concern for detail. The fear is that they will infect the organization with this unwanted culture.

In my roles as professor, consultant, and entrepreneur I go back and forth to different institutions, and have been struck by the differences. I feel as if I am going from Mach 1 to slow motion whenever I attend a meeting at a university. Some of my clients seem to operate at Warp 1. This shifting pace in different institutions is a real challenge as one gears up or down to the situations.

I recall being assigned to a Faculty Research Committee of five professors and the obligatory students. This committee had the charge of vetting requests for research money from a very small fund. It took a lot of effort to call a meeting and when we met the issues tended to be minor. One day, after hours of negotiating and many memos, we were called together to approve a request for $17.38 to reimburse a professor for the purchase of a book. I figured that this issue was worth 12 minutes of my time and even less of the entire committee's time. One of the members of the committee, who was always very thoughtful of the policy implications of any decision, brought up the larger issue of school policies. As soon as I heard him speak I knew that, unless some decisive action were taken immediately, I would be sentenced to a year of discussion of issues that were complex and profound. I took out a $20 bill from my billfold and said "Pay him this! Keep the change!" It worked, and I was able to get back to work. The policy-making professor never forgave me for depriving him of a marvelous opportunity to exhibit his intelligence. My "hostile act" was perceived as a challenge to the system. I have also found that passing out lollipops tends to shorten meetings, because mouths are occupied with the pleasure of taste rather than rhetoric.

One who designs organizations becomes fascinated with the variety of means for accomplishing work and justifying one's existence. It is always sad to see energetic and decisive managers drawn into prolonged organizational warfare. One wonders how they become ensnared and why they persist. The study of process and structural maladaptations has led to the capacity to recognize authority-task problems and their importance to organizational design. Later, it became clear that there was another whole issue, and that involved how a mechanism for adaptation to change had become an inhibitor of change through overuse. This led to a new analysis of the nature of power (cf. Pfeffer, 1981) and the arenas in which the struggle occurred. The key to this is the concept of a *virtual position*.

VIRTUAL POSITIONS

In Chapter 5, there was a discussion of official and actual positions which corresponded to the official-role system and the actual-role system. These positions could be easily spotted using the Organizational Responsibility

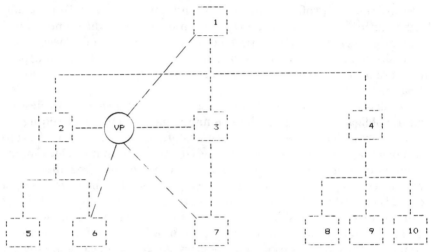

Figure 6.1.   An illustration of a virtual position.

Grouping chart. As different ORG charts were compiled, a phenomenon began occurring with marked regularity. There were task processes in which different positions in different chains of commands of the task processes led to a rash of P_1, S_1, and S_2 entries that were clearly maladaptive. Lots of persons were involved with the task process, but the task process was not connected in the Organizational Logic. There seemed to be a new type of position that "floated" amidst others, much as is illustrated in Figure 6.1. It is shown by the dotted circle labelled "VP" and the dotted lines to it from other positions.

The virtual position represents a composite of positions involved in a task process that is not tied to any immediate supervisor-subordinate chain. More precisely, a *virtual position* represents a set of task processes performed by a composite entity of three or more parties, and can be identified from the ORG chart whenever, for a given task process, the column representing the task process has:

a.   Three or more P entries
b.   Two or more P entries plus two or more X entries
c.   Two or more P entries, one or more X entries, and two or more S_1 or S_2 entries

Figure 6.2 shows the official organizational chart of a community bank in Louisiana. And Figure 6.3 shows the bank's 11 main virtual positions. The task process for each virtual position is listed in Table 6.1. The striking feature of the task processes of Table 6.1 is that they are nontrivial and vital to the bank. Figure 6.3 is a vast simplification of the actual organizational struc-

Table 6.1   Virtual positions for a community bank

Number	Brief Description
1	Operations Direction
2	Loan Coordination
3	Regulatory Compliance
4	Accounting Management
5	Due-From Management
6	Bookkeeping Direction
7	Deposit Service Management
8	Notes Processing
9	Branch Lending
10	Credit Collection
11	Information Systems

tures, because it *only* shows the 11 main virtual positions. The full drawing of the many process and structural maladaptations looks like a plate of spaghetti.

Once there was the ability to identify virtual positions, the questions of why they did occur and why they did persist became paramount, especially since they were identified only in those organizations I or my staff were studying. Given that structures represent need-satisfying interaction patterns, I had a clue to begin understanding virtual positions. I knew from earlier work on committees, task forces, and standing committees that these were instances of virtual positions. These are called regulated virtual positions. A *regulated virtual position* is a virtual position which has been officially recognized and a group has been set up to resolve the task process issues. But, in the case of the Louisiana bank, there were virtual positions on the list that fell outside the charges to the bank's committees. Hence, they are called *unregulated virtual positions.*

Once the concept of a virtual position was recognized, I found them in every organization. They seemed ubiquitous and important. The existence of unregulated virtual positions also presented a challenge to the underlying theory of authority-task gaps. The recognition of virtual positions and then efforts to understand them were the result of the strategy introduced in Chapter 2. Incidentally, the actual organizational chart for the Savings and Loan Association (Figure 1.1) shows the virtual positions by the junctions of the interactions.

Every virtual position has its own history of existence. Most of them are caused by changes in the organization's environments. The virtual positions listed in Table 6.1, for example, came as a result of changes in bank regula-

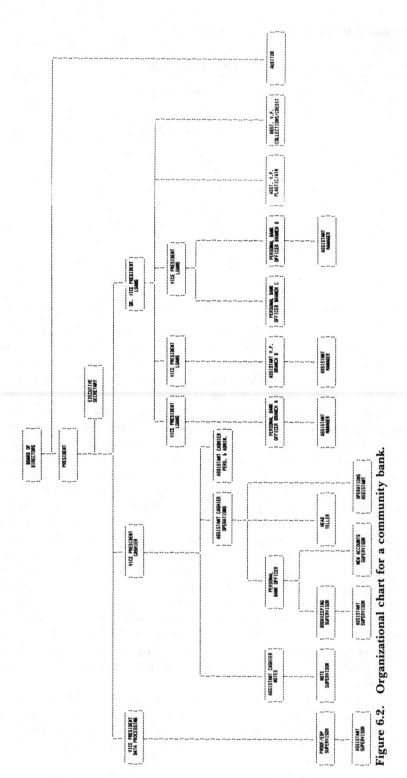

92

Figure 6.2. Organizational chart for a community bank.

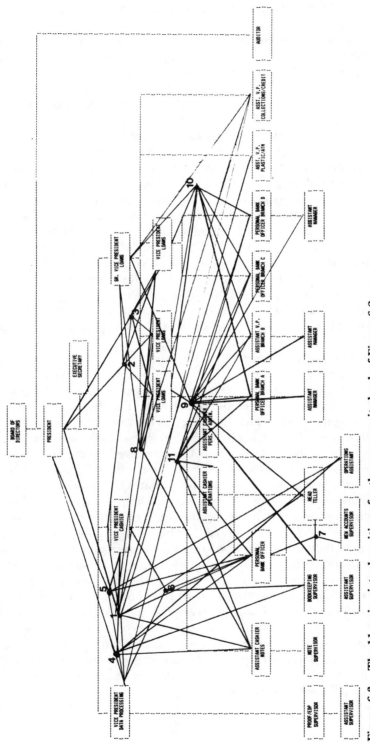

Figure 6.3. The 11 main virtual positions for the community bank of Figure 6.2.

93

tions, changes in technology, and a strategy of expansion by means of branch banking. A bank with one branch that opens up three more has the problem of coordinating operations, lending, credit, and information. Computers led to use of an external service bureau and the rapid install-ment of automatic credit machines. These changes created problems in reg-ulatory compliance, accounting, management, bookkeeping, due-from management, notes processing, and deposit services.

Each of the unregulated virtual positions began as a device for adapting to external change. An issue would come into the organization, and various individuals would begin to discuss it. This was usually informal and ad hoc. Some issues would go away and some became persistent. The informal ad-justments of the task-role system to deal with an unassimilated task process allowed the organization to function without disruption. Those who became involved had the opportunity to exchange information, engage in bar-gaining, and were able to "capture" the task process, thereby enhancing their own positions in the organization. Thus, the uncertainty about the new task processes and who would get them, as well as new opportunities for interpersonal influence, made these virtual positions arenas for power struggles. I began to see why they occurred, and why, once involved, people stayed involved.

If external changes were relatively infrequent, virtual positions would of-fer a mechanism for coping with change. Change could be dealt with with-out upsetting other task processes and, over a period of time, the discussions would lead to a workable solution which could then be installed into the or-ganization on a more regular basis. But, in the case of the community bank, the changes were occurring at such a rapid rate that the virtual positions were forming faster than they were being resolved. In the case of the bank, they could only be resolved by reorganizing the bank. The bank, organized traditionally by function, had an inappropriate Organizational Logic for the new environment. Strategy changes were leading to the conclusion to organ-ize for marketing and customer services rather than for the internal conven-ience of the specialists in the bank. When virtual positions start forming faster than they can be absorbed into the organization, the organizational processes and structures quickly become highly maladaptive. Issues tend to spread as the implications of the nature of the task processes involved be-come recognized. The widening vortex of influence attempts and power struggles tends to draw in all of the caring and ambitious members of the or-ganization. The resolution of a virtual position could have decisive effects on their own positions. It is no wonder that the bank president compared getting things done with "pushing a limp string across a rough table top." Virtual positions in the bank had reached the stage where they began to form virtual positions themselves.

It also became clear that the virtual positions were arenas for power struggles and, in fact, defined the issues over which the power struggles were involved. A lower-level person who captured a virtual position for himself or herself could leverage himself or herself to promotions, bigger budgets, and prominence. I noticed a dislike for virtual positions by bosses and a fondness for them on the parts of ambitious subordinates. Despite earnest oaths of purity, the same people always seemed to end up in the thick of any virtual position.

Once a system of unregulated virtual positions grabs hold of an organization and is growing, it takes radical reorganizing, in most cases, to eliminate them. Many of the task processes involved in virtual positions do not exist in the official- or the authority-role systems. One of the results of the absorption of a virtual position is the corresponding adjustment of the official- and the authority-role systems. But when they continue to grow and the issues spread to other task processes, the system of unregulated virtual positions must be dealt with by the organizational designer. To do this, he or she must look outside the normal task processes, the existing position descriptions, and the environmental changes to even find them. If the organizational designer is aware of the phenomena of virtual positions and is on the lookout for them, he or she will almost always find many in rapidly changing organizations which have lost control.

DESIGN PREMISES

A simple idea called the ABCE Model was introduced in Chapter 1. Block A contained the goals and strategies of an organization, block B the Organizational Technology, block C represented results, and E, which surrounds all three blocks, represents the environments in which the organization operates. The process of organizational design is described as a clockwise cycle through these boxes. The goals and strategies are used to define the Organizational Technology. The outputs from the organizational efforts are called "results," which are used to assess and modify the goals and strategies. All of this takes place in the context of the environments.

One must accept that all organizations will undergo change and that many of the changes are beyond the full control of the organization. No one knows exactly which changes will occur, or the magnitude and scope of their effects on the organizations. Accordingly, one must make assumptions about what one believes will happen. How the assumptions are made can improve adaptation if one's assumptions do not all turn out to be correct. It is helpful to organize these assumptions and make them explicit.

It is useful to consider three major types of assumptions that will be called "design premises." The first type of assumptions are those relating the goals with the environment, and are called *environmental design premises*. The second set of assumptions link the strategies of an organization with its environments. These are called *strategic design premises*. *Organizational design premises* are those made linking the strategies to the Organizational Logic. Organizational design premises define the macro-logic and represent the key assumptions about the basis for the Organizational Technology.

In order to illustrate these three types of design premises, consider what they might be for a community bank in the U.S.A. Environmental design premises would include assumptions about:

a. The basis for market segmentation
b. The impact of economic changes on the bank
c. The actions by competitors
d. The trends in competitiveness of the bank's market
e. The availability of low cost deposits.

Strategic design premises would include assumptions about:

a. The prime determinant of profitability
b. The key to satisfying customer needs
c. The nature and types of the bank's customers
d. The best way to create a good image
e. The timing and decisions to create new products and services
f. The basis for profitability
g. The importance of business development work.

Organizational design premises would include:

a. The basis for how the bank is departmentalized (by function, by market, by profit center, etc.)
b. How and where decisions should be made
c. How one obtains quality personnel
d. The problem solving process used
e. The basis for deciding about delegation
f. The role of committees.

Another way of thinking about design premises is to think about the vulnerabilities of the organization to changes. *Vulnerabilities* are events which can effect the organization's survivability. Some vulnerabilities are unique events such as hurricanes, strikes, loss of credit, cut off of supply, failure or bankruptcy of the organization's customers, and loss of key personnel. Some vulnerabilities are recurring, such as high persistent interest rates, shifts in distribution of costs, regulations created and imposed, new competitors, shifting technologies, ability of the organizational technology to implement a new strategy, liabilities to old contracts, legal actions centered on one's products or services, obsolete human resources, and changing economic conditions such as recession and high unemployment.

Vulnerability is a prime concern to the leaders of an organization. Should such an event occur, what would the response be? One-shot vulnerabilities are generally handled by ensuring that the organization obtains and is prepared to implement those task processes it controls to deal with the problem. For example, if being cut off from suppliers is a problem, efforts are made to set up relationships with other suppliers, increase inventory, redesign the product, create new contracts. One-shot vulnerability issues are handled within the normal Organizational Logic and Organizational Architecture. They may require a few new modules or bundles, but they usually do not result in major organizational changes. However, recurring, major vulnerabilities almost always change the Organizational Technology once they are recognized. The change is usually in the direction of placing the Chief Executive Officer closer to the positions capable of handling the vulnerability. The task processes for handling major, recurring vulnerabilities move closer to those performed or directly supervised by the CEO. And, as a one-shot vulnerability becomes recognized as being recurring, the position responsible for the task processes to handle it will be more and more in direct contact with higher officials and the CEO. In the language of the Organizational Responsibility Grouping chart of Chapter 5, the entry of S_k for the CEO changes to lower values of k.

The need for the CEO to have more direct access for major, recurring vulnerabilities results in major shifts in both the Organizational Logic and the Organizational Architecture. Often, new skills are needed, and so new opportunities arise. Many major, recurring vulnerabilities are handled first by means of the network of virtual positions. Competence, or the ability to create calmness about the task processes to handle a major, recurring vulnerability, means rapid promotion, at least within the task-role system. This ad hoc promotion will often result in a change in the offical-role system if the vulnerability persists and the position is successful in handling it.

Let's now go back to the community bank. Suppose it is organized about its traditional functions which separate organizationally the bank's assets and the bank's liabilities. Deregulation of interest rates meant that the bank now must manage its assets and liabilities jointly. Failure to manage one while managing the other can create disaster. The bank could, for example, have too many locked-in high interest rate deposits not matched by compensating high interest rate loans. Or it could have too many long term, low interest rate loans. Bankers call these new task processes asset/liability management. An officer of the bank who can manage assets and liabilities will be necessary for controlling this new major, recurring vulnerability. Another example is a change in banking laws permitting statewide branch banking. This can decimate the number of independent banks and vastly complicate how a bank positions itself. Thus, a one-shot legislative change sets into motion major, recurring vulnerabilities. Faced with the impending waves of mergers that will take place, there is the strategic puzzle of whether to acquire other banks or whether to be acquired by another bank. This may create a need to gain experience in mergers and acquisitions. A person having this expertise is going to become very important if the bank decides to become an acquiring bank. The same person is much less influential if the bank seeks to become acquired.

Major, recurring vulnerabilites are the tides that force major structural changes in organizations. Firms whose major vulnerabilities are sales usually have salesmen at the helm. Firms whose major vulnerabilities are finances become headed by financial experts. Public universities, whose major vulnerabilities are political, tend to have a set of top officials whose job is dealing with the government and public relations. A research-based enterprise may have its product design as its initial major vulnerability. Later, its major vulnerability may become the task processes of marketing the product. The shift from development to production and sales will rearrange both the Organizational Logic and the Organizational Architecture. Organizations that fail to adapt themselves to major, recurring vulnerabilities can deteriorate quickly as the vulnerabilities occur. Those that have adapted by reorganizing themselves have a much better chance of riding them out and even prospering as a result.

Changing design premises change the Organizational Logic, and, hence, are major concerns in selecting it. They may force the creation of new task processes and they may make it necessary to rearrange the old Organizational Logic. Major, recurring vulnerabilities affect the macro-logic directly and ripple down through the hierarchy of aggregation of task processes and change the location and content of planning and DCC task processes.

The Organizational Logic and the Organizational Architecture are normally determined jointly as the positions adjust to the work and as the work is modified because of the personnel capable of performing it. In designing organizations, I usually work out the Organizational Logic and then derive an interim Organizational Architecture called the Organizational Blueprint. The Organizational Blueprint is modified to fit the people, and these changes create changes in the Organizational Logic which, in turn, affect the Organizational Architecture, etc. There is an entity I call the Actual Organization which represents the task-role system. It evolves out of the Organizational Architecture.

Figure 6.4 shows the linkages among design premises, Organizational Logic, the Organizational Architecture, and the Actual Organization. These four elements make up the Organizational Technology, which is box B in Figure 1.2.

We are now in a position to redraw Figures 1.2 and 6.1 to show the more complete ABCE Model. This is illustrated in Figure 6.5, in which the Design Premises box has been divided into its three types: Environmental Design Premises, Strategic Design Premises, and Organizational Design Premises.

ORGANIZATIONAL CONGRUITY

The ABCE Model of Figure 6.5 represents the inclusion of an organization within a larger set of environments with which it must be adaptive. The means-ends linkages among the 10 elements are shown by the arrows, and the linkages of each element to the environment are shown by wavy lines. The organization is seen as a mechanism for converting goals into results by means of the selection of strategies and design premises, and then deriving an Organizational Architecture to implement these decisions. The arrows reduce the number of possible combinations of elements whose relationships need analysis. Results are seen as outputs from the Organizational Technology which are, in turn, inputs to the choice of goals and strategies. The cycle through the ABCE Model is assumed never to stop, because the environments keep changing from the viewpoint of the organization.

The task of the Chief Executive Officer is to ensure opportunistic adaptation of these elements in order to direct the organization. He or she must do this in the face of many uncertainties. Somehow, there needs to be a

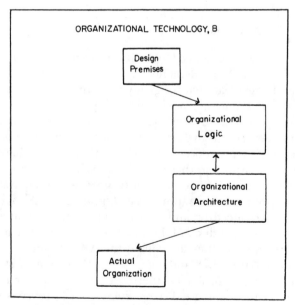

Figure 6.4. The Organizational Technology.

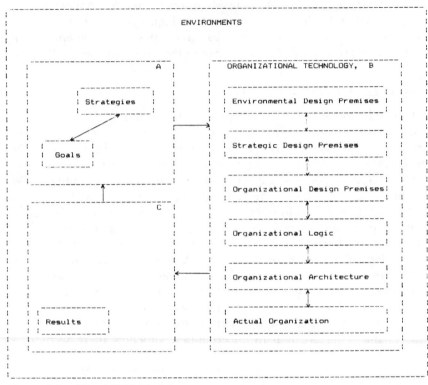

Figure 6.5.   The ABCE Model.

good fit among these elements. *Organizational congruity* occurs when, in the judgment of the CEO, all elements fit together and are consistent. The achievement of organizational congruity is assumed to be the prime objective of the CEO. Financial, performance, and other goals are seen as byproducts of the achievement of organizational congruity. For example, if the CEO has a return on investment goal of 25% and the results are only 12%, there must be some good reason. The number of possible explanations is potentially very large, and these explanations include inappropriate perception of the environment, an unrealistic goal, unworkable strategies, incorrect design premises, an inappropriate Organizational Logic, the wrong Organizational Architecture, and an actual organization that is out of control. Results, being byproducts of these choices, are seen as symptoms whose cause lies somewhere in the elements of the ABCE model.

In order to help the CEO (and his or her staff) be more systematic in the sensing and finding of problems, there are 11 organizational congruency conditions that can be analyzed. *Organizational congruency* is said to exist when, in the mind of the CEO, all 11 organizational congruency conditions are met. The 11 organizational congruency conditions are listed in order of importance in the analysis in Table 6.2. A more complete description of organizational congruency can be found in Mackenzie (1981b).

These conditions form a lexicographic ordering. If, for example, the goals do not match the environment, the lack of congruency will result in the lack of congruency in some or all of the remaining 10 congruency conditions. The savings and loan whose lending rate was less than the borrowing rate for funds created by a change by the U.S. Federal Reserve can expect to suddenly find its goals, strategies, design premises, the Organizational Logic and Organizational Architecture, the actual organization, and results to be incongruent. The automobile manufacturer who awakens to find the prices of gasoline and money suddenly increasing can expect many similar effects. If the goals and the environment are congruent, the next question is whether or not the strategies are congruent with the environment. Many times they are not. This incongruency sparks a cascade of subsequent incongruencies. Condition C_3, the congruency of goals and strategies, is important because, if they are not congruent, the Organizational Technology will be incongruent, as will be the results. The case study in Part 3 will show the effects when the goals and the strategies to achieve them are incongruent.

Congruency condition C_4 concerns the perceived agreement among senior management on the strategic options (choice of E, G, and S) chosen by the organization. If they are of one mind, they are likely to work together more effectively and have congruency in the Organizational Technology, B.

Table 6.2 Organizational congruency conditions

Condition Symbol	Condition of congruency	Relationship with ABCE Model
C_1	Goals and environments are congruent	A, E
C_2	Strategies and environments are congruent	A, E
C_3	Goals and strategies are congruent	A
C_4	Senior management agrees on goals, strategies, and environments	A, E, B
C_5	Environmental design premises and the environments are congruent	B, E
C_6	Strategic design premises and the strategies are congruent	B, A
C_7	Organizational design premises and the Organizational Logic are congruent	B
C_8	Organizational Logic and the Organizational Architecture are congruent	B
C_9	Organizational Architecture and the actual organization are congruent	B
C_{10}	Results are congruent with the Organizational Technology	R, B
C_{11}	Results are congruent with the goals	R, A

When, for any reason, the senior management disagrees on the strategic option, one can expect many adverse consequences including, but not limited to, creation of virtual positions, a lack of direction, control, and coordination, a slowing of adaptibility, and poor results. Condition C_4 reflects the wisdom of Jesus: "if a house is divided against itself, that house cannot stand" (Mark 3:25).

Conditions C_5, C_6, and C_7 relate the design of the organization to the design premises or assumptions made about the environment, the strategies, and the basis for the Organizational Logic. In 1983, there was a wave of bankruptcies and mergers in the airline industry in the U.S.A. which were traceable to the inability or unwillingness of senior management to adapt their organizations to the increases in costs and the new price competition created by deregulation.

Conditions C_7 and C_8 refer to the congruency of the organizational design premises and the Organizational Architecture to the Organizational Logic. These conditions are currently important to the banking industry in the U.S.A. because the traditional basis for bank organization by function is inappropriate to the new competition and technology due to deregulation and loss of low interest deposits. Condition C_8, the congruency of the Organizational Logic and the Organizational Architecture, is a restatement of the need for the organizational form to be consistent with the organizational functions. This incongruency is widespread in all organizations that I have analyzed. While important, it is seen as derivative from higher incongruities.

Condition C_9 is always incongruent because of the existence of authority-task gaps. The only question, in practice, is the size of the incongruities. Condition C_9 is one of the easiest to check. All that is necessary is to superimpose arrows on the organizational chart reflecting *how* the various task processes are actually performed. The overlay of the actual onto the official organizational charts will look like a plate of spaghetti.

Conditions C_{10} and C_{11} connect the congruencies to the Organizational Technology and goals with the results of operations. Condition C_{10} is a cause of incongruency for C_{11}. For example, a high-tech company just beginning to convert its technology into marketable products will have the problem of gearing up to respond to the demands of the market. This means expansion and change in the firm's task processes, and it takes time for the organization to learn how to do them well. C_{11}, the congruency of results and goals, is the most obvious of all 11 conditions of organizational congruency because most organizations have financial goals and financial statements whose comparison is easy. This incongruency, being easily spotted, leads to problem solving in the neighborhood of the symptoms. If costs have risen, the firm seeks to cut costs. If revenues are down, sales efforts are redoubled. If the football team loses too many games, hire better athletes or fire the coach. This narrow focus on the congruency of results and goals often leads to a "short circuiting" of the ABCE Model, with C going directly to the Organizational Architecture. Often, this short cut solution works well. However, in more turbulent environments it frequently leads to a type III error. Namely, management has focused on the wrong problem. Cutting costs, raising prices, and firing managers may be substituted for a more comprehensive examination of the organization's strategic options.

The achievement of organizational congruency is assumed to be the prime goal which, when met, ensures the achievement of the organization's other goals. The state of organizational congruency is only partially objective. The intuitive sensing of incongruencies is troubling and is assumed to worry the CEO. Often he or she cannot place a finger on the source of these worries. He or she senses them and the CEO eventually acts on these beliefs. He or she, alone, is in a position to see the entire organization and its relationship to the environments. Others, of course, have opinions and these are often voiced. But, the scope of the CEO's responsibilities and place in the flow of information and ideas, makes the CEO more aware of the whole organization than subordinate positions, who, by their nature, work on a more limited range of task processes. Furthermore, the CEO takes personal and political risks when voicing concerns and doubts. He or she must control the uncertainties in the task processes in order to be an effective leader. Public ventilation of doubt erodes his credibility. Others can offer advice, counsel, and support, but he or she is the one who has the responsibility for leadership. The position can be lonely and filled with doubt and guilt. It is the CEO's sense of organizational congruity that is vital because it governs his or her actions and inactions. The ABCE Model of the means-end linkages and these ideas of organizational congruencies are very useful tools to organize this intuitive sense more productively.

Furthermore, it is assumed that the attainment of organizational congruity will result in the attainment of a productive organization. As we shall see in Part 3, the first step in the design of an organization is the Organizational Assessment, which basically is a verification of the current organizational congruency and the examination of the future organizational congruency.

CHAPTER 7

Organizational boundaries

INTRODUCTION

The study of organizations can be made from many vantage points. One can approach the study of organizations in terms of different levels of aggregation, such as the individual, the group, the unit, the organization itself, and relationships across organizations. One can change lenses and examine the organization in terms of common processes such as decision making, goal formation, leading, planning, directing, coordinating, organizing, and many others. In any case, as one begins to study any real organization one is confronted with the reality that all organizations exist within a more extensive network. The environments in which an organization exists are affected by the actions of the organization and also constrain and influence the organization's behavior. Organizations change by the selection of how they choose to work with or compete with other organizations.

One small manufacturer launched his new product by subcontracting all manufacturing, advertising, and distribution task processes. This move allowed him to conserve capital and to concentrate on what he knew best. Another decided to sell its products by heavy television promotion and to distribute by means of chain stores. This firm's expertise was selecting good product ideas, specifying how they should be produced, developing television advertisements, and selling to retail chains. The firm subcontracted all of its manufacturing and distribution task processes. With only about 4% of the number of original employees, it increased its sales and profits. Its subcontractors also benefited, because they only had to do those task processes for which they had special expertise and advantage.

These two examples illustrate how an organization can think about its task processes as it would any other input of production. The analysis of contracting for a task process, selling task processes, or performing its own task processes is a new way to thinking through its productivity problems. Productivity can usually be raised by not performing task processes for which there is a supplier which can do them better and at lower costs. In this way, a company can concentrate on its special strengths and use the available markets to supply support for those task processes for which it has no special, comparative economic advantages.

The problems of determining what a company should produce and how to select its task processes are increasingly important to real firms. Even researchers have become interested in opening up the heretofore "trivial" problem of deciding, for the purposes of their studies, where one organization stops and another begins. The loci of all points where one organization stops and others begin are the organizational boundaries. Given the large variety and number of possible interorganizational relationships, the problem of defining each boundary and the set of all boundaries presents conceptual and theoretical puzzles which, as we shall see, lead to operationally and diagnostically interesting issues that are worthy of more serious attention (cf. Starbuck, 1976; Pfeffer and Salencik, 1978; Baligh and Burton, 1982). For example, what is the boundary between a union and a manufacturer, between a bank and a stock broker, between a vendor and a customer, between a company and the government? Where are the boundaries of firms in an automated office connected to others via electronic mail? There are combines, cartels, and trade associations whose relationships are not always "at arm's length." Increasingly, we observe subcontracting of major task processes, such as manufacturing of books by publishers, sales by direct mail order firms, and of services such as legal counsel, public relations, advertising, employment agencies, temporary help suppliers, engineers, accounting, data processing, fleet maintenance, food services, security, consultants of all types, computer service bureaus, janitorial work, industrial relations, and many others. We see new mergers and divestitures which change interorganizational relationships. We see vertically integrated firms subcontracting out major processes. Retailers move into wholesaling, and vice versa. We have interlocking directorates and leveraged ownership. Each changes the boundaries of an organization. The issue of defining each boundary and the set of boundaries is part of the general problem of selecting the goals and strategies of an organization (Baligh and Burton, 1982; Pennings, 1981). Thus, the problem of defining a boundary has begun to shift away from the arbitrary exercise of describing it for the purpose of special analyses to a class of important strategic choice problems (Baligh and Damon, 1980; Baligh and Burton, 1982). The selection of the boundary has become important to the operation of an organization and to organizational design (Pfeffer and Salancik, 1978). Clearly, organizational design involves the selection of the boundaries as well as improving the operations within one (Aldrich and Herker, 1977; Khandekar, 1983; Baligh and Burton, 1982; Pfeffer and Salancik, 1978).

An organizational boundary is neither fixed nor given. There is no shell or rigid membrane surrounding an organization. Organizational boundaries are flexible and changing, and an organization can lose control. "The problem of drawing the boundary around a social system has been a perplexing one" (Pfeffer and Salancik, 1978, p. 29). Organizational boundaries involve people and task processes within the organization, as well as with many other organizations. The people, the task processes, and the boundary relationships are fluid, and, hence, so are the organizational boundaries defining them. Judicious care in describing the stakeholders of an organization in order to make a first approximation in defining the organizational boundaries will always be incomplete because of the changes. The persons involved, and their task processes, dynamically adapt to one another. Care in describing the task processes and defining the boundary as the locus of task processes in which there are transaction-specific contracts is a little better (Williamson, 1975). But as soon as one begins to carefully describe these task processes and the concept of a contract, the variety of combinations becomes unmanageable, except to provide a second approximation to the concept of an organizational boundary (Baligh and Burton, 1982). For example, consider a company which has been organized by a labor union, has a labor agreement, and then files for bankruptcy under Chapter 11. Is the union still part of the boundary? Are the shop stewards in or out? What about the status of creditors and outside members of the Board of Directors. Consider a bank. Is the FDIC examining team part of a bank when the bank is placed on the list of banks in serious trouble? Static concepts of organizational boundaries can neither keep up with the changes that take place in most organizations, nor can they help an organization redefine its boundary as it adapts to its environments. Metcalf argues that "boundaries can be conceived of as regulatory processes which govern flows of transactions among overlapping subsystems" (1981, p. 205). Hence, as conditions change, so do the boundaries.

This chapter develops a concept of an organizational boundary which has the following attributes:

It can define the organizational boundary with another organization.
It can define the organizational boundaries within an organization.
It is capable of being specific.
It is capable of being changed as the organization changes.
It can be used to choose adjustments in the organizational boundaries.
It can be used to govern relationships spanning the boundary.
It can be used to analyze and inform organizational decisions.

The concept of organizational boundary is built upon a description of the structure of the task processes called the Organizational Logic (cf. Chapter 4). A special transformation of the Organizational Logic into component parts, called organizational plays (cf. Chapter 10), is then used to bring in the personnel. There are special organizational plays called boundary plays. *Boundary plays* involve mutual plays for at least a pair of organizations. Thus, the concept of a boundary as a sort of shell or membrane is replaced by a concept of overlapping sets of task processes and persons. Boundary plays can be used to describe interpenetration of organizations along the boundary (cf. Khandekar, 1983). Interpenetration is used to define the process of changing relationships along the boundary to stabilize relationships, and to exert power and control along the boundary. This general outline of the argument will be followed in the remaining parts of this chapter. The result is the conversion of the concept of organizational boundaries as objects into an open process capable of use in analyzing organizational behavior and for organizational design.

ORGANIZATIONAL BOUNDARIES

Most organizations can draw up rosters of their members. Most organizations have task processes that are executed only by these members. Thus there are organizational plays that can be considered as *internal* and, thereby, within the boundary. However, there are many individuals and task processes whose work extends into the organization's environments. All organizational plays involving some persons who are not members and some task processes that are not internal are called *boundary plays*. The set of all boundary plays defines the organizational boundary. Those members engaged in boundary plays are called *boundary spanning* members. Note that, because boundary plays involve both people and task processes, and people perform task processes, our concept of an organizational boundary involves both people and task processes, but will be described in terms of task processes.

A boundary between Organization A and Organization B can be illustrated by means of the type of diagram in Figure 7.1. Figure 7.1 shows the portion of the Organizational Logic of A by squares and that of B by ovals on the right. The notation within the boxes in Figure 7.1 is as follows: The letter I is an integrating task element, the letter E is an execution task element, B and M designate a bundle and a module respectively. The first number is the bundle being integrated, and the second number is the module number within the bundle. There are three plays at the bundle level and one at the group level for Organization A. There are two plays at the bundle level and one at the group level for Organization B.

In order to make Figure 7.1 more concrete, let us assume that Organization A is the First State Bank of Euphoria (FSBE) and Organization B is The Omni Systems Group (OSG). OSG sells and maintains software used by FSBE to analyze loans. The segments of the Organizational Logics for FSBE and OSG shown in Figure 7.1 can be described as follows:

First State Bank of Euphoria	*Task Processes in Figure 7.1*
Group Level: Loan Operations	IB
Bundle 1: Commercial Loans	IM1, EM11, EM12
Bundle 2: Consumer Loans	IM2, EM21, EM22, EM23, EM24
Bundle 3: Loan Processing & Administration	IM3, EM31, EM32, EM33

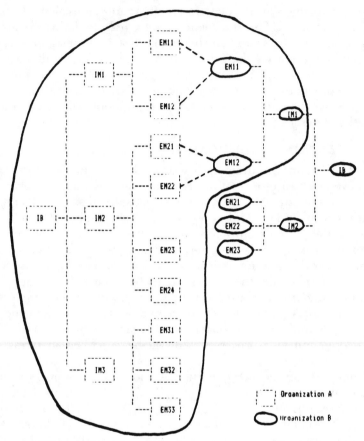

Figure 7.1.   A boundary between two organizations.

The Omni Systems Group	*Task Processes in Figure 7.1*
Group Level: Financial	IB
Institution Sales	
Bundle 1: Loan Analysis	IM1, EM11, EM12
Software Sales	
Bundle 2: Loan Processing	IM2, EM21, EM22, EM23
Systems Sales	

The boundary between FSBE and OSG begins with software sales for commercial loans and consumer loans. The direct links in the boundary between FSBE and OSG directly involve two boundary plays for FSBE and one play for OSG. There are four dashed lines which represent the linking of the task processes of both organizations. However, the relations extend beyond the four direct links. In order to also pick out the indirect linkages, the segments of the Organizational Logic of both organizations must be examined in order to locate the common predecessor task process for those task processes involved directly on the boundary. The boundary between FSBE and OSG includes the common predecessor task processes to the direct links and all its successor task processes for both organizations. Thus all of loan operations for FSBE (13 modules) and Bundle 1 (3 modules) of OSG are included in the boundary.

The Organizational Logic for FSBE can be depicted as the tree of its areas, group, bundles, modules, and activities as in Figure 4.8. From FSBE's viewpoint, its boundary with OSG can be thought of as covering a part of its Organizational Logic. Its boundary with OSG is analogous to Spanish moss in FSBE's Organizational Logic tree. (Spanish moss is an epiphyte or plant that manufactures its own food but grows on another. The long, slender, grayish stems look like human hair hanging from trees.)

There are many interesting properties of the boundary between any pair of organizations. These include the size of the boundary, the size of the boundary relative to the whole Organizational Logic, the task process leverage of the boundary for both organizations, the net advantage of each to establish and maintain a boundary, the stability and openness of the boundary, the vulnerability of each party to the other, and the dependency of one to the other. It is these properties that convert the problem of defining an organizational boundary into broader management problems. These properties are not always symmetric for both organizations.

Properties of a Boundary

Let us assume that any organization can be described by the task processes it performs. Further, let us assume that within limits that depend upon the circumstances, any organization has the right to select those task processes it performs and those which it acquires by creating boundaries. Thus an organization has the option of either providing task processes itself or creating a boundary with another organization. The decision to perform or to acquire a task process is a make/buy decision.

There are always two organizations involved in the creation and maintenance of a boundary. Each is assumed to have made its own analysis of the net benefits to forming a boundary. While the two parties may have different reasons for the boundary, it is assumed that a boundary will come into existence and be maintained if, and only if, both organizations perceive a net benefit. The net benefits are not, in general, identical.

Let β (A$\cap$B) designate the task processes contained in the boundary between organizations A and B. Let n_{AB} designate the number of direct links in β (A$\cap$B). Let T_{AB} and T_{BA} designate the common predecessor task process in A and B in β (A∪B) respectively. Let $R(T_{AB})$ and $R(T_{BA})$ denote the reach of T_{AB} and T_{BA}, respectively. Recalling the definition of "reach" in Chapter 4, the *reach of a task process* is the number of task processes at the same level of aggregation that flow from the task process (including itself) to the boundary or to its end points in the Organizational Logic.

The *size of the boundary* is $R(T_{AB})$ for A and $R(T_{BA})$ for B. *Example:* For the boundary in Figure 7.1, the size of the boundary for FSBE is 13 and 3 for OSG, provided we only count IB for FSBE as one module. The number of direct links, n_{AB}, is 4, as shown by the dashed lines.

Let M_A and M_B be the total number of task processes (at the level used to define the boundary) for organizations A and B. The potential task leverage from A to B is $R(T_{BA})$ - n_{ab} divided by n_{ab}, and the potential task leverage for B to A is $R(T_{AB})$ - n_{ab} divided by n_{ab}. In the example, the potential task process leverage from A to B is only $|\frac{3-4}{4}| = 0.25$, while the potential task process leverage from B to A is $\frac{13-4}{4} = 2.25$. Thus, OSG has more leverage in the boundary with FSBE than FSBE does with OSG. OSG greatly increased its leverage by providing software for both types of loans. For example, if OSG only supplied software for commercial loans, the leverages would be $\frac{3-2}{2} = 0.50$ and $\frac{3-2}{2} = 0.50$, respectively. Different sales strategies for creating boundaries can affect leverage, which can also be used for providing other products and services. For example, now that OSG is providing software for both commercial and consumer loan analysis, it is in position to enlarge its direct links by also offering loan processing software and contract programming.

The relative size of the boundary to each organization is also important. The *relative size of the boundary* for an organization is the ratio of the size to the total number of task processes. For example, suppose FSBE has $M_A = 100$ and that OSG has $M_B = 100$. Then the relative size is 0.13 for FSBE, and only .03 for OSG. Thus, relatively much more of FSBE is covered by the boundary with OSG than the other way around.

The determination of the net advantage for A to form a boundary with another organization is not the same as A's net advantage to form a boundary with another specific organization, provided it has alternative sources of supply. A buyer of task processes has different considerations than the seller of task processes. The estimation of net advantage of a buyer A to form a boundary to get a task process depends on at least seven factors: (1) Does it need these task processes performed? (2) Are these task processes currently available internally? (3) Could it acquire the task processes from another organization in time? (4) Is there an opportunity cost involved? (5) Is there an available outside source? (6) Is there "pressure" within to form the boundary? and (7) Does another organization offer significant advantage to performing these processes? A mapping function for describing how the seven binary variables lead to a determination of N_A can be found in Mackenzie (1984b). The estimate of net advantage N_A results in a five point scale from 0 to 4, with larger integers reflecting greater estimated net advantage to A.

The estimation of the net advantage to a seller B of a task process to form a boundary depends upon a number of factors. These include: (1) Does the organization need to provide the task process to another? (2) Does the organization have the capacity to perform these task processes? (3) Could these resources be obtained in time to perform these tasks processes? (4) Is there an opportunity cost to use the organizational resources in order to provide these task processes? (5) Is there a competitor? (6) Is there pressure to form this boundary? (7) Does forming this boundary create significant advantage to B? The estimate of the value of N_B also uses a mapping function to calculate a five point scale from 0 to 4, with larger integers reflecting greater estimated net advantage to B.

The values of N_A and N_B need not be identical. The asymmetry of the estimated net advantage to both parties affects the opening of a boundary, the negotiation of its terms, and the stability of the boundary once formed. For example, suppose FSBE believes that (1) the task processes available from B need to be performed, (2) it lacks its own resources to perform them, (3) it could acquire them from B in time, (4) it would suffer an opportunity cost in using its resources to perform them, (5) B could provide these task processes, (6) management has created pressure to form the boundary, and (7) another organization would offer significant advantages if it performed these task processes. In this case, the estimated net advantage to A, N_A, is 4. That means that FSBE perceives it has a strong net advantage to opening a boundary in order to acquire software for analyzing loans. On the other hand, OSG may believe that it has unique software, 12,000 potential customers, and does not really need the business of FSBE. In this case, the estimated net advantage to B, N_B, is 2. Consequently, OSG sees only a small net advantage to forming a boundary with FSBE to sell its loan analysis software. The result is a greater need for FSBE to form a boundary with OSG than for OSG to sell its software to FSBE. This will allow OSG advantages in its negotiations with FSBE.

The boundary depends upon both organizations desiring to create and maintain it. If both perceive very strong net advantages, the boundary will probably be very stable so long as the estimates remain high for both organizations. However, if one organization sees no advantage to the boundary, it probably will not be stable, no matter how the other organization perceives the net advantage. The *stability of the boundary* between organizations A and B is the value of min (N_A, N_B). In the example where $N_A = 4$ and $N_B = 2$, the stability is the minimum of 4 and 2 or min $(4,2) = 2$.

The fact that the organizations that are party to a boundary can perceive different net benefits implies that one could be more vulnerable than the other should the boundary be severed. The *vulnerability to A of the boundary with B* is the difference between N_A and N_B, provided $N_A \geqslant N_B$, and zero otherwise. In the example, the vulnerability of FSBE is two and zero for OSG.

One property of any boundary is how open one organization is to the other. The openness of the boundary is assumed to be identical to the net advantage. Thus, the *openness of the boundary* by A is N_A, and the openness of the boundary by B is N_B. Thus, any boundary is analogous to having two doors, one controlled by each organization.

Another important property of a boundary to another specific organization is the issue of how dependent one would be to the other organization. Pfeffer and Salencik stress these issues of dependency and control in their discussion of boundaries (1978, p. 32). The *dependency of organization A to B* is assumed to be (a) directly proportional to the value of N_A, (b) inversely proportional to the value of N_B, and (c) inversely proportional to the number of its alternatives. Thus, the dependency of A to the boundary with B is $(\alpha N_A)/N_B n_{AB}$ where n_{AB} is the number of alternative providers of the desired process and α is an unknown (but hopefully estimated) coefficient. It is assumed that $N_B > 1$ and $n_{AB} > 1$.

In the example, assume that $n_{AB} = 1$ and $n_{BA} = 12,000$. Then, if we assume further that the coefficients are equal to unity, then the dependency of FSBE to OSG is $4/(2 \times 1) = 2$ and the dependency of OSG to FSBE is $2/(4 \times 12,000) = .00004$. Of course, if OSG had a sales district in which FSBE was only one of five customers, then the dependency would rise to 0.10. In either case, FSBE is much more dependent on OSG than is OSG on FSBE. This asymmetrical dependency would affect pricing and the terms of a contract between the two firms. The more dependent organization would, *ceteris paribus*, have a weaker bargaining position.

The description of the boundary between Organization A and B for a specific set of task processes could be extended to other task processes *and* other organizations C, D, E, ..., Z, ... Using the Spanish Moss analogy, there is white Spanish Moss representing the boundary to B, blue Spanish Moss for the boundary to C, green Spanish Moss to the boundary with D, etc. A mature organization with lots of boundaries would look more and more like a "harlequin moss" of many multicolored patches of moss.

APPLICATIONS

There are numerous applications of this concept of a boundary and its properties. Some applications flow directly out of the underlying idea that an organization has the option of providing task processes internally or acquiring them by means of boundaries. One application is to examine current task processes to determine whether a boundary could be formed to improve productivity or the use of assets. For example, suppose a supermarket chain ties up too much of its working capital in stocking items whose volume is too low to be profitable. It could arrange for a wholesaler to handle these items for it. Similarly, it might have excess capacity in its perishables warehouse which could be used to provide wholesale services to another chain which is not a direct competitor but is a competitor of the chain's major competitor. Such a move would strengthen the main competitor's competition while providing a profit.

Another application is to plan expansion by first creating boundaries to acquire the fundamentals of a new technology or task process before providing it internally. Many small firms use public accounting firms until they are large enough to have their own accounting departments. Banks can now enter the stock brokerage business. A bank might first contract with a stock broker to provide services for the bank's customers. At a later time, the bank could absorb the stock broker or create its own internal stock brokerage service. Management consultants are often employed as an intermediate stage to help an organization acquire new task processes, especially in the new technology area. Gerlach and Palmer (1981) stress the value of evolving interdependence to foster adaptability.

We live in an era of subcontracting. Comparative economic advantages create many opportunities for selling task processes. Peterson (1981) discusses how such rearrangements can foster entrepreneurship within organizations. Some banks, for example, are learning to franchise special expertise to banks which are too small to support the costs of developing new services. A supermarket chain can sell its data processing expertise and its data to other supermarkets. Peters and Waterman (1983) provide examples of successful corporations using boundaries to improve productivity.

Another group of applications deal with "how to have one's cake and eat it" problems. These problems lie in how to manage a boundary to improve net advantage, decrease dependency, improve stability, and influence relative size. The applications include contracting, maintaining multiple suppliers, reorganizing to reduce dependency, retraining one's own personnel, reciprocal agreements to create double boundaries which, on balance, improve stability, and many others. Decentralizing, for example, tends to reduce the relative size of the boundary, because task processes do not reach as far into the interior of the organization. Reorganizing to eliminate task process maladaptions and virtual positions would limit interpenetration (Khandekar, 1983).

Supermarket Systems, Inc. had a particularly creative use of these ideas. During the Organizational Audit and Analysis stages of my involvement, SSI was under heavy pressure by a large national chain whose plan of expansion was aggressive. It would select a site and then construct a large new 43,000-square-foot store. The new store would open up by offering very low prices. The object (as seen by SSI) was to force weaker competitors to retire from competition. SSI was reeling from a succession of competitive new store openings and had decided to close a number of its stores. The national chain was using its financial muscle to change SSI's boundaries. SSI decided to fight back. It chose a location where it had just closed a store in reaction to the new store built next door by the national chain. SSI knew the strengths and weaknesses of the national chain and decided to create a new store format. The purpose of this store was to create a credible threat which would make the national chain reconsider before attacking SSI's stores. The new store format stocked staples and items for which SSI had large inventories. It was a box store with scanning devices at check outs. These changes allowed SSI to reduce its gross margins by about 6% and to reduce its labor costs as a percent of sales by 2%. The idea was to have customers shop first at the new SSI store and then go next door and complete their food shopping. The new SSI store competed aggressively and shocked the national chain. The vigorous action by SSI "sent a message." Because personnel move from chain to chain, SSI knew how the national chain would react, and it knew that the national chain would consider SSI's competitive reaction. SSI believed that this caused the national chain to shift its pricing policies in three states and to believe that SSI would react aggressively. SSI believes that the national chain changed some of its new store decisions to avoid opening against an SSI store. The counteroffensive by SSI also acted to distract the national chain which allowed SSI to open several new stores unmolested by the national chain. Having made its point, SSI then closed the new store. This process resembled a situation in a playground in which a smaller boy strikes back a bully. It acted to stabilize the boundaries between the two chains.

There are numerous applications to marketing (especially industrial marketing), wholesaling, and brokerage operations. For example, an industrial sale represents an opening of a boundary to the buyer. Some sales strategies penetrate deeper into the buyer's organization. It may take longer to make such a sale, but, once one has been made, the potential task process leverage and increased buyer dependency could become a highway over which one could march other products and services. IBM, for example, is a master of this longer-term strategy for sale of business computing systems. It has had to modify this strategy for sale of personal computers because of the limitation on the leveraging of the task processes. We know that firms in the same industry can have very different marketing strategies. It should be possible to study the effectiveness of these strategies by analyzing how they penetrate and maintain boundaries.

The problems of downsizing an organization present interesting boundary problems, because the organization may lose control of its boundaries due to forced sale of assets, departure of key persons who provide essential task processes, etc. (Hirschhorn et al., 1983). A theory of downsizing could be developed around the theory of organizational boundaries.

Boundaries can be used to study power and arenas of power struggles. There is no reason why the analysis in this chapter could not be used to analyze intraorganizational boundaries. Intraorganizational boundaries always invite process maladaptations which create opportunities to manage a set of boundaries to the advantage of a subunit. Virtual positions (cf. Chapter 6) are opportunities to change interdepartmental boundaries.

Organizational design is very helpful in establishing an organization's control over its boundaries. The organizational design can be used to decrease its dependency on, or vulnerability to, another and to limit the other's leverage on it. By identifying and eliminating excess interdependencies within the organization, the organizational design defines, limits, and can prevent conflicts due to intraorganizational boundaries.

CHAPTER 8

Organizational interdependence

INTRODUCTION

The concept of a system is built about the primitive concept of interdependence. Organization theorists recognize that there is something called interdependence in every organization. We now understand that, in some way, every organization not only has interdependencies within but also has some interdependencies with its environments. We realize that even these interdependencies are somehow interdependent. Organizational design can be viewed as a process for rearranging all of these organizational interdependencies. We lack a clear understanding of the meaning of the word "interdependence." We must be more precise if we are to design organizations.

There are different kinds of interdependence. There are interdependencies among the task processes. There are interdependencies among the task process resources characteristics. There are interdependencies among task processes and their resources characteristics. There are interdependencies among the positions in an organization. These interpositional interdependencies are linked to the task processes and task process resources characteristics interdependencies. There are interdependencies between an organization's task processes and resources characteristics and the environment. And there are the interdependencies, represented by the organizational congruency conditions, which affect all those already mentioned. For example, the goals and strategies of an organization are interdependent.

The purpose of this chapter is to shed some light on the concept of interdependence, types of interdependence, and how interdependence can be used to analyze organizational design problems. This chapter begins with a discussion of task process interdependence. Then it incorporates task process resources characteristics, and discusses their interdependencies. Next, the idea of "in-commoness" is introduced to bind three types of interdependencies (task process, task process resources characteristics, and positions). This discussion is called "intraorganizational interdependence." The next section examines environmental interdependence and binds organizational boundaries to the intraorganizational interdependencies. Then, interdependency is linked with organizational congruencies. This is followed by a discussion of a generalization of organizational forms called Data Base Organizations. The final section is a summary of numerous design principles that derive from these ideas.

Organizational interdependencies are necessary. However, there are often too many. The main problem with most organizations is too much organizational interdependence. For example, all process and structural maladaptations are additional interdependencies. Many of these are established to bind the personnel task processes by creating interdependencies that seem necessary in spite of the official organization. In fact, many of the interdependencies established by the Organizational Architecture are obsolete and maladaptive. The main reasons for analyzing organizational interdependencies are to determine which are necessary, to organize them so that they mesh, and to *eliminate excess interdependencies*. There is a proper level of interdependency that is necessary if the organization is to operate in a manner consistent with obtaining its goals. Excess interdependencies create waste and confusion, inhibit initiative, and generate political disputes. The best design defines and organizes the necessary organizational interdependencies while eliminating the excess.

Consequently, the idea that organization interdependency is necessary and good needs to be substantially modified. Instead of arguing that more interdependency is good, the argument becomes that the organizational design must both incorporate necessary organizational interdependencies and reduce those that are unnecessary. Thus, an organizational designer seeks to establish the minimum level of interdependencies over and above those that are necessary. In short, a good organizational design must recognize and encourage the necessary interdependencies to operate as simply as is technically possible. Much of the work of an organizational designer is concerned with clearing away these excesses. The idea of "keeping it simple and straightforward" (KISS) is the goal. An organizational designer seeks to identify and eliminate unnecessary complexity whenever possible. The idea is to free personnel to get their jobs done. Removing those unnecessary impediments and roadblocks in the paths of members which prevent them from doing their jobs is a sure way to improve their productivity.

TASK PROCESS INTERDEPENDENCE

No discussion of task process interdependence should fail to recognize the seminal writings of the late J.D. Thompson (1967) on this subject. His writings were based on long years of introspection about the nature of interdependence in the organization's task processes and how they might translate into guidelines for organizational design. Thompson's ideas of sequential, mutual, and pooled interdependence are historically important. In this section, building upon the description of task processes in Chapter 4, I shall develop a sequence of definitions and conclusions that allow sharpening of these concepts of organizational interdependency. The purpose is to make them usable for organizational design.

The concept of a task process introduced in Chapter 4 included five elements. These were: (a) the entities involved, (b) the elements or subtask processes, (c) the relationships among them, (d) the links to other task processes, and (e) the task process resources characteristics. As this chapter develops, each of these elements is built upon (b) and (c) by adding additional information until achieving organizational interdependence. In order to begin this development, I first use only the set of elements or subtask processes and the relationships among them. I want to begin with the most basic elements before extending the analysis.

Let T_i and T_j be two task processes belonging to a set of task processes, **T.** T_i is the *immediate predecessor* and T_j is the *immediate successor* if the outputs of T_i are inputs to T_j or if T_i immediately precedes T_j. The immediate predecessor–successor task process pair T_i and T_j is designated by $T_i \xrightarrow{1} T_j$. A *task process chain* has two or more task processes in **T** such that:

(a)   each task process is either an immediate successor or predecessor, and

(b)   none has more than one immediate successor or immediate predecessor.

The *length* of a task process chain is the number of immediate predecessor–successor pairs in the chain. Each intermediate predecessor–successor pair in a chain is called a *link*. The last immediate successor in a task process chain is called the *terminal task process*. A task process chain of length k is designated by $T_i \xrightarrow{k} T_j$, where T_i is the first predecessor and T_j is the terminal task process.

Two task processes are said to be in *parallel* if there exists a common predecessor to both and neither is the immediate predecessor to the other. If T_i and T_j are in parallel, we designate this by $T_i \| T_j$.

The number of different link relationships is summarized in Axiom 1, which states:

Axiom 1: For any T_i, $T_j \in$ **T,** there are exactly three possible link relationships:

(a) $T_i \xrightarrow{1} T_j$

(b) $T_j \xrightarrow{1} T_i$

(c) $T_i \| T_j$ or T_i and T_j are part of the same task process chain

An immediate result of these definitions and Axiom 1 is the following conclusion: There exists a single common predecessor task process $T^* \in$ **T.**

As we have seen in Chapter 4, the task processes of an organization have a structure called the Organizational Logic. The diagram of the structure of any constituent task process is called a *task process graph*. The *structure of a task process*, designated by S (T) = (T;L), where L = (l_{ij}), where

$$l_{ij} = \begin{cases} 1 \text{ if } T_i \xrightarrow{1} T_j \text{ and } i \neq j \\ 0 \text{ if } T_j \xrightarrow{1} T_i \text{ or if } T_i \parallel T_j. \end{cases}$$

The task process graph of T, designated by G(T), is the graph of S(T).

Two task processes are said to be *directly task process interdependent* if there is a link between them. Two *sets* of task processes are said to be *task process interdependent* if there are common task processes. Note that specific task processes belonging to a set of task processes (e.g., the modules of a task process bundle) are written with a subscript such as T_i or T_j. If there are sets of task processes under discussion, the sets are written with superscripts such as T^i and T^j.

Let T^I and T^{II} be two sets of task processes. T^I *and* T^{II} *are task process interdependent* if the intersection, $T^I \cap T^{II}$, is nonempty. For example, let T_1, T_2, T_3, T_4 be the task processes in a bundle, shown in Figure 8.1. T_1 is the DCC task process and T_2, T_3, T_4 are execution task processes for this bundle. Let T^I = (T_1, T_2, T_3, T_4) and T^{II} = (T_2, T_3, T_4). Then T^I and T^{II} are process interdependent, because $T^I \cap T^{II}$ = (T_2, T_3, T_4) Note that T_1 is the immediate predecessor of T_2, T_3, T_4, and that it is T_1 that creates the interdependence. Also note that $T_2 \parallel T_3$, $T_2 \parallel T_4$, and $T_3 \parallel T_4$ and $T_1 \xrightarrow{1} T_2$, $T_1 \xrightarrow{1} T_3$, and $T_1 \xrightarrow{1} T_4$.

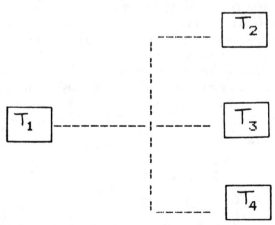

Figure 8.1. Simple example of task process interdependence.

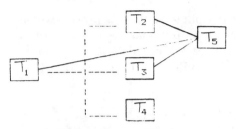

Figure 8.2. A process maladaptation created by T_5.

T^1 and T^{11} are said to be *task process independent* if $T^1 \cap T^{11} = \emptyset$. In Figure 8.1, T_2, T_3, and T_4 are task process independent.

The set of all task processes contained in the Organizational Logic or any part of it can be described by the structure of the task processes. For some purposes it is convenient to describe the set of all successors to a given task process and to count the number of them. To do this, the concepts of the range and reach of a task process must be introduced. The *range* of a task process, T_j, is the set of task processes in chains from T_j and includes T_j. The *reach* of T_j is the number of links plus one in the range of T. For example, in Figure 8.1, the range of T_1 is (T_1, T_2, T_3, and T_4) and the reach of T_1 is 4. If one has an Organizational Logic or if the graph of T is a hierarchy, then the reach of T is the number of task processes contained in the range of T.

A *process maladaptation* is any link or set of links that is not in a hierarchy of task processes. Process maladaptations increase task process interdependence. Figure 8.2 illustrates a process maladaptation.

For Figure 8.2, the range of T_1 is (T_1, T_2, T_3, T_4, T_5). The reach of T_1 is 7. If the links $T_2 \xrightarrow{1} T_5$ or $T_3 \xrightarrow{1} T_5$ were eliminated, the range would remain the same but the reach would become 5. The existence of a process maladaptation is a set, T^1, of task processes which is interdependent with another set of task processes, T^{11} and can compound the excess interdependencies as shown in Figure 8.3.

In the absence of T_5, the immediate predecessor of T_6 would have been T_2 and the immediate predecessor of T_9 would have been T_3. But the insertion of T_5 raises the reach of T_1 from 10 to 14. A rearrangement of the task

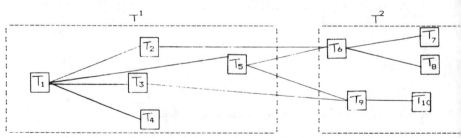

Figure 8.3. Process maladaptations created by T_5 in a compound task process.

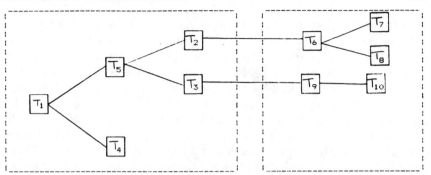

Figure 8.4.   An illustration of the impact of the rearrangement of a maladaptation task process.

process graph of T_1, shown in Figure 8.4, which makes T_5 the immediate predecessor of T_2 and T_3, reduces the reach of T_1 from 14 to 10.

There is another axiom that should be mentioned. *Axiom 2* states that any task process graph can be divided into hierarchial and maladaptative subgraphs. For example, the graph in Figure 8.3 is the combination (graphic summation, cf. Mackenzie, 1967) of the hierarchical graph of Figure 8.4 and the maladaptive graph shown in Figure 8.5.

The graph of Figure 8.4 is certainly simpler and less confusing than that of Figure 8.3. The simple reorganization of the work shown in Figure 8.4 cuts out four unnecessary links. The resulting task process could be easier to administer. Figure 8.5 illustrates another Axiom. *Axiom 3* states that any maladaptive subgraph can be written as a combination (graphic summation) of a set of hierarchical subgraphs with a common predecessor task process. Both range and reach of any task process graph is equal to the range and reach of its common predecessor task process. The range of any task process graph is the union of the range of the hierarchical and the maladaptive graphs. The reach of a task process graph with a hierarchical subgraph, G_1, and maladaptive subgraph, G_2, is the reach of G_1 plus the reach of the graph formed by the symmetric difference of G_1 and G_2. Thus, in Figure 8.3, the reach of T_1 is the reach of T_1 in Figure 8.4, which is 10, plus the reach of the task process graph in Figure 8.5, which is 4.

Figure 8.5.   The maladaptive graph to Figure 8.3 after reorganizing it as shown in Figure 8.4.

With these definitions, it is now possible to examine types of task process interdependence. Task processes T_i and $T_j \in \mathbf{T}$ are *immediately sequentially interdependent* if $T_i \xrightarrow{1} T_j$. Furthermore, the range of the graph of T_i includes the range of the graph of T_j. If T_i and T_j are immediately sequentially interdependent, they are a link. Task processes $T_1, T_2, \ldots, T_{k+1} \in \mathbf{T}$ form a *sequentially interdependent chain of k links*, designated by $T_1 \xrightarrow{k} T_{k+1}$ if: (a) each link in the chain is immediately sequentially interdependent, and (b) T_1 is the common predecessor for $T_2, T_3, \ldots, T_{k+1}$. Sequentially interdependent chains of k and k^1 links can be combined directly into a chain of $k + k^1$ links, provided that the last task process in the first chain is the immediate predecessor of the first task process in the second chain.

In an Organizational Logic there is a sequentially interdependent chain connecting every task process to the prime common predecessor task process. The *prime predecessor task process* in an Organizational Logic is that task process having no immediate predecessor. It is the T^* from Axiom 1. Note that an Organizational Logic is a concatenation of a hierarchy of sequentially interdependent chains. In this way, one can extend the simple idea of a sequential interdependence to the entire Organizational Logic.

Another type of task process interdependence is a pooling task process. Task process T_i is a *pooling task process* for $\mathbf{T}^1$ and $\mathbf{T}^{11} \in \mathbf{T}$ if: (a) $T_i \xrightarrow{k} \mathbf{T}^1, k > 1$, (b) $T_i \xrightarrow{m} \mathbf{T}^{11}, m \geq 1$, and (c) $\mathbf{T}^1 \cap \mathbf{T}^{11} = \emptyset$. A pooling task process is the common predecessor of two or more sequentially interdependent chains. Directing, controlling, and coordinating task processes are seen as pooling task processes. Many organizational staff task processes, such as Human Resources at the corporate level, are pooling task processes for related task processes at a lower division level. This pooling does not create process maladaptation if the pooling task processes have immediate predecessors and successors that pass through the positions in the chain of command. But, when the staff persons intervene directly, these interventions create a new type of interdependence.

Task processes $T_i \in \mathbf{T}^1$ and $T_j \in \mathbf{T}^{11}$ are said to be *osculated task processes*, designated by $T_i <\!-\!-\!-\!> T_j$, if: for $i \neq j$ (a) $T_i \cap T_j \neq \emptyset$ and (b) $\mathbf{T}^1 \cap \mathbf{T}^{11} = T_i \cup T_j$, (c) the range of T_i is not a proper subset of the range of T_j, and vice versa. Let $\bar{T} = T_i \cap T_j$. Then, $\bar{T}$ is the *osculating* task process causing the process osculation between T_i and T_j. Very often, staff groups as they gain power over line organizations create osculating task processes whose range and reach can be extensive. Many governmental regulations, such as those created for special interests groups (e.g., EPA, OSHA, FEPC), create osculating task processes which tend to inhibit operations, raise costs, and create more staff positions.

A pooling task process, T_p, for $\mathbf{T}^1$ and $\mathbf{T}^{11}$, is *correctly* placed if T_p is a common predecessor of $\mathbf{T}^1$ and $\mathbf{T}^{11}$. All osculating task processes are incorrectly placed. Every osculating task process creates extra interdependence.

TASK PROCESS RESOURCES INTERDEPENDENCE

The idea of task process resources characteristics was introduced in Chapter 4. There are eight identified TPRCs that are considered vital: location, personnel, technology, timing, knowledge, information, contingent others, and continuity of the direction, control, and coordination of the organization's task processes. Every task process that is performed requires resources. All of the task proceses at the execution level have predecessor task processes at the DCC or planning process law level to help allocate and regulate these resource flows.

For each TPRC there is a hierarchy. For example, the organizational chart is the hierarchy for personnel. A hierarchy for the TPRC of knowledge is described in Chapter 11. The use of room assignments and territories creates a hierarchy of location. The decisions about the use of technology form a hierarchy. The timing of the execution of task processes has a hierarchy formally embodied in a schedule of sequential task processes. An incompetent supervisor breaks the hierarchy of some of the TPRCs. Shared use of capital equipment without an agreement on allocation creates a violation of the hierarchy of its TPRC. When different units of an organization deal with the same vendors and customers, the TPRC of contingent others is broken. These violations of the hierarchy of the TPRCs create interdependencies among both the task processes and the positions. The result is always excess interdependencies. When the task processes, the TPRC, and the personnel form mutually congruent hierarchies, the magnitude of excess interdependencies is minimized.

This mutual congruence does not occur by accident. It comes about by decision. It is the job of management to effect this mutual congruence. The problems of management become greatly magnified whenever management must attempt to manage an organization riddled with excessive interdependencies.

Directing, controlling, and coordinating (DCC) task processes provide an integration of the execution task process level of aggregation above that of a module. If the execution task processes were shown as red blocks, the DCC task processes as green boxes, and planning task processes as blue blocks, an Organizational Logic will appear as a large set of red blocks, connected by green boxes which in turn are connected by blue blocks. The hierarchy of DCC and planning task processes regulates the interdependence and the execution task processes. They function much as the nervous system does to connect the muscles. In the language of the previous section, the integration of execution task processes is accomplished by creating common predecessor DCC task processes. The integration of DCC task processes is done by common predecessor DCC or planning task processes.

A key concept in a task process description of management is the notion of in-common task processes. Task processes T^1 and T^{11} are said to be *in-common* if they:

a. share the same task process resources characteristics
b. are on the same task process level, and
c. have a common predecessor, integrating task process (Usually DCC or planning task process level task processes).

Task processes T^1 and T^{11} are *compatible* whenever (a) one is the immediate predecessor of the other, or (b) they are in parallel and have a common predecessor task process not more than two levels higher. Two interdependent task processes are considered *maladaptive* if they are incompatible. Any two task processes are either compatible or maladaptive. Two task processes are *separable* if:

a. they are not in-common
b. one is not the immediate predecessor of the other, and
c. they are in parallel

Separable task processes are *integrable* if they share a common immediate predecessor *and* are compatible. Some task processes are integrable but are not in-common. Such processes are *directly integrable* if (a) there exists an integrating task process at the same level that creates in-commonness, or (b) one could be developed. An *integrating task process* is one that creates an in-common set of task processes.

The job of managers is to create in-commonness among the organization's task processes. This can be done by creating DCC and planning task processes that allow integration. Managers must cope with process maladaptations and especially nonhierarchical task processes, Duplicating and overlapping TPRCs, force excessive interdependencies. Understanding these maladaptations is an essential step that needs to be taken before attempting to perform an organizational design. As we shall see in Chapter 9, the Organizational Audit and Analysis technology has a sequence of stages to accomplish this. In every case that I have been involved with, the process maladaptations, once identified, spotlight management problems in organizations. If *management* is defined as the processes to manage organizational interdependence and to find, remove, and prevent process maladaptations in the presence of changing conditions, then this definition can be used, along with the concepts introduced in this chapter, to detect and diagnose management problems. The result of the task-process-oriented view of the organization is to operationalize the concept of management in such a way that it can be used for organizational design.

Position interdependence is created by task process and task process resources interdependence. Let x_1 and x_2 represent two organizational positions performing task processes T^1 and T^2, respectively. Positions x_1 and x_2 are said to be *position interdependent* if either (a) T^1 and T^2 are interdependent, or (b) the TPRCs of x_1 and x_2 are interdependent. Usually, if the task processes are interdependent, so are the task process resources characteristics. Figure 8.6 summarizes these ideas. *Intraorganizational interdependencies* consist of task process interdependencies, TPRC interdependencies, and position interdependencies. Figure 8.6 shows how each type affects the other. These interdependencies are interdependent.

It is the role of DCC and planning task processes to integrate these three types of intraorganizational interdependence. These integrating task processes are necessary because of both environmental and intraorganizational change. Most organizations are a mess because they have allowed authority-task gaps to become opened up by a failure to adapt management to change. The result is excessive intraorganizational interdependence whose resolution is the task of organizational design.

ENVIRONMENTAL INTERDEPENDENCE

The ABCE model of Chapter 1, and its elaboration in Chapter 6, illustrates how an organization is embedded in a larger set of environments. The changes in these environments change intraorganizational interdependencies. The impacts of the environments on the intraorganizational interdepenencies can be traced via the ABCE model.

The environments affect the goals, strategies, design premises, and results directly. Changes in the Organizational Logic and Organizational Architecture through the change in boundary task processes also impact. *Environmental interdependence* is the combination of interdependencies of the organization's task processes, TPRCs, and positions created and affected by the organization's environments.

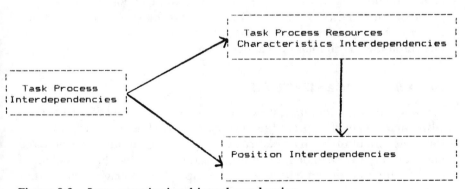

Figure 8.6.   Intra-organizational interdependencies.

The environmental interdependencies can be direct, depending upon their impact on the task processes interdependence or indirect as the impacts are filtered through a succession of changes in goals, strategies, design premises, Organizational Logic, Organizational Architecture, the Actual Organization, and the results. The environmental interdependencies can be managed by selecting and adapting task processes which allow intraorganizational interdependencies affected by the environment to be more in common.

The best way of managing environmental interdependencies is to first reduce the intraorganizational interdependencies and then to seek organizational congruence. Recalling the 11 organizational congruency conditions introduced in Chapter 6, this means achieving congruence in all conditions. For example, if the goals of an organization are incongruent with the environment, then the pressure from the environment will cause a succession of process maladaptations by increasing the intraorganizational interdependencies. The ABCE Model is a convenient way of tracing the impacts as they affect A, then B, and then C. As intraorganizational interdependencies are in B, the cycling of A$\longrightarrow$B$\longrightarrow$C$\longrightarrow$A$\longrightarrow$B$\longrightarrow$C can create waves of changes in the interdependencies when the goals and the environment are incongruent with each other. This cascading of cause and effect is cyclic, and the failure to manage the intraorganizational interdependencies due to environmental shifts can open up authority-task gaps and accelerate the creation of excessive intraorganizational interdependencies.

The Organizational Audit and Analysis technology for organizational design described in Chapters 9 to 12 is built upon the need to continually manage both environmental and intraorganizational interdependencies in the face of change. It is deliberate that the assessment of the organization's environments, its goals, and strategies is a factor of every stage of the OA&A technology. The idea is to assist management in controlling its intraorganizational interdependencies, even though it may have little control over its environments. It is also deliberate that the OA&A technology places a premium on the capacity of the organization to peform organizational maintenance. Organizational maintenance is a process of adapting the Organizational Technology to change.

DATA BASE ORGANIZATIONS

The scope of organizational interdependencies creates the need to continually manage them. The preceding sections described the interdependencies for firms with mostly stable task processes. Many organizations are new and many are rapidly changing. Such organizations have the dual problem of creating the interdependencies while attempting to manage them as they cope with change.

Consider a new company. As a new company starts up, its problems are staggering. Simple task processes, such as getting out a letter, are complex. For example, the company has to select its name, address, colors, design its logo, obtain stationery, business cards, sales brochures, etc. It must acquire capacity for producing and mailing the letter. To do that it may need to have a secretary and equipment. But to do that it needs to think about its salary system and about minimal personnel policies. Contrast this to a mature company. It has already solved these problems and it may already have the text of the letter stored on its word processor. The decision to send a letter may involve little more than a simple request to a competent assistant.

Every organization must adapt itself to changes in its environments. Managers control only a subset of the situation they must manage. Changes in regulations, technology, competition, and the economy are examples of environmental effects for which managers must adapt their organizations. Every organization has some control of its environments. But none has complete control. Organizations vary in the degree to which they control variations in their relevant environments.

Task processes vary in two basic dimensions with respect to change in a given time period. The first is stability and the second is regularity. *Task process stability* is defined as the percentage of all task processes that remain unchanged. New task processes, old task processes that are dropped and current task processes that are altered, decrease task process stability. *Task process regularity* is defined as the percentage of the time each task process is performed. Figure 8.7 illustrates the task process stability and regularity map.

Traditional management theory operates in the region of high stability and high regularity. This makes the management of interdependencies relatively routine and allows formalization. Many organizations, however, do not have this luxury. And to make matters worse, most texts on management have little to say about how to manage when the task processes are both unstable and irregular. Recently, Ellis (1984) has written a book to address such issues. All organizations can be viewed as operating somewhere between the two extremes of high stability and high regularity and instability and irregularity.

But all must manage, and this means managing the interdependencies to achieve the goals in the presence of change. All organizations must combine task processes, personnel, and resources. Each is analogous to a data base which allows management of these interdependencies. They differ primarily in the stability and regularity of their task processes. Hence, they differ in how they manage recombinations of task processes, personnel, and resources. Greater stability and regularity favor bureaucracies. Instability and irregularity require novel management which must act to continually

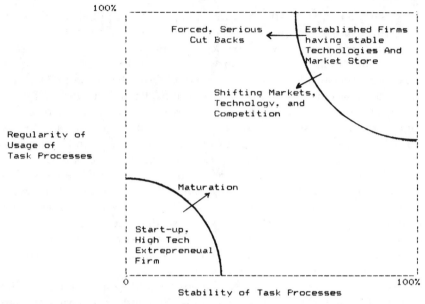

Figure 8.7.   Propositions on to distribution of task process levels and organizational stability.

recombine its task process, personnel, and resources much as a data base information system recombines its data.

A *data base organization* (DBO) is an organization that allows flexible recombinations of task processes, personnel, and task process resources in order to achieve the goals in the face of continual change. DBOs represent a general class of organizational forms based upon the stability and regularity of the task processes rather than features of the Organizational Architecture. There are many subclasses of DBOs, depending upon the stability, regularity, and type of management. One extreme case of a subclass of DBOs is the classic bureaucracy. Bureaucracies operate in the highly stable and regular part of Figure 8.7 and have hierarchical management processes. A matrix organization is a middle class in which stable and regular task processes are recombined by temporary direction, control, and coordinating mechanisms. A new start up organization (such as a new high tech firm) operates at the other extreme of stability, regularity, and systems of management. Some organizations, such as hospitals and research-centered universities, operate parallel organizations consisting of a stable, regular DBO for routine administration, an unstable, irregular DBO for basic research, and an intermediate class of DBOs for reconciling the two systems. Other organizations create combinations of DBOs to isolate the unstable and irregular from the more stable and regular. New product development teams, for example, are often allowed to form outside the bureaucratic DBO.

My organizational design work has uncovered many examples where the existing organizational form is the inappropriate type of DBO for current market conditions. This is especially true in community bank organizations, which typically have muddled through the wave of deregulations and technological changes by band aid, ad hoc adaptations of an old bureaucratic DBO. Such organizations need to acknowledge that chance circumstances have rendered the old DBO form obsolete and ineffective. Otherwise, the result is a growing inability to act.

Environmental changes and internal changes can be analyzed with respect to their impact on stability and regularity. One should expect that, everything being equal, the following propositions should hold:

1. All organizations, over time, tend toward greater stability and regularity.
2. The more a market is purely competitive, the more a firm loses stability over time.
3. Entrepreneurial, start up, and new high tech firms are relatively unstable and have many irregular task processes.
4. Forced cut backs in an organization decreases stability.
5. Environmental changes are more destablizing than internal changes.
6. Very stable firms require low stability units to react to and plan for the adoption of change.
7. Once a change has been defined and rationalized with respect to existing task processes, a stable firm is more likely to adopt and implement a change.

The Organizational Audit and Analysis technology has been used for firms whose task processes were relatively stable and regular. Recent work with a high tech start up has forced the OA&A technology to think through modifications in the OA&A technology. Such firms are different.

The distribution of task processes differs on both the task process level and in regularity and stability. Such firms have relatively more planning processes and fewer execution processes than do more stable firms. They have relatively fewer regular task processes and more infrequent and future task processes. They have to be taught about the calendar task processes. These firms are learning about processes they need and they are learning how to do them. Many of the personnel that are hired at the earliest stage will not be able to operate effectively as the company grows and matures. For example, it takes a series of stages to go from a part time bookkeeper to having a treasurer or controller. Making a few prototypes is not the same as manufacturing larger production runs. Early sales promotions are not the same as a carefully planned marketing program. Even the CEO may become a problem, because, although he has a good concept for the business, he may not necessarily be a competent manager.

These firms continually rearrange the interdependencies of the task processes, task process resources, personnel, and those involving the environment. These changes are usually ad hoc and are done more or less on a crash basis. As the firm operates, it begins to understand what it should do, how to do it, and how to begin managing its interdependencies. Many appear chaotic and confused. Most that appear this way are, in fact, chaotic and confused. Some like it that way.

One distinct characteristic is highlighted when an organizational designer sits down with the CEO to attempt to draw up an organizational chart. These firms usually don't have one because, for the most part, organizational charts are obsolete the day they are drawn. Furthermore, as we saw in Chapter 5, organizational charts are not accurate reflections of how an organization is actually run. At the earliest stages, about the only clear position is that of the CEO, who thinks in terms of individuals rather than positions. The sketched organizational chart usually is a hierarchy of boxes with names in them. The CEO is not sure what each person is supposed to do. The CEO, in many cases, would be hard pressed to describe what he or she does over a given period of time. The fluidity of the organizational interdependencies makes it very difficult to describe either the Organizational Logic or the Organizational Architecture. Operating in the area of low stability and low regularity, the CEO acts as a tactician who is continually redeploying the organization's assets. The CEO is not going to slow down and spend much time worrying about its past and the niceties of carefully constructed Organizational Logic or Architectures.

I have observed CEOs answering the telephones, emptying waste paper baskets, picking up the mail, fixing office machinery, organizing picnics, making sales calls, offering advice on design, writing checks, poring over advertising copy, programming computers, and performing routine personnel functions. The CEO will do what he or she believes needs to be done. This bias for action sets the tone for an organization, but it can also confuse the rest of the personnel.

But if one works with the CEO to think through a coherent strategy for growth and development, it quickly becomes clear that he or she has in mind many future task processes. An Organizational Logic can be developed at least to the bundle level of what the organization should be doing at the end of the first few years. A financial plan can be developed based on many key assumptions that allow one to verify feasibility. The use of spreadsheet software and specific product planning and analysis allows flexibility in thinking through the future. The assumptions and the relationships among the assumptions are more important than the actual figures for costs and profits. There really is not much value in very carefully constructed business plans, because of the wide range of unverified assumptions and the low quality of the information used. Nevertheless, a quick and dirty analysis usually is sufficient to verify feasibility.

What the CEO really needs is a way of examining changes that might occur if the assumptions or the information are changed. This type of plan is very valuable even if the plans are not very accurate.

Once the organizational designer and the CEO have reached a stable feasible strategic plan, the Organizational Logic can be specified for the future. Working backwards from it, one can describe more accurately the current Organizational Logic. Thus, the CEO can compare where he or she is with where he or she wants to go in the future. This guides the CEO's ability to create and manage the interdependencies.

Grouping the task processes around positions for the future leads to an ORG chart and an organizational chart. This helps define the ORG chart and the organizational chart for the current situation. When one does this, the current organizational chart looks very strange. First, some persons occupy more than one position. In one case, the CEO was also the director of R&D, the treasurer, and the field salesman. In another, the CEO was also a publisher, a R&D director, an editor, and the director of marketing. As we shall describe it in Chapter 10, many persons wear "multiple hats." The second characteristic is that many positions reflect organizational units that become activated when an infrequent or future task process is employed. If such positions are represented by dotted line boxes and the more regular task process positions are represented by solid line boxes, the resulting organizational chart is a mixture of solid line and dotted line boxes. The multiple positions almost always involve multiple hat positions.

A metaphor of Christmas tree lights is helpful here. The regular task process positions resemble those lights that don't blink. The dotted line task process positions resemble those that flash off and on. The infrequent task processes positions blink. The future task processes are like a string of lights that are not yet plugged in. An organization of 20 people can have 50 positions if it is operating in the low stability and low regularity area of Figure 8.7.

A third characteristic is that many organizational units resemble cadres about which the organization will expand as business improves. For example, one firm had a Sales Department that handled mail order business. It consisted of a supervisor and a clerk. As business grows, there will be more clerks and the roles of the clerks will become more differentiated. At a low sales volume, the clerk handles mail and telephone inquiries, does order processing, keeps some books, maintains inventory records, and does the shipping and receiving. But each of these task processes takes time and, as the sales volume grows, the present clerk will not have enough time available to get the task processes completed. So more personnel will be added. The new clerks begin to specialize—there may be a shipping/receiving clerk. The old clerk may become a supervisor of other clerks. And, as business continues to grow, the old supervisor may need several supervisors for different bundles and modules of these task processes. Thus, the old supervisor becomes a manager with several supervisors, each of whom supervises a group of clerks. Thus, the cadre becomes a base for expansion.

A fourth characteristic is the lack of management controls. Everybody pitches in and there are very few controls. Thus the DCC (directing, controlling and coordinating) task processes are poorly defined. As the organization grows and articulates its task processes and organizational architecture, the need for specifying the DCC task processes becomes clearer and clearer. For example, the original clerk who is now supervising five clerks is forced to think about how to organize their work and how this work should be coordinated with the others. The manager must begin to think about manpower planning, facilities, and personnel policies.

Task processes can be grouped into organizational plays, and the selection of the plays is the basis for the Organizational Game Plan. (These types are discussed in some detail in Chapter 10.) The main difference between organization in the unstable and irregular part of Figure 8.7 and those in the stable and regular part is the consistency by which the organizational plays are included in the game plan. For example, in a highly regulated public utility using an old technology in a stable population area, there is not much need to call plays, because almost all plays are regular and almost every position is normal. At the other extreme, the plays change daily as the organization lurches from crisis to crisis. The use of Organizational Playbooks and Game Plans provides a convenient way of directing traffic among the multiple hat positions and the interdependencies.

All organizations are DBOs. They differ primarily in how frequently and to what extent they actively rearrange the interdependencies. The pressure to convert infrequent and future task processes into regular task processes is very strong, as is the pressure to convert multiple hat into normal positions. But, when organizations become stable and regular, it is very difficult to regain the old flexibility. Many organizations I have worked with have factored the task processes and organizational units in order to separate the newer or more rapidly changing parts from the older more stable and regular parts. Thus, the same organization can have units of varying degrees of stability and regularity operating simultaneously and in parallel.

The use of Organizational Logics provides a convenient way of tracking and cumulating information about the task processes. This work generates an organizational memory that helps protect the DBO from the impact of employee turnover and helps it plan its growth.

ORGANIZATIONAL DESIGN GUIDELINES

It is tempting to enunciate decision rules such as "group contiguous task processes contiguously" or "create DCC task processes to manage sequential interdependencies." The list of possible rules and their exceptions would be extremely lengthy. Given the complexities of intraorganizational and environmental interdependencies and the interdependencies between them, the list would grow and grow. Creating such a general list would be impractical because of its length.

Instead of prescribing long lists of rules, it is more useful to describe a process for designing an organization in order to reduce its excess interdependencies. This is shorter and more powerful to use. There are three levels of guidelines to the process of designing the organizational interdependencies, which correspond roughly to the first three stages of the OA&A design technology (cf. Chapter 9). These three levels are:

1. Determine organizational congruency
2. Determine how the organization actually operates
3. Reconcile the actual organization by reducing excess organizational interdependencies by means of organizational design.

Many might argue that all one needs is (3). That is naive because: (1) one needs to know where the organizational interdependency problems are before reconciling them; (2) one needs to know where to start looking on a systematic basis; and (3) the interdependencies are interdependent, and one must be sure that solutions don't create more organizational interdependency problems.

The 11 organizational congruency conditions are first checked in Stage One (the Strategic Assessment); then they are rechecked in Stage Two (the Organizational Audit); and then rechecked again and again in every stage of the Organizational Audit and Analysis technology. The presence of organizational incongruency always signals the existence of excess or inappropriate organizational interdependencies. Checking and rechecking organizational incongruity allows one to focus in on where to begin looking when analyzing organizational interdependencies. Consequently, the first level of guidelines for this task is to determine organizational congruency.

The next level is to verify how the organization actually works by means of an Organizational Audit. This not only allows confirmation of the judgment for each organizational congruency condition, it also is the start of an analysis and documentation of the organization's task processes. This allows the task processes to be described and the task process interdependencies to be defined and verified. The task process interdependencies affect and are affected by the task process resource characteristics (TPRC). The interdependencies among the task processes and the TPRC taken independently usually give a good picture of the interdependencies between them. Then one reexamines the environmental interdependencies that the organization has with the task processes and the TPRC. This sets up another round to analyze and reconcile the interdependencies of the environment with the task processes (via boundaries) and TPRC (via resource flows). The result is more consistent and has fewer interdependencies between the task processes and the TPRC. These analyses allow one to understand the organizational interdependencies built into the existing Organizational Logic.

The next step is to examine how these task processes are assigned, directed, controlled, coordinated, and planned by the various organizational positions. The construction of an Organizational Responsibility Grouping chart (ORG chart) allows one to quickly spot all virtual positions and authority task gaps (cf. Chapter 6). This analysis pinpoints many of the excess organizational interdependencies.

The third level of analysis and reconciliation of the organizational interdependencies is the work done in Stage Three of the OA&A technology, which is to design the organization to reduce excess organizational interdependencies. This is done by reexamining the elements of the ABCE Model (cf. Figure 6.5) and looking for organizationally congruent solutions. Normally, the best approach is to develop an Organizational Blueprint (a prototype organizational design) that is both organizationally congruent and minimizes the total organizational interdependence. Almost always, the blueprints must be modified because of the interdependencies and commitments made to key personnel. The adjusting of an Organizational Blueprint to a working organizational design usually means designing in some excess organizational interdependencies. The main issue then becomes one of "trading off" possible excess organizational interdependency with the political reality which the CEO must recognize. Almost always, the more one has done the three levels of analysis first, the more the CEO can rationalize these practical adjustments. At the very least, it raises the issues of what changes must be made and provides a method of working them through in order to achieve a working organizational design.

This process of thinking through the problems of organizational interdependence is, in my opinion, more practical than a list of specific maxims. The best guidelines are to follow a process of identifying, documenting, and then reconciling the issues of organizational interdependence.

PART 3

The organizational audit
and
analysis technology

CHAPTER 9

Introduction to
the organizational audit and analysis technology

INTRODUCTION

The attempts to evolve a laboratory-based theory of group structure into a working field technology for designing organizations have continued without pause since August, 1976. Over the years, the laboratory-based theory has proven inadequate in many ways for organizational design. The research strategy described in Chapter 2 has proven very helpful in guiding these developments. The description of the Organizational Audit and Analysis technology in this chapter and those to follow is like a small oak tree compared to the acorn of the laboratory theory.

The development of this organizational design technology never stops. One is frequently reminded of the need for further development. This book should be seen as an intermediate report on the state of this technology as of 1984. More real-world adventures will continue to create needs for further development, and these, in turn, to improved theory. One must keep in mind that the real purpose of the organizational design work is the development of a general theory of organizational behavior.

Some of the basic ideas of this theory were presented in Chapters 4 through 8. The practical experience in designing companies lead to the 13 desiderata of Chapter 2. This chapter is a survey of the Organizational Audit and Analysis technology up to the end of 1984. Chapters 10 through 12 employ an example from the application of the Organization Audit and Analysis technology to the design for a supermarket chain. These chapters provide detail about the Organization Audit and Analysis technology in the context of an actual application. Every stage and step described in this chapter has been used in the field. The purpose is to present the Organizational Audit and Analysis technology in order that others might, by bringing to bear different perspectives, see ways of improving both the theory and the Organizational Audit and Analysis technology.

The reader should bear in mind that the Organizational Audit and Analysis technology is based on a scientific theory. It is a part of the development of a process-based theory of the firm. The evolving OA&A technology has been developed by applying it to the design of many types of organizations.

Each engagement has led to the evolution of both the basic process-based theory of organizations and the Organizational Audit and Analysis technology.

This chapter begins with an overview of the OA&A technology. This is followed by a description of how one conducts the process of an organizational design from the initial strategic assessment to the monitoring of the implementation. The chapter ends with a brief description of the later stages of the OA&A technology.

OVERVIEW OF THE ORGANIZATIONAL AUDIT AND ANALYSIS TECHNOLOGY FOR ORGANIZATIONAL DESIGN

Main features

There are currently nine major stages in the Organizational Audit and Analysis technology. Three of these stages have supplementary technologies, and two of them remain relatively untested. The creation of the stages flows from the 13 desiderata described in Chapter 2. These stages and steps are described in general terms in this chapter. Table 9.1 lists the stages and supplementary services in the OA&A technology. The discussion in this chapter will follow the main stages from the first to the ninth.

The first stage is the Strategic Assessment. It can also be called an Organizational Assessment. The purpose of the Strategic Assessment is to *identify* the organizational design problems. In some cases, the result of the Strategic Assessment is to recommend that the company not go any further. In the majority of cases, however, the result of the organizational assessment is to formulate what should be done to solve the organizational design problems. The basic idea of the Strategic Assessment is to use the ABCE Model for the means-ends linkages described in Chapters 1 and 6 to examine the organizational congruency conditions described in Chapter 6.

The Strategic Assessment usually involves only the senior management group. Sometimes, as in the case of banking, formal questionnaires are employed to gather the data that leads to the assessment of organizational congruencies. In cases involving a new industry, a special questionnaire may be developed for a specific company. In other cases, we do all this by means of personal interviews. In every case, one searches to examine the 11 organizational congruency conditions both for the present and for the near future. There are always some incongruencies, and these form patterns which lead to a diagnosis with recommendations for action. The Strategic Assessment is like a quick tour around the ABCE Model for the company. Later stages go deeper and deeper. Every stage has as its purpose the reaching of organizational congruency.

The second stage is the Organizational Audit. The purpose of the Organizational Audit is to *document how* the task-role system works and to compare

Table 9.1   Stages in the Organizational Audit and Analysis Technology

Stage	Description	Purpose
1	Strategic assessment	Find and identify the real organizational problems and formulate what should be done.
2	Organizational audit	Document exactly how the organization actually works. Build an initial model of the organization. Report on the state of the organization. Determine requirements for further stages and supplementary analysis.
3	Organizational design	Design organization to be more productive and to be more able to both implement strategies and improve employment of human resources. Develop position descriptions. Develop organizational manual.
	Supplementary services 3.1 Strategic planning 3.2 Merger/acquisition support 3.3 Market analysis and planning 3.4 Wage and salary system design 3.5 Job descriptions 3.6 Training 3.7 EEO compliance	
4	Implementation planning	Ensure smooth transition from old to new organizational design.
	Supplementary Services 4.1 Performance incentive systems 4.2 Performance planning 4.3 Performance management and review 4.4 Performance standards system 4.5 Manpower planning system 4.6 Management succession analysis and planning 4.7 Management development 4.8 Career planning systems design	
5	Monitoring the implementation	Ensure prevention of manpower waste during transition to new organization. Make adjustments and modifications to handle subsequent changes.
6	Organizational Playbook	Provide a planning and operating tool for management. Link human resources to operations.
7	Organizational Game Plan	Provide a tool for short term operating planning. Provide a tool for improved time management.
8	Organizational maintenance	Continue updating to adapt the organization to change and to prevent manpower waste.

continued

Table 9.1 continued

	Supplementary services	
	8.1 In-house organizational maintenance systems	
	8.2 Continue training and management development	
	8.3 Custom client software	
	8.4 Install micro computer software for client	
	8.5 Train human resources personnel	
	8.6 Crisis intervention	
	8.7 Executive counselling	
9	Systems review	Review entire organization to evaluate the organizational design and to eliminate or prevent manpower waste.
		Review progress and plans for organization.
		Assist, if necessary, the organization's internal staffs.
10	Educational services	Provide background for the OA & A Technology.
		Provide means for client to keep up to date.
		Provide custom seminars and workshops for the purpose of briefing senior management on recent developments.
11	Contract research and development	Develop custom analyses for clients.

it to the official-role system and sometimes the authority-role system. One looks for authority-task gaps and problems. During the Organizational Audit, one begins the development of the Organizational Logic. Along the way we cycle back through the ABCE Model and reevaluate the environments, goals, strategies, and design premises. The Organizational Audit is time consuming and results in a full report of the state of the organization. The results of the Organizational Audit become the basis for the organizational design. The main method of obtaining information during the Organizational Audit is personal interviews, but other methods are used to validate, verify, and evaluate the findings as they occur.

The third stage is the organizational design. This is the most exciting stage, because the results of the Organizational Audit are taken and used to develop an organizational design. This is an iterative process. Ideally, a set of strategic options is developed and evaluated from a viewpoint of resource flows. Then, the subset that seem feasible is selected. An Organizational Blueprint can be developed for each feasible option, and from this one can look for a robust organizational design. The Organizational Blueprint is a rough (and aggregated) Organizational Architecture with key positions plus an Organizational Logic at the bundle or group level of task processes.

Once the CEO has tentatively approved the Organizational Blueprint, the next step is to begin matching individuals to positions. Normally, key positions are examined first. Many individuals are easily assigned because there are usually only a relatively small number of new positions. However, trial assignments of individuals to the new positions progressively constrains and changes the choices as one fills out the Organizational Blueprint. Analysis of the problems for these trial assignments usually flushes out problems in the implementability of the organizational design. Changes are made in the Organizational Logic, and the design process cycles until a "better" solution is reached. Then, preliminary position descriptions are prepared. These are used to discuss the new positions with key officers, in order to fill them and to gain their acceptance and commitment. At this stage, one can expect many changes in the details of the Organizational Logic and the Organizational Architecture. The process continues until all of the positions are filled and the Organizational Logic stabilizes. Note that almost all of the adjustments have taken place within the general outline of the Organizational Blueprint. This reduces the combinatorial problems of fitting positions to people and vice versa. Soon the new Organizational Logic and the new Organizational Architecture are complete. Then "final" position descriptions are prepared and preparations are made to plan the implementation of the new design.

Stage four is called implementation planning. Its purpose is to "dot the i's and cross the t's" of the myriad of details necessary to ensure a smooth transition from the old to the new organizational design. There are problems of office layout, training, ensuring continuity of some projects, vacations, the information system changes needed to support the new organization, finalizing titles, examining compensation effects and many other personnel issues, planning the announcement party, public relations problems, business cards, stationery, etc. The implementation planning stage is a combination of detailed planning, selling, and education which is carried out during periods of some tension. One sees the best and the worst of people in this stage. Often, as the planning for the implementation proceeds, it is necessary to make further alterations in the organizational design. These iterations proceed from general to increasingly specific details. Sometimes, in the midst of this, there are emergencies created by environmental changes. In one case, this stage became complicated because the CEO was deciding whether or not to acquire an adjacent building. The purchase of the building would have changed the implementation plans. During this phase, consensus is building for the new design, and there are increasing pressures on the CEO and the key officers to cut over to the new organizational design. This pressure helps build consensus. However, individuals or groups who feel that they will lose power can and will act to pursue their interests. The implementation planning stage is probably the most exhausting stage of the whole organizational design process.

The fifth stage, monitoring the implementation, should be planned for during the implementation stage. Changes will continue to occur. For example, some persons will exceed what was believed to be their capacity, and some will prove disappointing. There will be numerous adjustments. Some, for example, will leave because of new opportunities. Sometimes, the new incumbents will uncover new problems as they settle into their new positions. Then there are the normal problems of injury, divorce, illness, and death that can upset the organizational design. The purpose of monitoring the implementation is to assist the organization in adapting the new organizational design to these changes as they occur.

Stages six and seven, the creation of an Organizational Playbook and Organizational Game Plans, are normally omitted from most organizational design projects. They will be discussed briefly later in this chapter, and more extensively in Chapter 10. These involve new ideas for linking human resources to management and for assisting in short-term operational planning. An Organizational Playbook and Game Plans are best suited to firms whose task processes are relatively unstable and irregular. New firms and high technology firms are especially appropriate for stages six and seven.

Stage eight is organizational maintenance. The object of organizational maintenance is to assist the organization in adapting its organizational design to change and to prevent manpower waste. This can be done by the organizational designer or by the organization itself or by some combination of both. Because of desiderata D_{11} and D_{13} of Chapter 3, it is important to assist the client organization to do this for itself as soon as possible, in order to reduce dependency on the outside organizational designer. In the case of the supermarket chain, computer software was provided along with special training in its use in order to assist the organization in developing the capability for handling most of its own changes.

At periodic intervals, it is helpful to review the operation in order to evaluate the effectiveness of the organizational design and, if necessary, aid it in making the necessary adjustments. Stage nine is the Systems Review. There is no precise formula for when to do this. Normally it should be done within the first year, but often, because of rapid changes that are impinging on the organization, it may be necessary to do this more often. For example, a change in the CEO, the installation of new technology, new problems and opportunities created by changes in the design premises, etc., could signal the need to conduct a review of the whole organization. The System Review does not take much time, because one is looking at the issues from a well-documented organizational design.

Stages one through nine constitute the main features of the Organizational Audit and Analysis technology. Stages three, four, and eight allow supplementary services. Most of these are in the Human Resources area and can be accomplished economically as a byproduct of the main work. Chapter 11 contains a description of some of these analyses.

Table 9.1 lists the stages and the supplementary analyses for the OA&A technology. There are several striking features of Table 9.1. The first is how the efforts made at each stage lead to the ability to perform the next. The second key feature is how the many supplementary services are seen as byproducts of the stages of the OA&A technology. The third key feature is the leverage of each stage in terms of how the efforts at each stage reduce the time and expense and each subsequent stage. Stage two, the Organizational Audit, is the most time consuming and expensive stage. However, once a model for the firm has been constructed, it can be used in the organizational design in every subsequent stage. The use of theory and computers to identify and process information as it evolves becomes an important reason why the swiftness desideratum (D_5) can be met. The application of the strategy for development of a theory and a technology of organizational design (described in Chapter 2), is a cause of the improvements in the OA&A technology. For example, what took 10 days in 1980 only took 1 day in 1982 for the Organizational Audit and design of a community bank. These productivity improvements in the application of the OA&A technology improve performance for the organizational designer and improve the swiftness and cost-effectiveness to the client organization.

Table 9.2 lists the desiderata met at each of the nine major stages of the OA&A technology. This table emphasizes the linkages between the OA&A technology and the commitments cited in Chapter 3 for achieving desiderata. Note that desiderata D_4 (Objectivity), D_5 (Swiftness), and D_{10} (implementibility) are involved in all nine stages of the OA&A technology. That is why, in Chapter 3, they are singled out as being especially important. The rolling nature of organizational design means that, during the design process and afterwards, the desiderata for selecting the best alternative are involved. D_6 (Fewer changes), D_7 (Simplicity), D_8 (specificity), and D_9 (robustness) come to play in the choices that are made in the organizational design (stage three), implementation planning (stage four), monitoring the implementation (stage five), organizational maintenance (stage eight), and the systems review (stage nine). The manageability of the organizational design is part of stages three through nine and are always part of the considerations as adjustments are made. Desideratum D_{12} concerns the provision follow up analyses and is involved directly in stages three, four, and eight. The desirability of reducing dependence comes to bear in stages four, eight, and nine.

The status of the Organizational Playbook and the Organizational Game Plan (stages six and seven) is more problematic, because of limited testing. However, they are seen as especially valuable in improving implementation (D_{10}), improving manageability (D_{11}), and reducing dependence (D_{13}).

Table 9.2   Stages and their desiderata for the OA&A Technology

Stage	Desiderata for the stage											
1. Strategic assessment	1	—	3	4	5	—	—	—	—	10	—	—	—
2. Organizational audit	1	2	3	4	5	—	—	—	—	10	—	—	—
3. Organizational design	1	2	3	4	5	6	7	8	9	10	11	12	13
4. Implementation planning	1	2	3	4	5	6	7	8	9	10	11	12	13
5. Monitoring the implementation	1	2	3	4	5	6	7	8	9	10	11	—	—
6. Organizational playbook	—	2	—	4	5	—	—	—	—	10	11	—	13
7. Organizational game plan	—	2	—	4	5	—	—	—	—	10	11	—	13
8. Organizational maintenance	—	—	3	4	5	6	7	8	—	10	11	12	13
9. System review	—	—	3	4	5	6	7	8	—	10	11	—	13

This section provided an overview of the OA&A technology. Stages one to five are described in more detail in the next section. This more complete description of the OA&A technology provides a guide of how the theory and technology is actually applied. Later chapters will build up these descriptions of the OA&A process to illustrate them in the organizational design of a supermarket chain.

STRATEGIC ASSESSMENT

The Strategic Assessment is designed to examine organizational congruency. Its purpose is to use the ABCE Model to guide an examination of the organization in order to identify what organizational problems, if any, need solving.

There are basically three task processes or methods followed in performing a Strategic Assessment. These three methods essentially seek answers to the same questions. They differ in how the Strategic Assessment is performed, and reflect the relative expertise of the organizational designer with a firm in an industry. The three methods are, in descending order of prior expertise:

1. Use of standard questionnaires
2. Use of custom-prepared questionnaires
3. Use of direct interviews

Method One, the use of standard questionnaires, is used whenever solid expertise has been achieved by previous experiences with problems in the industry. For example, in performing a strategic assessment for a community bank, I have developed a pair of manuals with approximately 113 pages. Method Two, use of a custom-prepared questionnaire, is used when the expertise of the organizational designer is relatively low in an industry and where one or more members of the client organization understands the OA&A technology. In the case of Supermarket Systems, Inc., the author had the good fortune of some prior experience and a client with an expert who could help with the preparation of the questions. Method Three is used when the expertise of the organizational designer in the industry is low and where the client's expertise about the OA&A technology is low. Method Three is common in high-tech, relatively new organizations such as a research and development company in linguistics or in a scientific, technical publisher and information company.

The typical strategic assessment involves the Chief Executive Officer and those officers who report directly to him or her. Sometimes, outside members of the Board of Directors are included. All three methods seek information about the following:

1. Questions on ownership and major problems for the Chief Executive Officer.
2. Profiling the environment. Examination of regulations affecting the organization's economic base, the growth or lack of growth, changes in the publics served by the organization, environmental characteristics, including some demographics, and industry trends in technology and services.
3. Profiling the market. Examination of geograhic regions served by the organization, an assessment of the strengths and weaknesses of competitors, customer profiles of the number, type, growth, and value of services provided, and a profile of the financial status of the organization.
4. Forecasting the environment. Essentially a verification of the Chief Executive Officer's judgments about how he or she profiles the present environment and that of the near future.
5. Forecasting the market. Essentially a verification of the Chief Executive Officer's judgment about his or her assessment of the current market and those of the near future.
6. Describing the organization. This includes key facts about the organization, its goals and strategies, its vulnerabilities, the Organizational Logic (official, actual, and desired), organizational charts (official, actual, and desired), the responsibilities of those directly involved in the strategic assessment, and the judgment of the responsibilities plus relative strengths of those in the program made by the other participants, a census of committees, information resources, technological resources, physical resources, and financial resources.
7. Strategic issues and problems. Here one looks into the environmental, strategic, and organizational design premises, the assignment of priorities for actions and strategies, an assessment of what is being done to ef-

fect the achievement of these high priority areas, and an open-ended request for each to list what are considered to be the three most important problems facing the organization.

8. Interpersonal judgments of strengths of those participating made by others and compared to self ratings.

The answers to the questions are tabulated and summarized, and then analyzed to examine organizational congruencies, both current and in the near future. Thus, there are 22 congruency condition tests. They form patterns which are part of the analysis and which lead to recommendations for the process for solving the identified organizational problem. Table 9.3 summarizes the organizational congruency test for a $135,000,000 community bank. This is a common pattern in a bank that is organized functionally and is beginning to understand that the increased competition caused by deregulation in the financial industries has made the current organizational design obsolete. In this case, the recommendation was to redesign the organization in order to organize itself for its markets. The Strategic Assessment also pointed out several market niches which the bank has comparative advantages in pursuing.

The results of the Strategic Assessment are put in the form of a formal report, which is usually lengthy because of the statistical summaries of fact and the interpretation of the reasons for the findings. This is first presented to the Chief Executive Officer and then later (usually the same day) to the whole set of persons participating in the strategic assessment. These discussions are opportunities to discuss the findings and the recommenda-

Table 9.3   Conclusions about organizational congruency for a community bank

	Conclusions	
Organizational congruency test	Current	Future (2-5 yrs)
1. Are goals congruent with environment?	Yes	Yes
2. Are strategies congruent with environment?	No	*
3. Are goals congruent with strategies?	No	*
4. Are senior management in agreement?	Yes	Yes
5. Are design premises congruent with the environment?	No	Yes
6. Are design premises congruent with the strategies?	No	Yes
7. Are design premises congruent with the Organizational Logic?	Yes	No
8. Is the Organizational Logic congruent with the Organizational Architecture?	Yes	*
9. Is the Organizational Logic congruent with the actual organization?	No	*
10 Are results congruent with the Organizational Technology?	Yes	*
11 Are results congruent with the goals?	Yes	*

* Answer is yes, if the bank takes appropriate action to redesign its organization.

tions. They usually help build consensus and commitment for taking action, if action is warranted. Every effort is made to preserve confidentiality. Almost always there is the side benefit that those participants feel that their opinions have been heard and that they have learned a lot about themselves and the organization as a direct result of the Strategic Assessment. Usually the CEO has a mandate and a consensus for organizational design, if one is warranted.

ORGANIZATIONAL AUDIT

The purpose of the Organizational Audit is to document how the organization operates. A detailed Organizational Logic and Organizational Architecture is prepared and compared to the actual organization. There is a verification of every element of the ABCE Model and the organizational congruency conditions. Requirements for proceeding to the organizational design, and for ancillary analyses, are determined. The results of the Organizational Audit are prepared in an extensive "State of the Organization" report exploring the findings, the judgments, the reasoning, and the recommendations.

The Organizational Audit requires intensive interviews and participation within the company in order to be successful. Most organizations have little systematic information about the various task processes and how the organization really operates. In cases where there are positions or job descriptions, they are usually of little value, because these records are out of date or were written and rewritten with other purposes than to faithfully describe the work of the organization. The Organizational Audit seeks to have an accurate description of the *actual* organization.

One important feature of the Organizational Audit is that it generates a common language in which key terms are defined in terms of the task processes involved. Words such as marketing, merchandising, strategy, goal, objective, environment, competition, regulation, production, personnel, finance, and data processing are subject to wide variation of meaning within any organization. These differences in meaning are often directly linked to organizational conflicts. Firms experiencing rapid growth, shifts in technology, changes in competitive practices, and changing markets often have great difficulty in their internal communications because the meanings of words change, and, as they change, so do the allocation of responsibilities. Words such as "direct," "plan," "coordinate," "allocate," "supervise," "cooperate," and "control" always create difficulties because of a lack of agreement on their definitions, and because of conflicting ambitions. Given the prevalence of conflicts involving these words, it should be no surprise that, when they are defined with respect to the task processes, many conflicts evaporate and others suddenly become clarified. Every organization develops its own dialects by which it communicates, and, often, different dialects exist within the same organization. It is helpful for the organizational designer to see himself as speaking his own dialect. Mine is "Org Struct." During the Organizational Audit, I must translate the organizational dialect(s) into "Org Struct" and then back again into the dialects of the organization. That is the only way I have found it possible to be understood and, more importantly, have them agree that I understand. Many position titles, names of departments, and descriptions of key task processes are semantically polluted. In one case, "materials managment" meant purchasing, inventory control, and data processing to the Manager of Materials Management, and nitpicking, second guessing, and useless computer printouts to the plant managers. The Manager of Materials Management used the word "control" as a noun (as in a system of control) and the plant manager used the word "control" as a verb (as in power). Efforts to "control" materials created all sorts of conflicts because of a basic misunderstanding of a seven-letter English word. Once this semantic puzzle is uncovered and resolved, cooperation rapidly improves.

Of course, only some of the problems are those of language. Most cannot be identified, solved, and implemented by clarifying meaning. Most process and structural maladaptions represent serious and systematic differences which lie at the heart of the goals, strategies, and Organizational Logic of the organization. But even these involve semantic "noise" which contributes to the confusion and shows up in the many organizational maladaptions. The Organizational Audit proceeds by well-identified steps in order to systematically construct a clear understanding of how the organization operates.

The first step is to plan how the Organizational Audit is to be performed. This usually involves ensuring that an individual such as the CEO or a committee (e.g., the Executive Committee) is prepared to act as a liaison between the organizational designer and the members of the organization. This individual or committee has to communicate who the designer is, what he or she is going to do, whom he or she is to see, and to assist in arranging for setting up interviews, obtaining needed information, and providing logistical support. The liaison also serves as provider of background information to help the designer understand the business and its usual business practices. A list of persons to be interviewed is drawn up and appointments are scheduled. A file folder for each person to be interviewed and facts for each type of information is set up from discussions. It is vital to the success of the Organizational Audit that the liaison person or committee be supportive of it. It is also important that the liaison be informed if the process of the Organizational Audit is to be changed.

There are six basic methods for gathering information during the Organizational Audit. They are:

a. Direct Interviewing
b. Reviewing Key Processes
c. Perching
d. Participation on a Key Project
e. Committee Census
f. Social Interaction.

The direct interviews are the most time consuming and important of the information-gathering techniques. Basically, the purpose of each interview is to understand the person's task processes. To do this, the person is asked what he or she does, how it is done, and with whom he or she works to do it. We also ask questions about the person's background and experiences, as well as an overall assessment of the important problems facing the firm. These interviews can take as much as a half day and as little as a half hour. Generally, the more senior positions require more time because of the broader scope of their jobs. I generally tape record these interviews, after obtaining permission. In only two instances out of hundreds has permission to tape been refused. The information is kept confidential. The reason for taping is that, as the designer becomes more knowledgeable about the organization, one may discover that one did not really understand what he or she was told during an interview. Also, inconsistencies and omissions will occur that need to be double checked. Reviewing a tape often eliminates the need for a follow up interview. Almost all persons seem to enjoy talking about their work and themselves. The data from the interview about the task processes and interactions is put together in the form of a part of an Organizational Logic which is usually reviewed at a later time with the interviewee in order to ensure that the task processes have been accurately described. If the interviewee speaks about using special forms, I generally get a copy of each in order to make the language as precise as possible.

One generally proceeds from the top of the organization down in conducting the interviews. How far down one goes into the organization will depend upon the needs of the designer to understand and to check opinions and assumptions, and on the time available. For example, a company can have 4000 employees and only about 150 different jobs. One does not need to interview all 4000. One may start by trying to see, say, 25. This number may grow as the interviews begin to reveal serious structural or process maladaptations.

The data for each interview can be triangulated with other interviews. If person A reports that he or she works with person B on a task process, but person B does not report that he or she works with person A, then there is a need to ascertain which is correct. Sometimes they are both correct, and sometimes neither is correct. Sometimes we identify persons who are bypassing their superiors and who don't make it known. The cross-checking of the interview data is very valuable in identifying such issues, and can be used to locate virtual positions. One must avoid jumping to conclusions too early as a result of the interview data, because there may be issues that lie beyond the individual conflicts. One should try to understand what is happening and how it is happening. As the Organizational Audit unfolds, a more complete picture is pieced together. Many times, the inconsistencies and omissions are only *symptoms* of more serious organizational design problems.

During the personal interviews, various management processes are identified. Some of these, such as quality control, budgeting, capital investment decisions, and reward systems may appear to reflect serious organizational problems. These key processes are then carefully described. A process review means verifying how the task process works. For example, one company had a complex process for converting a customer inquiry into a price quotation. I took a blueprint from a customer and "walked" it through the organization, following the official procedure. This process review quickly established that the official process was not followed, that persons involved did not really understand the process, and that the computer was systematically avoided until the last moment. I learned, for example, that the industrial engineers had never seen the product and were just going through the motions, that the plant managers ignored the voluminous computer output, and that the method of determining the mark up for the parts and materials, labor, and overhead was not the one that was supposed to be followed. These inconsistencies meant redoing some of the earlier interviews and digging deeper into other parts of the organization. It became clear during the process review that the members of the organization had evolved very different procedures, and, as a result, the elaborate computer systems were obsolete. Process reviews are very helpful in pinning down task processes that cut down units of the organization. The results are vital clues in designing organizational design issues.

A third method of obtaining information is called "perching." In perches, the organizational designer spends every minute of a full day, every minute, with the CEO and a few other key officers. Perching gives much more information about how the work is done and about the problems of interruptions and crises, and provides insights into the styles of management and the corporate culture. Perching allows one to verify the task processes from the interviews, and almost always opens up a wider variety than those identified in the interviews, even after all of the cross checking.

Describing the job of a CEO is difficult, because of its wide scope. Many of the CEO's task processes flow out of his or her theory of how to manage. This theory is often implicit, and it takes time to understand it. Perching helps fill in the holes in one's understanding of these task processes. One learns quickly that different problems and different individuals are handled in diverse ways. For example, during a perch a CEO was interrupted by a call from an irate consumer. Observing how this was handled changed the entire description of how the process of customer relations was described. It also became fascinating to trace how the CEO's actions triggered responses that had thus far been missed. Sometimes a perch begins at a 6:30 A.M. breakfast and extends on through to dinner and then to some evening event. Perches should be done after the organizational designer has become a "fixture." People streaming in and out of the CEO's office know the organizational designer as do those at meetings, and, in principle, there is less disruption due to his or her presence.

Participation in a key project is a fourth means of gathering information during an Organizational Audit. The designer sits in on all of the meetings and gets involved. He or she picks those projects cutting across organizational lines and which involve poorly understood task processes. A key project for a retail chain might involve a new store opening. A key project for a bank might involve the development of a new customer service. The acquisition of new computer facilities is always a prime candidate in any organization. Observation and participation in a key project for a period of time gives the designer a clearer picture of what is done, who is involved, and what is involved, and a sense of the individual strengths and weaknesses, as well as many interpersonal relationships, that may be needed during the organizational design stage.

Committee census is a fifth way of obtaining information during an Organizational Audit. One makes a list of all the organization's committees, what the charges to each are, who is on each committee, and how often and how long each meets. Because committees are regulated virtual positions, and because they reflect authority-task problems, the census of committees provides an excellent check on the rest of the Organizational Audit. One can usually work backwards from the committee census later to identify authority-task gaps and who is involved. This is a very useful way of validating other findings and developing leads for more interviews, in order to understand how the organization operates.

The sixth method is to observe social interactions, usually off premises. These might involve receptions, parties, dinners, or visits to a local recreation site with members of the organization. In a more informal setting, an observant designer can learn a lot about interpersonal dynamics, strategic issues, and lots of other information that tends to improve his or her understanding of the organization.

By now it should be clear that gathering information never ceases and that each new piece of information, when added to what has been learned before, helps improve one's understanding. The integration of these data takes place while the information is gathered. Eventually a stage is reached where new information has decreasingly marginal importance. At this point, it is time to organize and interpret this information into a full Organizational Logic.

The designer begins by constructing an overall macro-logic of areas and groups for the entire organization and for each of the major officers. This is done in conjunction with an attempt to define all of the design premises of which one is aware. This macro-logic has been evolving since beginning the organizational assessment. During the application of the OA&A technology, the Organizational Logic becomes clearer and more precise. The macro-logic should be checked with key officers, and especially with the CEO. This helps the designer verify his or her work and also helps to teach the CEO and the officers about how to think about organizational design issues. It also builds trust.

Once the macro-logic is clear and drawn out on horizontal graphs, one can then proceed to subdividing each group of task processes into its constituent bundles, modules, and activities. The result is a full activity list for the Organizational Logic. This activity list may have up to 10,000 lines. It is very detailed, and every effort has been made to make it as accurate as possible. Parts have been verified during the interviews. But the step of putting it all together yields gaps which usually involve the DCC and planning processes. These gaps are filled in and there may be some renumbering and even shifting of existing bundles and modules. These insertions continue until the whole of the Organizational Logic "hangs together" as one coherent whole.

All during the Organizational Audit, the designer has been improving the organizational chart to show more detail about the positions, the titles, and the names of the incumbents. These organizational charts are kept up to date and are drawn in descending hierarchies in order to show the details of each organizational unit. These must be maintained because, during the Organizational Audit, there are promotions, transfers, new hires, and terminations which are the everyday part of any organization. After the Organizational Logic has become solidified, the current positions are then used to define the Organizational Responsibility Grouping chart. The ORG chart matches the positions with the task processes, and uses interview data to record the many entries in the ORG chart. This allows easy display of organizational maladaptations, because these show up as virtual positions, overlapping responsibilities, and task processes spread over more than one organizational unit. Inspection of the entries in the ORG chart typically suggests many organizational design issues that need to be resolved during the Organizational Design stage of the OA&A technology.

At this stage, the major maladaptations are superimposed onto the existing and most current version of the organizational chart in different colors of ink for different major processes. The virtual positions are placed and drawn in, as well as numerous cousin and uncle–nephew relationships. The resulting overlay is a depiction of the actual organization. Generally, it is helpful to describe the actual organization at different levels within the organization in order to sharpen the focus on specific and important processes and structural maladaptations.

The lines, the task processes they represent, and the positions that are connected by the lines are very specific, with real names and actual processes. Anyone looking at it can verify immediately if the designer has shown the information correctly. One can be sure that all position holders will study the part of the organization of which they are members very critically. Thus, the main findings about the process and structural maladaptions are quickly verified. Their reaction is generally swift and binary. One either has it right or one does not. The designer will quickly be informed if something isn't right. Sometimes one is dead wrong and sometimes one is right as far as he or she has gone, but not totally accurate. Often one is right, but people don't like the implications of what they are reading. Usually the members of the organization are delighted to see someone take their job seriously. One crusty VP actually wept with aesthetic pleasure in seeing his operations carefully and fully described.

Before writing the report on the results of the Organizational Audit, which is called the "State of the Organization," it is a good idea to preview these preliminary results with the liaison person(s) and other key individuals. When there are errors of fact or interpretations, the designer should take steps to validate what is true by more fact finding. The designer must bear in mind the responsibility of describing the organization as accurately as possible.

The writing of the "State of the Organization" moves swiftly. The description of the key results, how the study was done, who was involved, the details of the results, and the summary and recommendations are included in the report. Generally, the full activity list of the Organizational Logic is placed in a separate volume. There is a report on the organizational congruency conditions and often analyses of data such as a tabulation of the key problems seen by those interviewed and other supplementary evidence that has been gathered. The resulting report can be centered on a general theme which represents the major findings, of which the other findings are supporting elaborations. The recommendations are generally obvious, given the facts and the interpretations.

The "State of the Organization" is presented first to the CEO and then to those who served as liaisons and, generally, all involved in the Organizational Assessment. This meeting can be tense, because there is a mutual concern among those involved about the conclusions and the possible assignment of blame. Usually, it is a waste of time to place blame, because of the structural nature of the findings. If A is involved, so are B and C, because they are involved, so are D and E, etc. The tone of the "State of the Organization" is objective. The facts are mostly accepted. It is the interpretations and recommendations that become important. Usually, for the first time, the members of the organization can really see the whole of their organization and understand the reasons for the recommendations.

The recommendations are usually intended for resolving the maladaptations by means of an organizational design, and not for any specific solution. The discussion of the findings in the "State of the Organization" generally helps build a consensus to solve the underlying problems. Another possibility is to stop the OA&A process, but this is rare. If the designer had not seen any purpose in proceeding with the OA&A, the study would have been discontinued earlier. If the study was no longer cost effective, the CEO would generally have seen it immediately.

The "State of the Organization" report is read seriously. When a consensus is reached to take action, this report then becomes more or less a museum piece, or part of ancient history. The attention turns to the next state—the organizational design.

THE ORGANIZATIONAL DESIGN

The Strategic Assessment identified the organizational design problems. The Organizational Audit defined the actual workings of the organization and verified the identity of the problems. Both considered all parts of the ABCE Model and the organizational congruencies. The greater precision of the Organizational Audit can now be used to move from problem identification, verification, and documentation to the solution of the organizational design problems. Stage three is organizational design.

The organizational design, unlike the Organizational Assessment and the Organizational Audit, is not conducted with widespread participation. Typically, the designer and the CEO work intensively together before bringing in other persons. The organizational design is the responsibility of the CEO, and the designer's role is to act as midwife to aid in the rebirth of the organization. The early phases of the organizational design are not made public.

The first step is to once again examine the organizational goals and strategies. A list of strategic options is generated and evaluated for feasibility. This usually involves a financial analysis and an assessment of the organizational capability to implement. A *strategic option* is defined as the triple (E,G,S) where E is the environment, G the goals, and S the strategies on the ABCE Model. Those strategic options that appear feasible and desirable are then analyzed more intensively.

For each strategic option, the designer derives an Organizational Logic and, from it, a proforma organizational chart. This helps the CEO scan the possibilities. Usually, some are eliminated and others are generated. This process iterates rapidly until a subset (usually five or less) of the strategic options are left. The designer then compares the Organizational Logics of each and finds all of the task processes that are common to all. This is called the core Organizational Logic. Because the different strategic options represent different combinations of assumptions about environments, goals, and strategies, the design premises for each become very important. Each strategic option represents a different future for the organization. However, no organization has full control over the validity of its assumptions. A key question that arises in the mind of the CEO is how to hedge choices, given these uncertainties. An analysis of the different Organizational Logics in terms of the core Organizational Logic highlights the differences among the strategic options. Usually, the CEO and the organizational designer can make modifications in the Organizational Logics that result in a larger core Organizational Logic. Robustness is the percentage of the union of the task processes in the Organizational Logics for the viable strategic options that is in the core Organizational Logic. The refining of the Organizational Logics for the viable strategic options generally increases the robustness of the solutions. The more robust the Organizational Logic, the less change it takes to modify the organizational design when there are changes in the environment. Achieving greater robustness is a desideratum (D$_9$ of Chapter 3).

The result of these iterations is the Organizational Blueprint. The Organizational Blueprint is the selection of the Organizational Logic and Architecture that is seen to be the best solution to the organizational design problems. Every effort has been made to derive the Organizational Blueprint without considering which individuals will fill each position on it. The Organizational Blueprint represents what would be desirable for the best interests of the organization, without specific regard for each possible incumbent. It represents an "ideal" solution. In some cases, an Organizational Blueprint is derived to solve the existing organizational design problems. In others, it is derived as an intermediate organization which is seen as a stepping stone to a future organization. For example, a firm may wish to decentralize, but it lacks general managers, and so it must first organize itself to allow this to happen. Or, it may wish to set up special units for planning how to prepare the organization to launch new strategies.

This process of thinking through the future with the CEO is greatly aided if the CEO has confidence in the judgments of the organizational designer, and if the organizational designer is not seen as a rival. One simple test is for the designer to ask the CEO if he or she thinks that the designer knows enough about the business and the organization to be able to run it. If the CEO does not agree that the designer has the necessary knowledge and judgment, then the designer has not done a very good job. The design phase must be conducted in an atmosphere of mutual trust and respect for it to be successful.

The Organizational Blueprint is not as detailed as the final design. The Organizational Logic is not yet fully defined. The aggregation levels of the task processes are usually never higher than the bundle level, and the organizational chart usually contains only the more senior positions. It is only an ideal. It represents what the CEO believes is the outline of the best solution. It also represents the judgment by the designer that it can be accomplished.

The next step is to analyze the Organizational Blueprint. Names are tentatively attached to key positions, and these questions are asked: "Could he or she do it?" "Will he or she accept it?" "Is it right?" Answering these questions usually causes changes in the Organizational Blueprint. By now the CEO is beginning to zero in on both the desirable features of the Organizational Blueprint and the problems he or she might have in implementing it.

An Organizational Responsibility Grouping chart is made to analyze the features of the Organizational Blueprint. Shifts are made to accommodate key individuals, all of whom have strengths and weaknesses. This initial effort to achieve congruency between the Organizational Logic and Organizational Architecture generally results in modifications of the Organizational Blueprint. These iterations continue until an Organizational Blueprint is reached that is both robust and workable. Based upon my experience with many firms, the iterations described in this paragraph take about a half day for larger firms and longer for smaller firms. For firms whose task processes are unstable and irregular, this step could take much longer, because each choice is seen as "betting the company."

The "final" Organizational Blueprint tends to be very stable. The remaining steps of filling in all of the details only result in minor modifications of the Organizational Blueprint. Usually, the steps to reach this "final" Organizational Blueprint are very exciting and rewarding for the CEO and the designer. A decision has been made and the outline of the solution is clear. There is a sense of relief. The remaining steps are more tedious. They are analogous to "hard yardage" in American football.

The existing Organizational Logic needs refining. There are many new DCC and planning task processes that must be described and incorporated into it. Some of the execution task processes are modified. The designer then constructs an ORG chart showing the assignments of task processes to the new positions in the Organizational Blueprint. These are then used to develop a set of new position descriptions which show the position titles, the supervisors, those directly and indirectly supervised, committee assignments, and a listing of the direct and indirect task processes. These new position descriptions from the Organizational Blueprint and the new organizational chart or charts are then examined. This examination always results in minor modifications. Luckily, the data are on a computer which can quickly handle such changes. By now, the CEO is clear about what he or she wants to do. It is now time to begin the process of reconciling the new organizational design to the individuals.

The next step is to call in key persons whom the CEO wishes to place in the key positions. He or she "sells" the idea of the Organizational Blueprint and attempts to win their consent and commitment. The designer is present at those meetings to answer technical questions and to be ready to examine changes if they are necessary. This step in the organizational design process is tense. If there are major position changes, the persons involved will often not understand what they are being told by the CEO because of their nervousness. Even though every effort is made to achieve understanding and agreement, it is often necessary to have a separate meeting to answer questions. Changes that are seen to be promotions go smoothly. Transfers created by elimination of the person's old position and the creation of a new one are tense. Perceived demotions are difficult and are generally handled with utmost diplomacy. No one is fooled. After the first level reporting to the President is handled, there will always be several iterations as the position descriptions are studied. But now, all of the changes fall within the guidelines created by the Organizational Blueprint. Bundles are modified, modules are rewritten, traded, etc., but the main features remain in place. The new organizational design has begun to "lock in." Please note that it is the CEO who presents the solution. This process helps the CEO gain confidence in it.

Before each of these meetings, the CEO and the organizational designer have worried over the titles and likely changes in compensations. A CEO has two key decisions: Is anyone going to be terminated? Are salaries going to be maintained? Most answer "no" to the first and "yes" to the second. These answers help obtain consensus and commitment. Often the organizational designer must help the CEO avoid "title inflation."

Once those who report directly to the CEO have agreed to accept their positions, they now become involved in selecting the second tier of their immediate subordinates. If the new organizational design is mostly a minor modification of the existing one, there are usually few surprises. But when the design represents a major change, the CEO can expect a lot of surprises. The first line usually have strong preferences for certain people and strong reservations about others. This creates the need for some negotiations and consensus before the next level is approached. For major changes the process can resemble the National Football League draft, with executives bargaining and trading personnel.

The process at the second level is like the first, except that, while the CEO introduces (and blesses) the new design, the first level appointees now explain the new design and the role of the individuals in it. The process creates changes in the activity lists and position descriptions, but at each stage the solution is becoming more prescribed. Again, understanding, consensus, and commitment are being formed.

Most organizational designs do not change much at the lower levels, and so the series of meetings and iterations tapers off. The rumor mills are operating, and the overall design begins to leak out, even though every person swears to keep the meetings confidential. This rumor mill is the ally of the CEO, as it spreads the innovations represented by the new design throughout the organization.

And at every step modifications are made, and every effort is made to keep lines of communications open. The value of having done the Organizational Audit becomes crystal clear, because it has provided the information and the data for handling all of the many changes and adjustments. The "State of the Organization" report allows the CEO to explain why there was a problem and how the new design is a solution. The fact that the task processes have been carefully validated creates a sense of competence and caring that builds the trust necessary to make the changes and have them accepted.

During these iterations, pressure begins to mount for the CEO to implement the new design. As the pressure to implement gathers momentum, the organization is beginning to adopt the new design. This impatience is leading to adoption. But, until the "i's are dotted and the t's crossed," the new design is not yet ready for implementation.

The designer now prepares a report on the organizational design that explains what it is, why it is necessary, and how the new design intends to operate. This report includes both the new Organizational Logic and the position descriptions. The report on the organizational design becomes an organizational manual.

To go through these steps, it is absolutely necessary for the CEO to believe in the organizational design. It is necessary for the CEO to be strong enough to make the many decisions, and it is very helpful if the technology and support to negotiate adjustments and compromises is available. The desiderata of minimizing the number of changes (D_6), preferring simpler designs (D_7), specificity (D_8), and robustness (D_9) described in Chapter 3 are helpful. The desideratum of ease of implementation (D_{10}), when met, helps the process of reconciling the Organizational Blueprint with the personnel. The desideratum of allowing provision for maintenance and updating is a requirement in order to handle the iterations and adjustments.

IMPLEMENTATION PLANNING

The new organizational design is a prescription for how the organization plans to operate in the future. Even though there may be consensus and enthusiasm, implementing the transition from the old organization to the new one can be hard, detailed, and exhausting work. There is a need for prudent planning on how to achieve implementation. The implementation planning stage of the OA&A technology is very important to the success of the new organizational design.

Each organizational design has its own implementation problems. And the implementation problems depend very much on both the new and the old design. Thus, there are no magic prescriptions. The most important concern is how to ensure a smooth transition from the old to the new organizational design.

The earlier stages have done much to help the members of the organization prepare themselves to adopt the new organizational design. Efforts have been made to achieve a new organizational design that meets the desiderata described in Chapter 3. Despite all of these efforts, it is important to realize that, as the date for "cut over" approaches, every member of the organization can be assumed to be concerned with his or her own interests and specific relationships. Many questions and problems will emerge that need to be anticipated and resolved if the new organizational design is to be implemented.

Each person will be concerned about job title, reporting relationships, responsibilities, authority, relative and absolute salary, office facilities, and expected performance. Many of those directly affected by the new design are going to worry about their ability to do the new job. Some will need training. Most will require emotional support. There will be questions about why someone else is perceived as being benefited more or less than others. The desiderata of simplicity, parsimony, specificity, and implementability, if met by the new organizational design, will help prevent many of the possible counter-adoption processes that can upset the adoption of the new organizational design.

There are numerous issues involving facilities. Some organizational designs will require a rearrangement of office facilities, and these must be planned for in advance of the cut over. Office assignments, choice of furniture and office equipment, ensuring that the internal communication system is changed to meet the needs of the new organizational design, are all issues that must be solved. There may be need for new business cards and new signs for the offices.

Customers and suppliers need to be informed about the changes, if they affect working boundary relationships. It may be necessary to prepare new brochures and information packets for them. Many employees will not be directly affected, but they need to be fully informed so that they can do their work and understand the new organizational design and how it affects them.

It is not uncommon for the new organizational design to also launch a new organizational strategy and even a change in the corporate name. These changes will require new graphics and signs. They usually involve issues of institutional advertising and the conduct of public relations. Planning is necessary to achieve success in implementing these changes.

Often, the organization's internal reporting system for accounting and data processing must be changed in order for the new organizational design to function. It is my experience that planning to meet these needs is met with resistance unless the heads of the organizations for these reporting systems are strongly in favor of the new organizational design. It is very difficult to get an accounting system and M.I.S. System to work properly. Changes create more work for these personnel. However, the reporting systems are vital to the control of the organization, and when the reporting systems are inconsistent with the new organizational design the results can be serious. Consequently, an important issue in implementation planning is to ensure that there is a clear schedule for adapting the reporting systems to the new organizational design.

Most organizations have ongoing projects such as opening new stores, publications, product development projects, sales efforts, and others that must be continued during the transition. In some cases, these projects will involve different organizational units after the change. Care must be taken to ensure the continuity of such projects.

In more radical organizational design changes, such as moving from a functional to divisionalized organizational structures, there are problems in training new position holders to do their jobs. For example, in functional organizations the managers are all either revenue or cost centers. The only profit center is the CEO. The creation of new profit centers involves the balancing of revenues and costs, which is very difficult for most functional specialists. It may be necessary, as part of the implementation planning, to provide concurrent training and support to these officers. The new responsibilities in such cases involve the rapid acquisition of newer ways of thinking and problem solving.

Even though great care has been taken during the organizational design stage to pick the best persons for each new position, one must realistically expect that not all will be able to meet the new challenges. Others will exceed expectations. Part of implementation planning is to think through what will happen if such problems occur, and what should be done if new opportunities arise during implementation.

The foregoing discussion is a realistic description of some of the problems and issues that must be considered during implementation planning. The real benefits of having gone through the stages and styles carefully and thoroughly before reaching the implementation stage become increasingly clear as one moves from the basic idea to the details of the new organizational design. The use of the computer to process the many adjustments that are *always* needed help the organization keep on top of the problems.

It is essential for the Chief Executive Officer to be firm, consistent, and enthusiastic about the new organizational design in order not to undermine it. Vacillations, capricious changes, and indecisiveness create uncertainties that can rapidly undo the carefully built concensus. Organizational design changes are a real test of the CEO and the management team. The skills and the knowledge of a good organizational designer can do much to help the CEO through this trying period.

Pressures by the members of the organization to cut over to the new design mount with every passing day. The CEO can be brought under heavy pressure to announce the new organizational design before the implementation planning has been completed satisfactorily. The CEO can expect to have less time than is needed. He or she can also expect political pressure being brought to make alterations. In one case, a Manager of Customer Relations went around the President to her friends on the Board of Directors so that her title could be changed to Vice President and Director. These kinds of "end runs" mount as the interval between the new design and its implementation lengthens. Some who were earlier enthusiastic begin to sense that they can improve their lot by lobbying. Woe to a weak CEO during the period.

Although I have no objective data to support what I am going to say next, I still think it is important. Organizations tend to resemble tribes, and the CEO is the chief. The CEO role is more than the technical exercise of expertise. He or she occupies a position with tribal responsibilities. The CEO also is the custodian of the corporate culture, and must act to strengthen and preserve these values if he or she is to be successful in mobilizing the energies of the members of the organization. Organizational design changes have an imprint on this complex web of social interrelationships. It is vital that the CEO personally gives public approval of the new design in order for it to be legitimate.

I have found that it is necessary and beneficial to arrange a public ceremony to announce and bless the new organizational design before it is implemented. The planning for the ceremony must be a part of implementation planning. Members of the Board of Directors, the CEO, the officers, and the organizational designer are involved in these ceremonies. The Board of Directors sanctions the new organizational design much like tribal elders. The CEO and his or her management team give it legitimacy. This public ceremony is important to all the stakeholders. I am always amazed at the soothing effect it has on the CEO who, up to this time, has been subjected to so many pressures. The public announcement and the ceremonies help bind together the new organization. This cut over ceremony is a rite of passage for the organization. It is necessary to do it, and it is almost always emotional and satisfying to all who participate.

MONITORING THE IMPLEMENTATION

Following the cut over ceremony, the organization converts to the new organizational design. There will always be problems in the implementation which must be monitored and resolved. The environment will not stop changing, and there will be numerous adjustments and modifications as the organization adapts itself to those changes. In addition, there is the normal employee turnover, illnesses, and personal emergencies that exist in all organizations. Change never ceases to impact the organization.

The monitoring of the implementation stage is part of the OA&A organizational design technology. Its purposes are to ensure success in implementing the new organizational design and to assist in the necessary adjustments and modifications as they occur. Make no mistake, it is necessary to do this, especially when the new organizational design is a major departure from the old organizational design.

One can expect to be surprised by the ability of those in the organization to respond to the new organizational design. Some, for example, will succeed beyond reasonable expectations. Some will disappoint the CEO because, for a variety of reasons, they will not or cannot adequately perform their new jobs. There will be pressures to revert back to the past. It takes time to establish new equilibrium among the task processes, the personnel, and the resources. There is a natural inclination to remember fondly the old organization and to look for the shortcomings of the new. Usually the initial enthusiasm begins to fade and criticisms of the new design begin to crystallize about certain individuals or policies.

The CEO must be ready to accept this and the necessity of adapting the organization during the implementation phase. In my experience, a high percentage of the criticisms are really just bids for attention and a result of the jockeying to achieve new equilibria. But some of the criticisms are valid and require resolution. Many times the criticisms, when resolved, improve the organizational design. To view such problems as only requiring emotional support or firmness underestimates the capacity of the member of the organization to be responsible. The attitude should be: If we can improve it and if it will benefit the organization, let's try to get it done. Monitoring the implementation is thus a continuation of the organizational design.

Stage five, monitoring the implementation, has four major steps. The first is to review the organizational design. This review is to assess how well the new organizational design is working and to identify any special implementation problems. The second step involves specific analyses of the identified problems in order to reach a decision about how to solve the problems and how to implement required changes. The third step is to update the organizational design. This means updating the Organizational Logics, the Organizational Architecture, and relevant position descriptions. The fourth step is to investigate requirements for any supplementary services as might be needed. There are 22 supplementary services that are part of the OA&A technology that might be helpful to the organization listed in Table 9.1. For example, there may be need for systematic management development or for in-house organizational maintenance systems. In other cases, problems identified but not dealt with during the earlier stages such as developing a manpower planning system get resolved during stage five.

STAGES SIX THROUGH NINE

Stage six is the Organizational Playbook, and Stage seven is the Organizational Game Plan. Organizational Playbooks provide a planning and operating tool for management which directly links human resources to operating in a novel way. Organizational Game Plans are a tool for short term operations planning and for improved time management. Both are new and relatively untested in direct application. Organizational Playbooks and Game Plans will become more central to organizational design in the future than they are now for the OA&A technology. I wanted to mention them here in what I believe is their proper placement in the OA&A technology. These new tools are discussed in detail in Chapter 10.

Stage eight is the organizational maintenance stage. Its purposes are to provide continual updating to adapt the organization to change and to prevent manpower waste. There are ten key elements to the organizational maintenance system (OMS). These are:

a. Position descriptions
b. Activity list
c. Organizational Logic
d. Organizational charts
e. Organizational Responsibility Grouping chart (ORG chart)
f. Procedures for maintaining and updating position descriptions
g. Procedures for maintaining and updating the activity list and the Organizational Logic
h. Procedures for maintaining and updating the organizational chart
i. Procedures for maintaining and updating the ORG chart
j. Procedures for reviewing organizational consistency and for using organizational documentation.

The organization will change when there are (a) shifts in the environments, (b) changes in goals and strategies, (c) shifts in key personnel, and (d) changes occuring over a period of time that are generally minor but which tend to accumulate and create, over time, significant structural changes. An OMS is very helpful in tracking, updating, and generally maintaining the organization. The main purpose of an OMS is to ensure that there is overall guidance to documenting and approving changes, that they be made fairly with logical integrity,and that there is review and control of all of these changes.

Major changes due to shifts in the environments and changes in goals and strategies require the direct involvement of the CEO, because the decisions can affect every part of the organization. This means that the design premises may change, and, when they change, so does the Organizational Logic and the organizational design. Changes in key personnel often reflect ad hoc shifts in strategies, and, when they do, there needs to be some rethinking of the organizational design. But most changes are rather minor in terms of their effects on the rest of the organization. These include promotions, transfers, new hires, and personnel departures. They also include many small adjustments in the assignments and descriptions of work.

The bulk of the many changes can be handled by maintenance of the organization's position descriptions. Position descriptions contain information about the formal working relationships and the duties and responsibilities of each position. Position descriptions are the primary working document for handling most organizational maintenance issues. The general procedure is for the CEO to assign the responsibility for OMS to a staff unit, such as the Human Resources Department. This staff unit does more of the actual maintenance work under the supervision of the CEO, who must ensure that major changes are reviewed and approved. A typical division of responsibilities involves six key task processes.

1. All organizational changes will be reviewed and approved by the CEO.
2. The creation of most organizational changes is the responsibility of the officer whose organizational unit is affected.
3. The staff officer is assigned the responsibility for reviewing the organization in every area of the company with the officer in charge *each quarter*. He or she is to ensure that the changes are processed.
4. The staff officer is responsible for checking the format of the changes, ensuring approval has been obtained, processing and distributing them, and for providing guidance and consulting as required.
5. The staff officer is responsible for providing departmental organizational manuals as requested.
6. The staff officer will maintain a log of organizational changes and their status.

The basic procedure for most changes is to proceed bottom to top. Any person becoming aware of a change in any position or in departmental activities shall notify the Area Head. The Area Head then prepares or delegates to another the preparation of the change, and notifies the staff officer of the forthcoming change. The staff officer provides forms and guidance as required. The Area Head then forwards the change to the staff officer, who reviews the format of the change, advises on revisions, and prepares a draft of the change. The staff officer then forwards the draft change to the initiator and/or the Area Head with an update approval sheet. The Area Head signs off on the change and obtains the approval of the CEO. The CEO then notifies the staff officer, who then prepares a quarterly report to the CEO summarizing changes approved during the period, those awaiting approval, and those in process.

Typically, we find that staff officers rarely understand the task processes of most of the operating units of a company, and that operating unit leaders rarely understand the OMS details. There is often a game played in which individuals seek expansion of their responsibilities, which often is not recognized by the staff officer. Although the procedure described in the previous paragraph may seem cumbersome, it at least provides the opportunities for checking and controlling the changes. The quarterly review helps the CEO and the staff officer to spot trends. Typically, operating officers do not like the work involved in making the changes and dislike the implied control by the staff officer and the CEO. The process helps build some understanding and at least keeps the CEO informed. One should expect to be surprised by the lack of detailed knowledge of the CEO and his or her staff about operations. For example, a university president only has the vaguest idea of what all the units of the organization are doing.

Over a longer period of time, despite the routine processing of many minor changes, it becomes necessary to review the whole organization. Stage nine is the Systems Review. A System Review is an abbreviated Strategic Assessment, Organizational Audit, and organizational design. Its purpose is to evaluate the organizational design, to review progress and plan for the organization, and to assist, if necessary, the organization's internal staffs. It also provides a review and a quality control for evaluating the OMS. A Systems Review is a time for ensuring that the effects of changes in the environment, changes in goals and strategies, changes in key personnel, and the accumulation of many smaller changes are maintaining the organizational congruency.

The ABCE Model, the definition of organizational design, and the theory of group structure stress change and the need for maintenance of the organization. Desiderata D_{11}, manageability, was concerned with the capacity of the organizational design to allow provision for maintenance and updating. Stages six to nine are directly concerned with meeting this important desideratum. That is why they are a part of the OA&A technology.

CHAPTER 10

Organizational playbooks and game plans

INTRODUCTION

Football coaches are no dummies. They have invented a management tool called a playbook. The playbook describes how each player performs his assignments in every offensive and defensive play. The head coach and his assistant coaches recruit players needed to perform the plays, and then they train the players until they not only know the plays but can also execute them. They videotape practices and all games, and then grade the players according to how well they execute their play assignments.

Most American managers follow football. Yet I have never met one that has ever developed a playbook for his own organization. They know about playbooks, but they have never thought of doing one for their own organizations. They routinely praise teamwork and team building. Given the talent and energy of so many executives, this omission has always surprised me. We have the technology and tools to produce Organizational Playbooks routinely.

Most organizations have position descriptions which describe the role of each position within the organization. These are used for many decisions (hiring, paying, promoting, EEOC, compliance, etc.), but they are difficult to use for managing. Consider the football coach who has a position description for every position on the team. Would the coach study the position descriptions for each individual and then construct a play? No. A football play is defined in terms of what the *set of players* on the field are to do. A football play is defined with respect to the group of players. It shows what each is to do and how he is to do it. When each carries out his assignment, they are to work together as a team. I doubt whether most football managers have position descriptions (except for people in the office staff). They are not very useful for teamwork. The play is the natural unit of action of a football team, because football is a team sport whose participants operate as a team rather than as a collection of individuals.

Since most managers praise teamwork and since most know about playbooks, why don't they build teamwork by using Organizational Playbooks? Probably the main reason is that they have never thought about doing so. Even if they did think about it, they lack the necessary tools. I also believe that the existing theory could not be used to define the playbooks. Information on position descriptions is too imprecise to construct plays. However, once an organization has its Organizational Logic, the organizational chart, and the ORG chart, it is a routine exercise to develop an Organizational Playbook.

Playbooks for football teams are living documents that are repeatedly updated and refined in order to make each play more productive and in order to keep them up to date. The playbook is used to develop a game plan for each game. Selecting the plays and practicing them before each game is necessary for the success of the team.

Management, too, has a need for a playbook and game plan, and it needs one that is flexible and easily understood by all the members of the organization. Most managements must continually cope with change. A lot of the change is brought into the firm by its environment. Environmental changes include new technology, shifting economic conditions, new regulations and laws, competition, and social values. However, there are many changes that occur within the firm, such as employee turnover, new goals and strategies, corporate policies, application of research and development, bargaining over resource allocations, and many on going crises and emergencies. These environmental and internal changes create the need to have an up-to-date playbook upon which the organization can develop a game plan so that the team can achieve its goals.

Many of the secrets of a successful firm involve knowledge of key management plays that have never been written down and communicated. The memory of the organization often resides in the heads of experienced personnel. When the key persons leave, or are promoted or transferred, important information about the organizational processes becomes lost and must be reinvented at high cost. The costs of turnover should include the loss and the disruption of Organizational Plays.

ORGANIZATIONAL PLAYS

The reader was introduced to task processes in Chapter 4, to structures and Organizational Responsibility Grouping charts (ORG charts) in Chapter 5. We need to return to some of the ideas presented in these chapters in order to define a play.

A *play* is a set of task processes which includes the directly integrable task processes and their directly integrating task process. A play is a unit of task process combining managing task processes (DCC and planning) with execution task processes. The play is usually defined with respect to an organizational unit, such as a head teller and the tellers who work for him or her. The tellers perform execution task processes, and the head teller directs, controls, and coordinates the tellers. The main task of the head teller is to bring integrable task processes into "in commonness." To do this, the task processes, the personnel, and the other task process resources characteristics must be reconsidered. Despite the atomistic pressures brought to bear by position descriptions, and performance appraisal methods which emphasize the individual worker, the basic unit of behavior for managers is the play itself.

The levels of aggregation of high task processes were introduced in Chapter 4. These included the macro-logic, areas, groups, bundles, modules, and activities. In the OA&A technology, every bundle is a play of modules, every group is a play of bundles, every area is a play of groups, and the macro-logic is a play of areas. Thus, the Organizational Logic is a hierarchy of its constituent plays. The other dimension of task process hierarchy was the level which included planning, directing, controlling and coordinating (DCC), and execution task processes. Planning task processes change DCC and execution task processes, and DCC task processes integrate execution task processes. Hence, we can speak of planning, DCC, and execution plays.

A task process can also be classified temporarily, according to whether it is a regular task process, a calendar task process, and an infrequent or future task process. Consequently, we have regular plays, calendar plays, infrequent plays, and future plays.

There is a two-fold classification of organizational plays. The first dimension concerns the *timing* of the play. We use four categories:

1. *Regular plays* occur continually and are the normal part of the functions of an organization. Most line functions are regular plays.
2. *Infrequent plays* are more plays that are only executed when some specific contingency occurs. However, law suits, working with OSHA inspectors, assembly line breakdowns, etc., are examples of (hopefully) infrequently occurring plays. Contingency planning for handling infrequent plays can improve adaptability. It is not an uncommon organizational design to have regular plays considered as infrequently occurring plays and thus not adequately incorporated into the organizational design.
3. *Calendar plays* are a type of regular play that are only executed for specific time periods. A common calendar play is the preparation of the payroll at the end of the month, the filing of quarterly tax statement, and the annual stockholders meeting.
4. *Future plays* are planned plays for future task processes that are not yet in the repertoire of the organization but are planned to be included in the future. They are written for launching new units and task processes for an organization.

The second dimension of a play is its *level*. Plays are broken into three levels:

1. *Execution plays* describe how an execution task process is to be performed.
2. *DCC plays* refer to the directing, coordinating, and controlling plays made to ensure completion and scheduling of execution plays. DCC plays are made by supervisors and managers.
3. *Planning plays* describe the processes by which plays are selected and coordinated. Senior management spends more time on planning plays than on execution plays, because they typically manage through managers rather than directly.

The two dimensions of play, timing and level, with each having three categories results in 12 types of plays, is shown in Table 10.1.

The classification of each play is used to describe each play in the Organizational Playbook. Generally, senior management spends more time on planning plays than on DCC plays, and more on DCC than on execution plays. Generally, staff persons spend more time on calendar, infrequent and future plays than on execution plays. The distribution of type of play will depend upon the specific contingencies found by each organization.

TYPES OF POSITIONS

It is in the nature of many jobs that there resides potential for misdirected or broken plays. As presented in Chapter 5, there are three basic patterns that show up in carefully drawn organizational charts.

a. *The Normal Position,* in which there is a position X and this position is performed by a specific person, A.

Many organizational charts are drawn as if all positions were normal positions when, in fact, many are not. This lack of accuracy becomes entombed in formal position and job descriptions, performance incentives, and the allocation of responsibility. It is misleading to consider positions as normal when they are not. At the very least, this makes it difficult to manage systematically because the implied playbook is simply incorrect. This is especially acute in unstable and irregular DBOs (cf. Chapter 8).

b. *Parallel Positions,* in which there exists a position X which is performed by more than one individual.

Table 10.1 Play classifications

	Play level		
Play timing	**Execution**	**DCC**	**Planning**
Regular	R,E	R,DCC	R,P
Infrequent	I,E	I,DCC	I,P
Calendar	C,E	C,DCC	C,P
Future	F,E	F,DCC	F,P

Many positions such as salesmen, professors, doctors, nurses, bank tellers, and machinists, are parallel. Parallel positions are common in industry. Problems occur for a team when positions considered parallel are not so, and when the execution of the task process in parallel position does not have consistent direction, coordination, and control. Employee turnover creates a real need to ensure that all of the parallel players know how to peform their plays. When they don't, there are little "huddles" to either provide on-the-job training or to work at coordinating problems in spite of management.

c. *Multiple-Hat Positions*, in which an individual is performing more than one position.

A common occurence is the *combination* of parallel and multiple-hat positions as shown by:

Position S	Position Y	Position Z
A	A	A
	B	C
	C	D

Such combinations create real problems in coordination and control. These types of positions are common in entrepreneurial firm management, firms going through rapid change, firms under changing regulations, and firms where the customers expect personal service from an individual even though that individual's job has changed. In one case, the president of a firm acted as:

President
Director of R & D
Purchasing Agent
Salesman

As purchasing agent, his job fell under the job of a manager and, as salesman his job fell under the VP of Sales. Both the manager and VP Sales reported to the President. Thus, the peculiarities of this firm and its history of growth had created the possibilities of many broken plays, along with confused lines of authority and responsibilities. In many cases such multiple-hat roles are necessary and should be recognized and acknowledged.

Multiple-hat jobs are common in matrix organizations where many of the participants wear two hats. For example, Philips has a matrix organization with sales and technical persons in dual control at every level of management. In one R & D firm, there were four stacks of multiple-hat jobs reflecting the type of talent required. The same person developing the fundamental technology is also involved in conversion to a development project, the development project, and the project to enable commercial application. Matrix organizations exhibit a double stack. Stacks of higher order are not only common but are often desirable because of unique talent, shortage of personnel and capital, and because of personal interests. They can create excessive organizational interdependencies, which leads to confusion and waste.

The existence of multiple-hat and parallel jobs demands a mechanism for allocating the human resources as needs arise. These not normal jobs also involve restrictions on the allocation of other task process resources such as facilities, equipment, and working capital. The existence of multiple-hat and parallel jobs creates the necessity for setting forth priorities and periodically developing who is supposed to do what this period. An Organizational Playbook and a Game Plan provide a system for making these types of decisions in an orderly and effective manner.

COMPONENTS OF A PLAY

Every play has four components regardless of the type of play. These are:

a. The Players. Each play has a play leader as well as the players. Usually the distinction between play leader and players follows the chain of command. But for parallel and multiple-hat jobs, infrequent or calendar plays, and planning plays, the selection of play leader and player may be more complex and subtle.
b. Player Assignments. The specific functions or tasks performed by each player in every play is specified.
c. Play Logic. The play logic describes how the bundle is broken into its modules and the modules into their constituent activities.
d. Play Location. The play location describes how the play fits into the overall Organizational Logic.

Play Organizational Responsibility Grouping (Play ORG)

The players and player assignments can be summarized in a table with the players listed as rows and the modules of the bundle describing the play logic as columns. The entries in the play ORG are:

P—Player Performs the Module
S_1—Player Supervises directly a player with a P
S_2—Player Supervises a Player with an S_1
S_n—Player Supervises a Player with an S_{n-1}
X—Player works with a player with a P but is not a regular player

Every play in the Organizational Playbook has a play ORG at the bottom of the page describing the play.

Organizational Playsheets

An organizational play sheet is a form with the following information:

Play Title:
Play Location:
Play Type:
Play Logic:
Play ORG Chart:

Example of an Organizational Play Sheet

This example is taken from a scientific technical information brokerage firm whose customer service constitutes an important organizational play within the Document Sales and Service Division. This play is written at the bundle level. It is the first bundle of Group 303 in Area 3 of the company. It is a regular, execution organizational play.

The play leader is the Manager of Document Sales and Services (DSS). The players consist of his three clerks (mailing lists/fulfillment clerk, DSS clerk, and the shipping/receiving clerk). The modules involve two players outside the DSS department: the bookkeeper who tracks and records all cash transactions, and the research librarian who helps out on Module 303-01-04 for special requests/order processing. The research librarian is involved because handling special requests requires special expertise that resides in the research department. One of the responsibilities of this person is to act as a resource in support of Document Sales and Services. The shipping/receiving clerk is involved with two modules because he maintains the inventory and assembles orders. Sometimes an order cannot be filled from inventory, and must be assembled as the documents arrive from various publishers. The Manager of Document Sales and Services acts as the direct supervisor for each of the seven modules. However, for module 303-01-04 he is involved because this module requires special expertise.

As the organization's sales increase, Bundle 303-01 may become a group and the modules may become bundles, because there will be a need for DCC task processes to direct, control, and coordinate many clerks and the workload. Organizational plays must change as the organization changes. The playsheet for Bundle 303-01 is shown in Figure 10.1.

THE ORGANIZATIONAL PLAYBOOK

The Organizational Playbook is a manual which has seven sections. These are:

1. Introduction
2. Executive Summary

Play Title: TRS Customer Services

Play Location: 303-01

Play Type: R. E

Play Logic

    Module -01: Receipt of Customer Inquiries and Orders
    Module -02: Routine Customer Order Processing
    Module -03: ABC Product Customer Order Processing
    Module -04: Special Requests/Order Processing
    Module -05: Inquiry Services
    Module -06: Mailing Lists Maintenance
    Module -07: Customer History File Maintenance

Players	Play Logic						
	1	2	3	4	5	6	7
Manager, Document Sales and Services	S_1	S_1	S_1	S_1/P	S_1	S_1	S_1
Clerk, Mailing List/ Fulfillment	O	P	P	O	P	P	P
Clerk, DSS	P	O	O	P	P	O	O
Clerk, Shipping/Receiving	O	X	X	O	O	O	O
Bookkeeper	X	X	O	X	O	O	O
Research Librarian	O	O	O	X	O	O	O

Legend of Entries into the Play Logic Table

    P   Directly Performs the Task

    S_1 Supervises the Position Performing the Task

    S_1/P Acts as Both a Supervisor and A Performer for the Task
    S_2 Supervises the Position Who is the S_1 for the Task

    X   Works with Others in Performance of the Task
             (Usually provides information necessary for support)

    O   Position is not Directly Involved with the Task

Figure 10.1.   The playsheet for TRS customer service.

3. Lists of Plays by Play Timing
4. List of Plays by Organizational Logic
5. Organizational Playsheets
6. Organizational Logic
7. System for Updating Organizational Plays

The Introduction essentially describes the concepts of organizational plays. The executive summary provides an overview of the Organizational Playbook in terms of the needs and uses of a specific organization. It also has an organizational chart and a complete list of all players. The list of plays is a listing of play location, play title, play timing, play level, play leader, players, and play period if a calendar play. The Organizational Playsheets are listed in the order of the Organizational Logic. The Organizational Logic gives the details of every module's activities. The system for updating organizational plays describes how to update the Organizational Playbook. The Organizational Playbook is essentially arranged in increasing order of task process detail. It is designed to facilitate search for developing Organizational Game Plans. This separation by timing helps sort out priorities in the Organizational Game Plans. For example, calendar plays can be used for planning, and a "tickler" file can be set up to ensure that monthly plays, such as payroll and billing, quarterly plays such as budgeting, quarterly statements, and tax payments, and annual plays, such as stockholder meetings and business plans, do not fall by the wayside.

Updating the Organizational Playbook

The basic source of the Organizational Playbook is the Organizational Logic and the set of play ORGs. Any change in the play logic or play ORG should be made in the Organizational Logic, and vice versa. The table below describes what to update for each change. In every case of a change, all of the playbook should be updated and the changes disseminated to those involved.

Playbook Changes and Update System

Change	What to Update
Play Classification	Play File, Play Lists
Play Logic	Organizational Logic, Play Lists
Player	Play File, Play ORG, and Executive Summary
Play Location	Organizational Logic, Play File, Play Lists, and Play ORG

The employment of a system for Organizational Game Plans is usually a quicker source of information about needs for updating the Organizational Blueprint than is the Organizational Maintenance System described in stage eight in Chapter 9. Whenever a manager calls a play and can't find it in the Organizational Playbook, it points out the need to update the Organizational Playbook.

RELATIONSHIPS AMONG ORGANIZATIONAL PLAYBOOKS, POSITION DESCRIPTION SETS, AND JOB DESCRIPTION SETS

The Organizational Playbook is not the same as a set of position or job descriptions. It is more fundamental because it focuses on the management of plays or processes. This emphasis on the functions or processes is very different from the emphasis at the individual level embodied in position and job descriptions. The Organizational Playbook can be used to generate the set of position descriptions, but the set of position descriptions cannot generate the Organizational Playbook. Job descriptions are built up from position descriptions, plus information about wage and salary ranges for each position and qualifications for each position.

The following example will illustrate how a play contains information lost when one completes position descriptions:

Let the play ORG be given by:

	Play Logic					
Player	1	2	3	4	5	6
President	P	S_1	S_1	S_2	S_1	S_1
VP	O	X	P	S_1	P	P
Supervisor	O	P	X	P	O	O

We can draw this play ORG logic as shown in Figure 10.2.

The entries in each circle include the module number and the player. For example, 2/S designates module 2 performed by the supervisor. The box

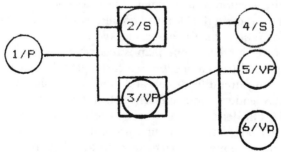

Figure 10.2. A play ORG logic.

around the circle refers to the "works with" relationship in a play. The network describing the play illustrates the Organizational Logic of the play. This diagram contains a lot more information than a position description summary. For example, the VP's and Supervisor's position descriptions would read:

Title: VP	Title: Supervisor
Supervises: S on 4	Supervises: None
Reports to: P on 3,4,5,6	Reports to: P on 2
	VP on 4
Job: Performs	Job: Performs
3	2
5	4
6	
Works with: VP on 2	Works with: VP on 3

Note that the individual position descriptions lose the essence of the play and the information about the play logic. And, as the number of plays increases, the loss of information becomes greater as one relies on position descriptions.

The relationship among the Organizational Playbook, the sets of positions, and the job descriptions are described in the following three tables: Table 10.2 gives comparisons according to the types of inputs, Table 10.3 provides comparisons according to uses by management, and Table 10.4 lists comparisons according to qualitative aspects.

ORGANIZATIONAL GAME PLANS

An *Organizational Game Plan* is the selection of organizational plays from the Organizational Playbook for a specific time period. It specifies the play leader, the players, the priority of each play, a time deadline, and specific comments or instructions for each play. The called plays are usually listed in order of their location in the Organizational Logic on a form generated by a word processor. This form also has an empty column labeled "results" which is filled in before the next game plan is described.

The basic procedure is to meet to select the plays for the next period. At this meeting, those attending discuss and then decide what plays to perform. They select play leaders and players, establish the play priorities, and agree on a time table. The decision procedure to select the plays starts by reviewing the previous period's game plan, the upcoming calendar plays, the need to meet a crisis, and the need to perform postponable plays. The review and the upcoming calendar plays are key ingredients in play selection. In the

Table 10.2 Comparisons according to types of inputs

Items	Organizational Playbook	Position Description Set	Job Description Set
Inputs			
Activity list by individual	Can be generated	Yes	Yes
Activity list by play	Yes	Information lost	Information lost
Individual tasks	Can be generated	Yes	Yes
Player tasks by play	Yes	Information lost	Information lost
Structural relationship: individual summary			
Supervision	Can be generated	Yes	Yes
Works with	Can be generated	Yes	Yes
Liaison	Can be generated	Yes	Yes
Structural relationship: by each play			
Supervision	Yes	Information lost	Information lost
Works with	Yes	Information lost	Information lost
Liaison	Yes	Information lost	Information lost
Salary ranges	No	No	Yes
Qualifications	No	No	Yes
Play Classification			
By timing	Yes	No	No
By level	Yes	No	No

Table 10.3 Comparisons according to use by management

Items	Organizational Playbook	Position Description Set	Job Description Set
Use by management			
Line management			
Operational Planning	When in the form of Game Plan		
Setting Priorities	Yes	No	No
Allocating Personnel	Yes	No	No
Play Selection	Yes	No	No
Play Scheduling	Yes	No	No
Time Management	Yes	No	No
Conflict Prevention	Yes	No	No
Improving Operations			
Updating Activities	Yes	No	No
Improving Plays	Yes	No	No
Changing Plays	Yes	No	No
Communicating Changes			
Individual	Yes	Yes	Yes
Play	Yes	Information lost	Information lost
Staff			
Human Resources			
Salary & Benefits	No	No	Yes
Selection, Promotion, Hiring	Indirect	Yes	Yes
Evaluation	Indirect	Indirect	Indirect
Training & Development	Yes	Yes	Yes

Table 10.4. Comparisons according to qualitative aspects

Items	Organizational playbook	Position description set	Job description set
Qualitative aspects			
Dynamic	Yes	Too Static Information Lost	Too Static Information Lost
Used For:			
Directing Operations	Yes-In Game Plan Form	Possible	Possible
Controlling Operations	Yes-In Game Plan Form	Indirectly Possible	Indirectly Possible
Coordinating Operations	Yes-In Game Plan Form	Indirectly Possible	Indirectly Possible
Tool For:			
Active Management	Yes	No	No
Staff Work	Yes	Yes	Yes
Used For:			
Emergencies & Crises	Yes-In Game Plan Form	No	No
Separates Calendar, Infrequent, and Regular Plays	Yes	No	No
Acts as Active Mgt. Memory of Task Process	Yes	No	No

case of multiple-hat positions, parallel positions, or combinations of these two types, the selection of play leader and player helps management "direct traffic," plan for overloads, and balance the workloads more evenly. For example, if a member of the research department is also the play leader for some new product development, the selection of plays in both parts of the Organizational Logic may overload this member. If the priority of the research is low relative to the product development, the play leader may be assigned both with an understanding about the relative priorities. But, if both are huge priorities, he or she may only be able to get one done. In this case, another may be appointed as the play leader for one of the plays. Thus, he or she may be assigned the role of a player in a play for which he or she would normally be the play leader. The preparation of the game plan helps spot these problems and achieve an understanding for how to solve them. Some persons will take on more than they can handle. The review of the person's game plan quickly builds up a record of accomplishment which can be used both to select the plays and to review the plays and play leaders. Persons who are unable to complete the assigned plays according to the game plans are easily spotted. This information provides vital clues about the Organizational Technology. Sometimes, for example, the organizational play is out of date. In others, the estimate of time for completion was unrealistic. But, in other cases, the failure to meet deadlines is a cause for review of the person's capabilities. The records of results for the Organizational Game Plan are very useful in performance appraisal. These records guide the CEO in managing. Often, the CEO underestimates the difficulties in executing plays, and unrealistic expectations cause others trouble. The CEO can use this analysis to soothe hurt feelings.

The decision process to select the plays for the Organizational Game Plan also provides clues about the adequacy of the plays in the Organizational Playbook. For example, if a play is called for, but it does not exist in the Organizational Playbook, a new play needs to be written. There will always be one-shot special plays that need not always be incorporated into the Organizational Playbook. But if, period after period, the same general type of play is called for, this is good evidence of the need to update the Organizational Playbook. Virtual positions become identified as a by-product of selecting plays.

Calling the plays begins with a review of the previous game plan. Normally, completed plays are dropped and regular plays are not listed. The regular plays are supposed to be completed as a matter of course and do not need to be called. Crises must be dealt with swiftly, and organizational plays that are seen as ways of handling a crisis are automatically listed in the Organizational Game Plan.

After calling the crisis handling plays, the next step is to review the plans for the next period. All calendar plays falling in this next period are automatically included in the new game plan. The next question is to review uncompleted plays for the previous period and to decide if they are still necessary. The next step is to look for special plays (usually infrequent or future plays) that might be useful to complete. Another list of possible plays that is part of the plans for the next period is listed. The crisis, calendar, and planned plays are called required plays. The other possible plays are only listed tentatively. The next step is to examine resource conflicts to select plays for those on the tentative list. The result of those choices is the preliminary Organizational Game Plan. Priorities are set, players assigned, and a due date is established. This information is recorded on the form and given to a word processor which produces the next period game plan. This is reviewed and, if approved, is sent to the play leaders.

I have personally been involved in developing Organizational Game Plans for some time. It works very well. Each successive planning session is faster than the last, as persons learn to prepare and use an Organizational Game Plan. It clarifies expectations, sorts out priorities, allows review of operations and performances, provides information needed to update and maintain the organization, and is easily communicated. The exercise is a very powerful method of time management for the organization involved.

The preparation of Organizational Playbooks and Game Plans are stages six and seven of the OA&A technology. They are very useful to flushing out needs for organizational maintenance (stage eight) and, together with the Organizational Maintenance System, they are very valuable in conducting a system review (stage nine).

The CEO, or the manager in charge of a section of an organization using an Organizational Playbook, benefits from the discipline of working through an operational game plan. It helps the CEO communicate and work with key subordinates. It helps the CEO recognize present conflict issues. It is very useful in detecting deficiencies in the playbook and in deciding what plays require special effort to improve. For example, a busted play that does not seem to work is not unlike a football play that does not work. Developing Organizational Game Plans helps the leader become more effective.

CHAPTER 11

Supplementary human resources analyses in the OA&A technology

INTRODUCTION

Chapter 9 contains a description of stages one to five, and eight and nine, of the OA&A technology. Chapter 10 describes stages six and seven, which, while part of the OA&A technology, are relatively untested. Table 9.1 provides an overview of every stage in the OA&A technology, plus a listing of 22 supplementary analyses. Of these 22, there are the following supplementary analyses that directly support the management of a human resources program. These include:

3.4   Wage And Salary System Design
3.5   Job Descriptions
3.6   Training
3.7   EEO Compliance
4.1   Performance Incentive System
4.2   Manpower Planning System
4.3   Performance Management Review
4.5   Management Succession Analysis and Planning
4.7   Management Development
4.8   Career Planning Systems Design
Plus related services for organizational maintenance (stage eight).

The purpose of this chapter is to explain how selected human resources analyses can be performed as a byproduct of the main stages in the OA&A technology. The main emphasis is placed on those analyses for which there are distinctive features that are directly a result of viewing an organization in terms of its task processes, and for which the OA&A technology offers improvements to existing methods. The goals of these services are (1) to improve the usefulness and responsiveness of the human resources staff, (2) to assist the integration of the senior management and the human resources staff in order to prevent manpower waste (Mackenzie, 1982), and (3) to improve utilization of human assets.

These supplementary human resources analyses make four major assumptions. First, the primary data for any human resources management system begins with an accurate description of the task processes, the Organizational Responsibility Grouping chart, the organizational chart, and a full set of position descriptions. Second, human resources departments lack current information about the work of the organization. It is vital that these primary data be kept current with actual operations to the extent possible. The main reasons are: (1) the existence of change creates authority-task gaps between the official-role system enshrined in the human resources department and the actual task-role system; (2) the human resources departments do not process systematic descriptions of the work because they lack Organizational Logics; (3) the human resources departments lag the actual task-role system in adapting to change; and (4) most human resources departments are, despite appearance and logic to the contrary, not central to the way most companies manage themselves. After 8 years of working with many companies, I have never run across a human resources or personnel department that was integrated into critical, strategic, and operation decisions. Most, frankly, are treated as service departments which are considered cost centers, whose purposes are to manage the minutiae of personnel issues such as payroll, benefits, managing the union-management relationships, defending and protecting the corporation from government regulations, assisting in recruiting, selecting and training, and appraising performance. Third, the human resources departments desire to contribute more to the organization. Collectively, these departments perform very important duties. Nevertheless, to the extent to which those duties are seen as tedious and boring, most CEOs will avoid too much involvement. Fourth, the CEOs I've met would like to improve this situation.

I have never met a CEO who does not believe in the importance of his organization's human resources. I have never met one who would not ascribe to and affirm the linkages among human resources issues and the eventual success of the organization. I have also never met a Director or Manager of Human Resources or Personnel who is not frustrated by the gap between these beliefs and commitment to what is actually being done to improve the management of human resources. It seems as though both sides are caught in a logical trap. There is really no good reason why this muddle cannot be improved.

The methods used by human resources departments to perform those important functions are basically antiquated, for seven reasons. First, the basic information does not exist in most companies about how the various jobs are designed. The texts by Davis and Taylor (1979) and by McCormick (1979) provide useful guides to job design and job analysis. Second, there are usually two personnel systems: one for senior officers, and one for the rest of the organization. The one for the officers is often managed by the CEO. Third, they lack the technology to update the systems as change occurs in the task processes and organizational interdependence. Fourth, most of the staffs in human resources or personnel departments do not really know the business they are entrusted to help. The training and experience that most receive does not include knowledge of the specific operating problems in a firm. The concept that personnel management is a profession whose techniques and ideas are universal encourages most I have met to act like technicians. Fifth, most of the work done is under the law, and is technician work with great emphasis placed on accuracy and compliance. Most CEOs I have met think that all of this detail is a bother because it is not central to the strategic management of the firm. They want to be fair and they want to stay out of trouble. Sixth, the CEO's emphasis on the bottom line is usually directed to cutting or containing personnel costs rather than to improving usage of human talent. This means that the prime information required by the CEO is not normally supplied by the human resources department except for counts of various types of personnel and a range of compensation for each position. The aggregation of these data into budgets generally lags the strategic management of the firm. Lastly, I believe that most Directors of Human Resources or Personnel Managers are viewed as having a vested interest in continuing the problems rather than in solving them. This attitude on both sides is unfair and certainly unfortunate. This creates a wall which further erodes cooperation. This lack of cooperative partnership serves to increase the time lags between the needs of senior management and those of the human resources staff.

The OA&A technology can provide new tools for modernizing the management of human resources. It is an open question whether or not most human resources staff are the ones to manage the human resources of an organization. There are many barriers that must be broken down, including changing attitudes on all sides and retraining both senior management and the human resources staff. I am pessimistic about the current ability of the typical human resources staff to do this, because its members rarely have operational experience in sales, production, finance, etc. These issues lie behind the descriptions of the Organizational Maintenance System and systems review procedures described in Chapter 9 and in the need for Organizational Playbooks and Game Plans described in Chapter 10. However, I am very optimistic that, with the OA&A technology and with continued development of its methods, this unfortunate gulf between human resources staffs and senior management can be narrowed. It should be.

WAGE AND SALARY SYSTEM DESIGN

The design and use of wage and salary systems is the bread and butter of most professional personnel departments. There are many systems, ranging from pure market to fully administered systems. The text by Bowey and

Lupton (1973) will provide the reader with the basics. The methods used in most cases take longer to develop, update, and use than for the underlying relationships to change. This violates desideratum D5 for which $T_A < T_C$ (cf. Chapter 3). Generally, methods are used which are appropriate when the task processes are regular and stable. These methods usually are not agile enough to keep pace in more rapidly changing circumstances. This is one of the reasons they are often used for lower level positions. The main idea behind most wage and salary systems is to develop fair and defensible systems which facilitate cost containment.

The OA&A technology can be used directly to define, develop, implement and update wage and salary systems. The organizational design provides the primary information about task processes and the organizational structures. The position descriptions accurately describe each position and the system of intraorganizational interdependencies. The procedures for organizational maintenance allow frequent and timely updates to the primary data. Thus, the OA&A technology offers the opportunity to improve the effectiveness of human resources management programs, especially in developing and maintaining wage and salary systems.

Most wage and salary systems attempt to evaluate each position according to key factors. The list of factors describes incumbent attributes that are believed to apply across the full range of positions. Factors typically include (a) knowledge aspects required by the position, (b) personal qualities of an incumbent, (c) the functions performed by an incumbent, and (d) management requirements required of an incumbent. These four groupings of factors are usually subdivided into subfactors. I find that, in most organizations with which I have worked, there will be between 20 and 25 factors. For example, in a supermarket chain the management factors include: (1) leadership, (2) judgment, (3) planning, (4) delegation, (5) training and development, and (6) accountability. Personal factors included: (1) integrity, (2) initiative, (3) communication, (4) commitment, and (5) diplomacy. Knowledge aspects will be discussed in the next section. The factors for a bank may be very different from those of a supermarket chain.

The list of factors are assigned relative weights. It is usually easiest to have all of the weights total 100%. The assignment of factor weights usually leads to adjustment of the list of factors, and is best characterized as a negotiation process. The factors and factor weights apply to every position. The next step is to develop a scoring procedure for evaluating each factor. Thus, each factor has its own scoring method. For example, the management factor called Level of Accountability Required might have the following scores.

Factor: level of accountability required by an incumbent of a position	Score
Incumbent is accountable for bottom line profitability, growth, and survival of the organization.	100
Incumbent is accountable for the bottom line profitability, growth and survival of a division.	80
Incumbent is accountable for bottom line profitability and growth within a division.	70
Incumbent is accountable for allocations of major resources as identified by one or more line items in the income statement or balance sheet of the company.	50
Incumbent is accountable for level of specific line items in the financial statements.	30
Incumbent is not directly accountable for any specific line items.	0

Some firms use education as one of these factors. A community bank used the following scores:

Factor: level of education required by an incumbent of a position	Score
Masters degree in field related to banking	100
Ph.D. in Business or Economics	80
Bachelor's degree in field related to banking	70
Bachelor's degree not in field related to banking but with some business and economics training	60
College level courses (60 hrs.) yielding a working knowledge of a useful and relevant field needed by the bank	55
Vocational/Technical education in an office skill	35
High school graduate	20

This bank did not find a Ph.D. as valuable as an MBA. The factor weight for accountability was 7%, and was only 1% for education. Another company might have a very different set of factors and factor weights. A regional bank would probably place more weight on education than a community bank. The selection of factors, factor weights, and scores for each factor depend upon the goals, strategies, beliefs and judgments of each organization. In a wage and salary system, all positions are evaluated with the same factors, factor weights, and factor scores. For example, consider a CEO and a head teller. An example of factors, factor weights, and the scores are presented in Table 11.1.

Table 11.1. Sample factor and factor weight

Factor	Factor weight	Score	
		CEO	Head teller
Level of responsibility	.07	100	30
Education	.01	70	20

The product of the factor weight times the factor score summed over *all of the factors* is the *job rating* of the position. For example, the job ratings of the CEO and the head teller were 98.71 and 24.36, respectively.

Almost always, the calculation of job ratings creates subsequent iterations in the factors, factor weights, and factor scores until the scores "make sense" and are consistent with each other. It is very important to ensure that the position, and not a particular incumbent, is rated. The next stage is to plot current salary ranges against the job rating numbers. The resulting compensation curve can be quickly scanned for exceptional points. Almost always, some men will be higher than the compensation curve and some women will be lower than the compensation curve. These outliers create concern and often result in shifting the factors, factor weights, and factor scores to bring about more consistency. But, almost always, these changes still yield others.

Once these iterations are over, a salary range (minimum, maximum, and medium) can be defined for each position. The salary ranges are often taken from a compensation survey for peer organizations for "standard" positions. Unique position salary ranges are a mixture of current salary and a best guess at the closest category from a compensation salary.

Those paid below the minimum for a position are due for management action to bring the incumbent into the salary range. This might mean an immediate raise or a program of raising the salary over a period of time. The salary of those incumbents over the maximum are generally frozen. It is always helpful to consider market prices, because an internally consistent salary system will tend to inflate over time. It is always useful to compare the compensation curve of an organization with its competitors.

Some organizations maintain relatively flat compensation curves but allow reasonable incentives to operate differently for different level positions. Bonuses, profit sharing, and other incentive systems can reward more compensation to higher level positions and yet keep fixed personnel costs low. One can be reasonably sure that, left to its own devices, a firm's human resources staff will tinker with the job rating system until its own salaries and benefits are high. This tinkering is a major reason for the "corruption" of most position descriptions, which, when unchallenged, become modified to increase the job ratings. And when those responsible are not knowledgeable about the work of the organization, the entire wage and salary system can become out of control and will tend to rise as rapidly as permitted. For example, regulated and quasi-monopolistic industries tend to have very high salaries, because they can pass along these costs to the consumers. Continental Airlines, before it declared bankruptcy, paid the average employee $47,000 a year. After deregulation of the airline industry, it became clear that these salaries were exorbitant.

There are many "bells and whistles" one could consider in describing a wage and salary system. For example, there is the issue of comparable worth, in which a job rating system may be used to replace market prices for labor. There are problems in employee benefits. There are employee stock option programs. There is the issue of the shape of the compensation curve. The list is very long. There are special circumstances and prior commitments that must be dealt with. The existence of an up-to-date Organizational Logic and ORG chart is a real help in defining the position descriptions which are used to establish the job ratings. The creation of a wage and salary system is a natural byproduct of an organizational design. Attempts to design jobs and to evaluate jobs *after the fact* rather than as a part of an Organizational Logic are less effective and inherently less consistent, despite elaborate methodologies.

Wage and salary systems need to be adapted to changes in the Organizational Logic. Slowly, changing organizations can get good service out of traditional wage and salary system design methods, because their task processes are stable and regular. However, for more swiftly changing organizations, the wage and salary system cannot keep up, because it is not built upon the Organizational Logic and the ORG chart. Consequently, wage and salary systems tend to be used most in the slow-moving parts of an organization and least in the areas where a good wage and salary system would be of most use to management. They are especially good where there are many individuals holding the same stable jobs. They are especially inappropriate for unique, novel, and fast moving positions. I think that is the main reason a parallel personnel system for salaries is set up outside the normal channels of the personnel department for senior officers, and why it is difficult to create and administer wage and salary systems for high-tech, entrepreneurial start-ups. Because wage and salary systems are normally not based on an Organizational Logic and an ORG chart, they are difficult to adapt for changes. Consequently, despite the importance of rewarding employees for working well, and despite the importance of being fair, I believe that most wage and salary systems act as a type of organizational novocaine which anesthetizes responsible managers from the pain of making these decisions. Procedural rules replace thinking. As this is unreasonable, the gap and mutual frustration between the CEO and the staff in personnel remains.

With the OA&A technology, changes in the environment, goals, and strategies leading to new design premises and hence to Organizational Logic, changes can be easily incorporated and used to generate new ORG charts and position descriptions. There is no technical reason why the impact on job ratings could not be a mostly routine computation exercise. From there, the salary and wage implications of a design change can be calculated.

QUALIFICATIONS

Assuming that the organization possesses accurate valid position description, the natural question is, What qualifications does an incumbent need to effectively occupy his or her position? Specifying qualifications is very important, because of the following types of decisions: Recruiting, Selecting, Hiring, Promotions, Transfers, Training and Management Development, EEOC Compliance, Performance Incentives, Manpower Planning, Career Planning, and others.

Each of these has both operational and legal consequences, and so care must be taken in defining qualifications. Outside of the obvious admonishment not to waste talent through racial, ethnic, religious, and sexual discrimination, there is the problem of how to specify qualifications.

The system for creating job factors, factor weights, and factor scores to develop a job rating scale contains information that can be used to define most of the qualifications. This information can be used as a "first cut" in defining position qualifications. However, more refining may be necessary because of special technical requirements for many jobs. For example, a corporation's attorney must be a law school graduate, the Treasurer should be a C.P.A., a plant manager an engineering graduate. In industries such as health care and education, there are legal specifications of qualifications. Sometimes the qualifications are specified so precisely that only a previously picked candidate will be hired.

A whole book can be written about how to specify qualifications and it still would be incomplete because of change. I should like to leave that task to others, in order to present a few ideas about how to describe knowledge requirements. These ideas were developed during the course of an engagement with Supermarket Systems, Inc.

Supermarket Systems, Inc. has a Personnel Department which does a credible job in administering a wage and salary system for nonofficers. The Personnel Department is headed by a Vice President whose duties range from managing a union contract in the Distribution/Transportation System to planning and conducting training programs for new store managers and heads of produce and meat departments. The officers are not part of the wage and salary system except for routine maintenance issues. The CEO, for example, negotiated and set salaries for all of the officers personally after consultation with the Treasurer and his Executive Committee.

Most officer and staff positions (including the CEOs) did not have position descriptions, and the personnel files for the staff were extremely sketchy. For example, it was not recorded anywhere in the work records that the CEO had an M.B.A. degree. In some cases, the files contained information about the person's experience and training, but the data were hit and miss. It was known that Mr. Jones worked 2 years for another chain, but it was not clear what he did there. The files did contain the information needed to perform payroll and benefit functions and to determine eligibility for the ESOP plan. There were few performance appraisals for officers and staff people, while there were full reports of disciplinary actions for union employees.

The VP had, for years, been attempting to upgrade the Personnel Department into a Human Resources Department. I believe that he wanted to do this in order to improve the ability of Supermarket Systems, Inc. to make better use of its human assets. But he was so busy with union grievances, OSHA, and NLRB issues that this was never done. The dual track personnel system was a frustration, because he knew that he could use his knowledge to improve cost control and enhance his contribution to the firm. Being a tenacious professional, he applied steady pressure on management in order to accomplish his ideas for a human resources department, one piece at a time.

The CEO also realized the need to improve the service of human resources and was a supporter, but he was also very busy with more pressing matters. For example, I remember working with him one day when some bad mushrooms had to be recalled from all the stores and warehouses. This emergency brought in the local press and television. Signs had to be made warning the customers, and he had to consult with legal counsel about liabilities. The development of a Human Resources Department took a back seat. It was a postponable action which did not really affect the viability of the firm. Because it was not seen as a matter dealing with a major, recurring vulnerability, the issues were put off.

The new organizational design created positions for four new general managers who were responsible for the gross profits of a group of stores. The changes made it clear that SSI was going to need a much better system of evaluating, training, and developing personnel. There was a further need for more college graduates and for manpower planning in order to manage the expected growth of SSI. The CEO wanted a system for which no computer was needed and which could be used by nonspecialists. To do this, the CEO had to have a better idea of what each incumbent needed to know in order to perform his or her job, *and* what he or she needed in order to become qualified as a back up or successor to another position. He also wanted to know more systematically who knew what about each major task process. In short, he needed to know knowledge qualifications. My job was to invent a system for this.

To my knowledge, it is not possible to go to a university and take an advanced degree in supermarket management. It was not clear that an MBA was very useful for most jobs in SSI. For example, running a store means running a $5,000,000 business with many employees. It is hard work with many long hours, and the work is certainly not classified as high tech. A produce buyer needs specialized product knowledge that is learned on the job. Except for a few staff positions such as accounting, data processing, real estate, and personnel, most of the positions require actual experience. The relevance of college degrees was certainly a question mark, and the validity of requiring such a degree as a position qualification was considered very low in this business. These considerations, combined with the absence of information in personnel files, made it necessary to rethink the problem of specifying knowledge qualifications.

Fortunately, because of the organizational design and ongoing Organizational Maintenance System, SSI had current and accurate position descriptions. These were analyzed to uncover the type of knowledge that was needed. This preliminary analysis resulted in a classification scheme or code for different types of knowledge which was verified and amended through interviews with officers of SSI.

These discussions led to a realization that there were four main aspects of knowledge to be considered. These aspects were: (1) level of knowledge usage, (2) scope of the application of the knowledge by a position, (3) the relative value of the knowledge to the company, and (4) the source of the knowledge. The *level of knowledge* refers generally to the expertness of knowledge required. *The scope of application* describes the range of the Organizational Logic for which application of this knowledge had an impact. The *relative value* of the knowledge refers to the importance and usage of a type of knowledge to performance. The *source of knowledge* examines how the knowledge was gained. For example, knowledge of accounting is viewed differently for a store manager than it is for a controller. Knowledge of data processing had different aspects for the CEO and a member of the Personnel Department. These four aspects seemed to capture the elemental distinctions about knowledge for the many positions at SSI.

These four aspects of knowledge were considered generic to all positions. These aspects could be applied to each type of knowledge for every position. The four aspects can be displayed by quadrants: a *knowledge grid* as shown in Figure 11.1.

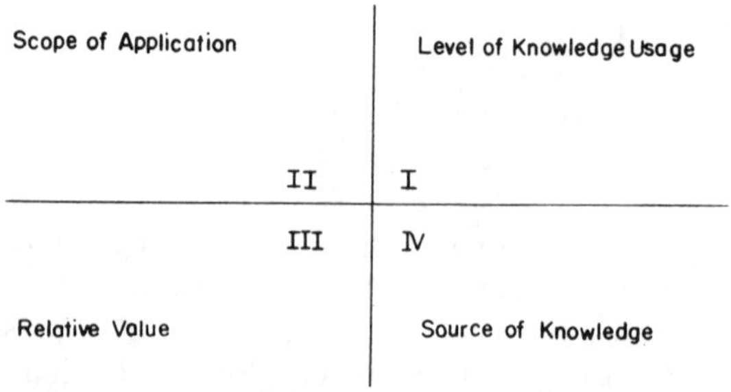

Scope of Application		Level of Knowledge Usage
	II	I
	III	IV
Relative Value		Source of Knowledge

Figure 11.1. The knowledge grid.

Table 11.2. Knowledge grid scales

Level of knowledge usage

Aware of the knowledge area; able to recognize problems, to handle them independently, to solve novel problems.	5
Aware of the knowledge area; able to recognize problems, to handle them independently, and to solve most nonroutine problems.	4
Aware of the knowledge area; able to recognize problems, and able to apply knowledge independently.	3
Aware of the knowledge area and able to recognize problems.	2
Aware of the knowledge area.	1
Unaware and unexposed to the knowledge area.	0

Scope of application of knowledge

Knowledge is used directly in planning and in the directing, controlling, and coordinating of task processes at the macro-logic level.	5
Knowledge is used directly in the planning and in the directing, controlling, and coordinating of task processes at the area level in the Organizational Logic.	4
Knowledge is used directly in the planning and in the directing, controlling, and coordinating of task processes at the group level in the Organizational Logic.	3
Knowledge is used directly in the planning and in the directing, controlling, and coordinating of task processes at the bundle level in the Organizational Logic.	2
Knowledge is used directly in the execution of task processes.	1
Knowledge is used only as background information in order to inform the execution, directing, controlling, and coordinating or the planning of other task processes.	1
Knowledge is not used at all.	0

Relative value of the person's knowledge

Knowledge is very important and is frequently employed.	5
Knowledge is important and is frequently employed.	4
Knowledge is very important but is only used infrequently.	3
Knowledge is important but is only used infrequently.	2
Knowledge has only marginal importance but is frequently employed.	1
Knowledge has only marginal importance and is only used infrequently.	0

Source of knowledge

Person has or position requires both experience and formal course work in the knowledge area.	5
Person has or position requires both expeience and systematic on the job training.	4
Person has or position requires experience but neither formal course work nor systematic on the job training.	3
Person has or position requires formal course work and systematic on the job training but not experience.	3
Person has or position requires formal course work but neither experience nor systematic on the job experience.	2
Person has or position requires systematic on the job training but neither experience or formal course work.	1
Person has or position requires no experience, no formal course work and no systematic on the job training.	0

Table 11.3. Knowledge grids for "front end operation"

Position	Knowledge grid	Comments on level of knowledge
CEO	5 | 2 2 | 3	Did not need specialized expertise about front end operations to be CEO.
SVP of Sales and Merchandising	4 | 5 4 | 3	Person in charge of all of the stores and staff product group. Knowledge of front end problems were applied to solve only the nonroutine. He then has to work with other senior officers such as accounting and data processing to effect a solution.
VP and General Manager	3 | 4 4 | 4	Supervises the territory supervisor. Front end knowledge is important to him.
Territory Supervisor	2 | 5 5 | 4	Direct supervisor of store managers. He is the man in the field who must keep stores operating.
Store Manager	2 | 3 4 | 4	Most store managers rely on head cashier and the staff specialist to handle nonroutine problems.
Manager of store financial services	2 | 5 5 | 5	Staff specialist who helped select equipment and to train store cashiers.
Personnel Clerk	0 | 0 0 | 0	Not involved in front end problems.

A scale was developed for each of the four aspects. The scale for each is given in Table 11.2. There is a six-point internal scale for each aspect. Consider the type of knowledge called "Front End Operations." Its knowledge grid for seven positions are displayed in Table 11.3.

The second aspect, scope of application, follows the Organizational Logic. The CEO applies his knowledge to the entire organization and has a 5. The SVP of Sales and Merchandising applies his knowledge to a whole area of the Organizational Logic, so he has a 4. The VP and General Manager has a group of activities and he has a 3. The Territory Supervisor, the Store Managers, and the Manager of Store Financial Services operate within a group of task processes at the bundle level, so they have a 2. The personnel clerk is not involved with front end operations, and has a value of 0.

The third aspect, relative value, reflects the combinations of importance and frequency of use of this knowledge. Knowledge about front end operations is important to the CEO, but he applies it infrequently. This knowledge is considered both very important and frequently used by both the Territory Supervisor and the Manager of Store Financial Services. To the other three positions, this knowledge is considered both important and frequently used.

The fourth aspect, source of knowledge, shows how the incumbent should be trained. Only the Manager of Store Financial Services required formal training in front end operations. Experience is seen as required for the VP and General Managers, Territory Supervisors, and Store Managers. Neither the CEO nor the SVP of Sales and Merchandising needed either formal course work or systematic on the job training.

The values for each aspect tabulated in Table 11.2 can be represented by a mapping function for each, as shown in Figures 11.2-11.5. The mapping function is very easy to use in direct interviews, because it directs the questions to determine the value of each aspect of a position. The interviews attempted to establish the necessary level for each quadrant for each position.

Coding knowledge by types is complicated by hierarchies of knowledge. Consider knowledge of Personnel Policies and Procedures. At the highest level, the type of knowledge is "Personnel Issues Formulation." A notch below is "SSI Personnel Policies and Procedures." A similar hierarchy occurs for knowledge about pricing. At the highest level the knowledge required is "Pricing Policy Formulation." Next is "Knowledge of SSI Pricing Policy." Knowledge about "Trends in Merchandising" divides into "Knowledge of Merchandising for Product, In-Store, and Store Layout." It further subdivides into "Knowledge about Meat Merchandising."

Knowledge types were classified by what was needed by every area of activities within the Organizational Logic, and then by each group within an area. This further refinement shortened the list of types of knowledge, and was helpful to organize them for collecting values for the four aspects of positions by direct interview with experts within the company. Table 11.4 lists the number of types of knowledge used.

Application of the knowledge grid

Let α_1 be the value of an entry in the first quadrant of the knowledge grid. The knowledge grid, in general, appears as:

$$
\begin{array}{c|c}
\alpha_2 & \alpha_1 \\
\hline
\alpha_3 & \alpha_4
\end{array}
$$

The values of α_1 and α_4 are determined by the individual's experience, education, and ability. The values of α_2 and α_3 are determined by the organizational location of the position and are more a property of the organization than the person holding the position.

The worth of the knowledge represented by a knowledge grid, designated by W, is given by:

$$W = \alpha_3[\alpha_1 + \alpha_4].$$

194

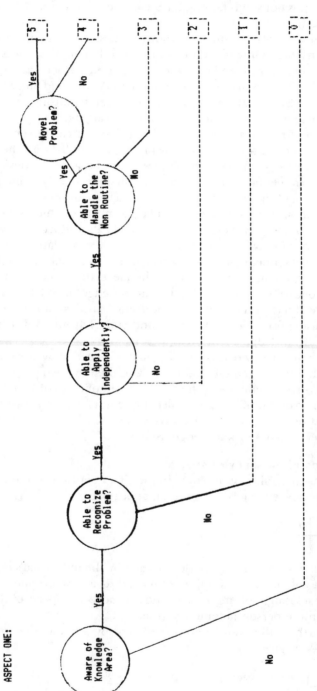

Figure 11.2. Determining the level of knowledge usage.

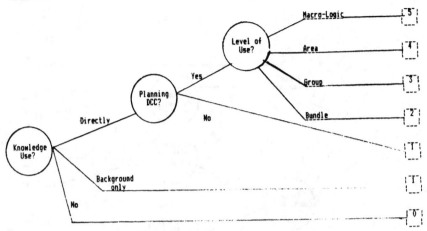

Figure 11.3. Determining the scope of application of knowledge.

ASPECT THREE:

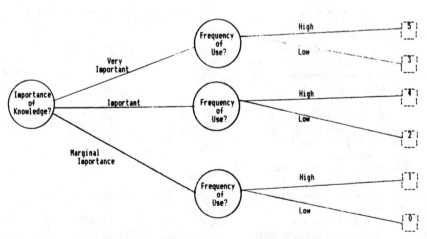

Figure 11.4. Determining the relative value of the person's knowledge.

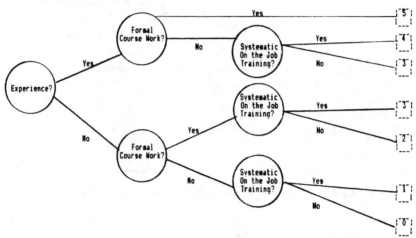

Figure 11.5. Determining the level of the source of the knowledge.

Table 11.4. Tabulation by area of number of types of knowledge at SSI

	Area of SSI	Number of types of knowledge used
A1.	Direction of SSI	
	Corporate administration	32
	Corporate administration support	14
A2.	Sales and merchandising	
	General	42
	Meat operations	41
	Produce operations	28
	Grocery operations	20
	Store group operations	11
	Store operations	28
	Marketing and communication	15
A3.	Store support	37
A4.	Distribution/transportation	40
A5.	Personnel	23
A6.	Finance and accounting	35
A7.	Management information system	22
	Total	308

Calculating W for each knowledge grid converts the knowledge grid into a number rather than a matrix of numbers, and is the easier to use. It must be noted that the formula for W is from the point of view of the organization rather than a position or a person. W can only be calculated for an incumbent because α_1 and α_4 are personal properties, and α_2 and α_3 are position properties. The value of W ranges between 0 and 50. Note that the second aspect, scope of application, is considered irrelevent to W because of the hierarchy of the types of knowledge already built into the code. The values of W for "Knowledge of Front End Operations" knowledge grids of Table 11.2 are given in Table 11.5.

Note that the CEO's value of W is only 10, and the staff specialist in the area has a value of 50. The value for the Personnel Clerk position is zero. These values do not imply that the CEO is not an expert on front end operations, or that the Personnel Clerk does not have this knowledge from a prior position. The values summarize what an incumbent should have to be competent in his position as the CEO or as a personnel clerk.

The coding of knowledge into types involves three classes: technical knowledge, managerial knowledge, and professional knowledge. The general pattern of the values of W by different levels of positions are illustrated in Figure 11.6. W tends to drop as position levels increase for technical knowledge, and increases for managerial knowledge. Professional knowledge does not compare systematically with organizational rank at SSI, because these are all staff positions located in the middle ranks of the organization. For example, there is an architect, an industrial engineer, and a real estate specialist. These persons reported to a senior officer, but had no subordinates.

The value of the second quadrant, the scope of application, is determined entirely by the position's organizational level. As the level rises towards that of the CEO, so does the value of α_2. One way of thinking about α_2 is to consider that the task processes of the subordinate tend to be subsets of those of the superior, who must consider other task processes. For example, a produce Vice President has a broader range of activities than does a buyer in the

Table 11.5. Example of worth of knowledge about front end operation

Position	Worth of knowledge
CEO	10
SVP	32
VP	32
Territory supervisor	45
Store manager	28
Mgr. store financial services	50
Personnel clerk	0

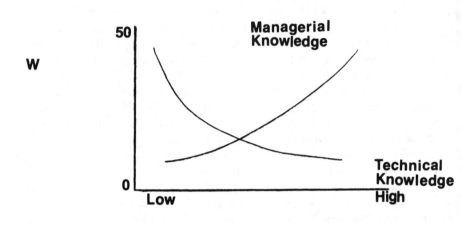

Position Level in Organizations

Figure 11.6.   Comparing W with position level.

produce department. The Senior Vice President of Sales and Merchandising has a larger set than the product Vice President.

The knowledge grids for each position can be compared directly. First, one must code the many different types of knowledge in order to develop a composite code for the entire organization. These types of knowledge can be subdivided by the various areas, groups, and bundles in the Organizational Logic. Then, the code can be displayed on a large sheet of paper, such as the one on the next page. This sheet is called the *Position Knowledge Profile*. One tabulates the values of W for each position, and then transfers these values from the knowledge grid onto this sheet as is shown in Exhibit A.

A *position knowledge template* can then be constructed by punching holes above the lines in the knowledge profiles with nonzero entries of W. Then, by simply overlaying one position knowledge template over another position knowledge profile, one can compare any two positions by inspection. Where the jobs overlap in their knowledge, the entries in the profile show through the holes of the template. But, wherever the holes in the template have no entries on the other position profile, they indicate where the knowledge is inadequate. By consulting the position knowledge profile of the position knowledge template, one obtains the values of W for each type of knowledge

Exhibit A. Position Knowledge Profile Sheet for S.S.I.

Position Title_____ Approved By:_____ Date_____

Name_____ Approved By:_____ Date_____

Corporate General Administrative:

1-001	1-002	1-003	1-004	1-005	1-006	1-007	1-008	1-009	1-010	1-011	1-012	1-013	1-014	1-015	1-016	1-017	1-018	1-019	1-020	1-021	1-022	1-023	1-024

1-025	1-026	1-027	1-028	1-029	1-030	1-031	1-032																

Corporate Administrative Assistance

1-101	1-102	1-103	1-104	1-105	1-106	1-107	1-108	1-109	1-110	1-111	1-112	1-113	1-114										

Sales and Merchandising - General

2-001	2-002	2-003	2-004	2-005	2-006	2-007	2-008	2-009	2-010	2-011	2-012	2-013	2-014	2-015	2-016	2-017	2-018	2-019	2-020	2-021	2-022	2-023	2-024

2-025	2-026	2-027	2-028	2-029	2-030	2-031	2-032	2-033	2-034	2-035	2-036	2-037	2-038	2-039	2-040	2-041	2-042						

Meat Operations

2-101	2-102	2-103	2-104	2-105	2-106	2-107	2-108	2-109	2-110	2-111	2-112	2-113	2-114	2-115	2-116	2-117	2-118	2-119	2-120	2-121	2-122	2-123	2-124

2-125	2-126	2-127	2-128	2-129	2-130	2-131	2-132	2-133	2-134	2-135	2-136	2-137	2-138	2-139	2-140	2-141							

Produce Operations

2-201	2-202	2-203	2-204	2-205	2-206	2-207	2-208	2-209	2-210	2-211	2-212	2-213	2-214	2-215	2-216	2-217	2-218	2-219	2-220	2-221	2-222	2-223	2-224

2-225	2-226	2-227	2-228																				

Grocery Operations

2-301	2-302	2-303	2-304	2-305	2-306	2-307	2-308	2-309	2-310	2-311	2-312	2-313	2-314	2-315	2-316	2-317	2-318	2-319	2-320				

Store Group Operations

2-401	2-402	2-403	2-404	2-405	2-406	2-407	2-408	2-409	2-410	2-411													

Store Operations

2-501	2-502	2-503	2-504	2-505	2-506	2-507	2-508	2-509	2-510	2-511	2-512	2-513	2-514	2-515	2-516	2-517	2-518	2-519	2-520	2-521	2-522	2-523	2-524

2-525	2-256	2-527	2-528																				

Marketing and Communications

2-601	2-602	2-603	2-604	2-605	2-606	2-607	2-608	2-609	2-610	2-611	2-612	2-613	2-614	2-615									

Store Support

3-001	3-002	3-003	3-004	3-005	3-006	3-007	3-008	3-009	3-010	3-011	3-012	3-013	3-014	3-015	3-016	3-017	3-018	3-019	3-020	3-021	3-022	3-023	3-024

3-025	3-026	3-027	3-028	3-029	3-030	3-031	3-032	3-033	3-034	3-035	3-036	3-037											

Distribution/Transportation

4-001	4-002	4-003	4-004	4-005	4-006	4-007	4-008	4-009	4-010	4-011	4-012	4-013	4-014	4-015	4-016	4-017	4-018	4-019	4-020	4-021	4-022	4-023	4-024

4-025	4-026	4-027	4-028	4-029	4-030	4-031	4-032	4-033	4-034	4-035	4-036	4-037	4-038	4-039	4-040								

Employee Relations

5-001	5-002	5-003	5-004	5-005	5-006	5-007	5-008	5-009	5-010	5-011	5-012	5-013	5-014	5-015	5-016	5-017	5-018	5-019	5-020	5-021	5-022	5-023	

Finance & Accounting

6-001	6-002	6-003	6-004	6-005	6-006	6-007	6-008	6-009	6-010	6-011	6-012	6-013	6-014	6-015	6-016	6-017	6-018	6-019	6-020	6-021	6-022	6-023	6-024

6-025	6-026	6-027	6-028	6-029	6-030	6-031	6-032	6-033	6-034	6-035													

that is lacking to perform the other job. The analysis of what is lacking, and the value of W, leads to defining the questions to be asked about the readiness of an incumbent of one position to occupy the other.

An incumbent, because of prior experience and education, may know more than is required in his or her current position. Therefore, there must be an individual knowledge profile for each person containing this information, if one is to use this data to make judgments about his or her suitability for being a back-up or promotable to another position. The *individual knowledge profile* has check marks everywhere the individual has experience or expertise for a type of knowledge not covered by his or her current position, plus the values of W for the current position.

No one is ever truly a substitute for another, and there are more factors to consider than knowledge for promotion, training, or transfer decisions. Nevertheless, a comparison of an *individual knowledge profile* to a position knowledge template leads to a judgment about a person's qualifications for a position movement in terms of what the person knows. The discrepancies between what a person knows, as indicated by the individual knowledge profile, and the position knowledge profile, is used to define what is needed to render him or her qualified for the position change.

The discrepancies across many such comparisons have been used to systematically define what knowledge is lacking across an entire set of persons in a career planning program. For example, what does a store manager need to know to become qualified for the position of Territory Supervisor, or a Territory Supervisor to become a VP and General Manager? These composite comparisons can be used to define requirements for management development or training.

For example, suppose a company has a choice of having a course in management information systems or a course in accounting and finance. Upon completing such a course, new entries would be added to the student's individual knowledge profile. Some might need the knowledge in accounting and finance to become more qualified for promotion, some might only need the MIS course, and some might need both. This information can be used to select students for the training, the type of training, and the expected benefits of the training. Thus, the management of training and management of development can be tied logically and precisely to the needs of the company. Ideally, all training should at least result in new checkmarks in the individual knowledge profile of the trainee.

The values in the knowledge grids for each position reflect the judgment of either the incumbent or his or her superior. These values may change as the application of this system proceeds. The values in each person's individual knowledge profile are more prone to inaccuracy. The existing personnel records may not contain such information, and the entries must be inferred. Successive use of these data, however, should, over time, add accuracy and

precision. Those in charge of managing a career planning program understand that these data are not yet precise, and that the entries in the profile
will be improved over time as experience is gained.

At the beginning of the application of knowledge grids, the individual
knowledge profiles contain two types of entries: Numerical values of W
from the position profile held by the person, and check marks referring to
knowledge acquired elsewhere. Clearly, the vague data of check marks
needs to be improved. It will be the task of those managing career development to balance the cost of obtaining more data and the value of such information in making judgments about the qualifications for movement along in
a career path.

Care must be used in the application of the individual knowledge profiles
because of several factors:

a. The data are not precise.
b. The entries in a profile are not independent of one another. (For exam-
    ple, knowledge of 1-006 implies knowledge of 1-029 and 1-032.)
c. The requirements may shift over time.
d. The incumbent may not be qualified for his or her current position. A
    "grandfather" rule was used to give every incumbent the benefit of the
    doubt.
e. Personal qualities, such as integrity, energy, initiative, leadership, judg-
    ment, and health, are not indicated on the knowledge profiles.

The value of α_4 indicates the desired source of knowledge. In some cases,
formal education is important. In others, experience or systematic on-the-
job training is important to increasing both α_1 and α_4; this analysis effects
both the recruiting policy and the selection of method for training and management development. For example:

If formal course work is required, choices are to select courses or to recruit more selectively and systematically.

Value of $\alpha 1$	Indicated Background
5	More generalized training about basic theory plus proven talent
4	More generalized training about basic theory
3	More thorough training directed to job peformance
2	Short course of needed skills
1	Brief introduction
0	None

Value of $\alpha 4$	Indicated Training
5	Formal course work plus direct experience
4	No formal course work but both experience and OJT
3	Direct experience required
3	Formal course work plus OJT
2	Formal course work
1	Systematic OJT
0	None

Value of $\alpha 3$	Need for Training	Level
5	Very Important	Intensive
4	Very Important	Intensive
3	Important	Moderate
2	Low importance	Survey
1	Very low importance	Survey
0	Not necessary	None

The information contained in the knowledge grid of a position can be used to develop simple statements of qualifications. The rules used are based on combinations of α_1, α_4, and α_3. The value of α_3 was used to define the noun in the noun phrase indicated by the blank:

It is ___ for the incumbent to have:

The blank is completed according to these rules:

$$\alpha_3 = \begin{cases} 5 & \text{Essential} \\ 4 & \text{Very Valuable} \\ 3 & \text{Valuable} \\ 2,1 & \text{Useful} \\ 0 & \text{Drop Knowledge Grid Item.} \end{cases}$$

Next, combinations of α_1 and α_4 were considered for the construction of nine standard phrases. The phrase number corresponding to the combination of α_1 and α_4 is shown below:

The nine phrases are:

1. Proven ability to solve novel problems involving:
2. Ability to solve novel problems involving:
3. Proven ability to handle non-routine problems involving:
4. Ability to handle non-routine problems involving:
5. Proven ability to handle routine problems involving:
6. Ability to handle routine problems involving:
7. Training in handling routine problems involving:
8. Ability to recognize problems involving:
9. Ability to recognize and obtain assistance in solving problems involving:

Given a knowledge grid:

$$\begin{array}{c|c} \alpha_2 & \alpha_1 \\ \hline \alpha_3 & \alpha_4 \end{array}$$

and the above rules, one can construct a sentence which describes the knowledge grid in simple English.

Example (a). Suppose the type of knowledge is "Knowledge of Personnel Policies and Procedures" and, for it, the knowledge grid is:

$$\begin{array}{c|c} 3 & 5 \\ \hline 5 & 4 \end{array}$$

Then the statement of qualifications concerning it would read: "It is essential for the incumbent to have proven ability to solve novel problems involving knowledge of Personnel Policies and Procedures."

JOB DESCRIPTIONS

A job description is a position description (cf. Chapters 5 and 10), plus information about the salaries and benefits and qualifications to perform the task processes of the position. Job descriptions are a natural byproduct of the OA&A technology. The position descriptions are generated in stage three (Organizational Design) and updated in every successive stage of the OA&A technology. The wage and salary system is based on the position descriptions, and various methods can be used, including knowledge grids, to complete a statement of qualifications *based upon the task processes* involved with a position. The conversion of the knowledge grids into simple English sentences yields a structured set of qualification statements of each position.

This step-by-step development of job descriptions allows for updating and maintenance. Everything is tied directly to the organizational design. Each analysis builds upon the previous ones into an easy-to-use system. In my experience, it is as fast to do the Organizational Assessment, Organizational Audit, and Organizational Design and then generate salary and qualification data as quickly as it is to start with an existing organization and try to perform position descriptions from scratch. Preparing position descriptions without doing the organizational design has several drawbacks. First, those preparing them generally do not understand how all of the task processes and positions go together. Second, the data in the formal system is always out of date, and so the effort would tend to enshrine the status quo. Third, because the position descriptions will not be as good, and because they do not reflect the current goals and strategies, senior management (including the CEO) will not have much faith in them. This tends to maintain the gulf between senior management and the human resources staff. Fourth, because they are imprecise and often bloated, it is much harder and it takes longer to update them. The result is that they really are not part of the active management system in an organization. Fifth, one loses the opportunity to use the ideas of Organizational Playbooks and Game Plans discussed in Chapter 10. The main advantage of more traditional ways of creating position and job descriptions is that they perpetuate the status quo and are, therefore, "safe." Rapidly changing and growing organizations, as a consequence, place little importance on position description except as a documentation used for hiring and protecting the company from complaints and government agencies. On the other hand, firms enjoying quasi-monopolistic control of a market with a stable technology can rely on traditional position and job descriptions because, over the years, they have been refined many times and there is usually experience in using them. Personally, I have never seen an example of an organization where the position and job descriptions are either accurate or valid. This is especially true for academic institutions.

TRAINING AND MANAGEMENT DEVELOPMENT

No knowledgeable observer of organizations could reject the importance of training and management development. Training can improve on-the-job performance, perfect skills, be used to qualify personnel for promotion and transfer, improve the value of the organization's human assets and accomplish much for both the individuals and the organization. Training is an important part of every manager's job. The OA&A technology can add little to the existing knowledge about training. While training is built into the OA&A technology, it is mostly training in how to think about organizational problems and in implementation planning. The bulk of the task processes involved in training falls outside the scope of the OA&A technology.

However, the use of knowledge grids and their application to defining position knowledge profiles, position knowledge templates, and individual knowledge profiles is very helpful for designing management development programs within a company. Tying a management development program to a career planning system can yield large returns.

The first step is to develop a list of persons whose development is considered vital to the future success of the organization. This list must be tied to the strategic requirements of the organization for qualified and experienced personnel, and must reflect the current capacity of the organization to support an internal management development program. For example, if the company is just getting started with management development programs, it must set priorities on who is to be included and how much time and resources are to be allowed. Some organizations cannot afford very much and must be content with a small program. How the persons are selected, and the conditions under which the training and management development program is to be conducted, are important.

At SSI, the problem was that most of the managers, supervisors, and senior officers had little or no college training. Even the Management Information Systems personnel were not college graduates in computer programming. The second problem they found was that they decided to operate divisionally but had no cadre of general managers to choose from. Thus, they had to develop their own out of functional specialists. The third problem was that the CEO wanted to deepen his management team from the top down. Thus, he decided to tie the management development to the career planning program that was just being installed.

The second step is to determine what subjects need to be covered in a management development system. This is done at SSI by establishing a list of successors to each of the 150 key positions. The individual knowledge profile was compared with the position knowledge template to uncover what types of knowledge were lacking for each of those on the list, with all possible positions to which they might aspire in the future. This quickly gave us information about who could be considered as having the knowledge to be as a successor to another, even if the position involved was not in the individual's functional department. An organizational chart showing the qualified successors was prepared. Many of the key positions did not have any successors. However, it quickly became clear that there were clear patterns in what knowledge was lacking. For example, the self-made line employees generally lacked any formal instruction in finance and accounting, in computer science, and in human resources. The staff persons on the list generally had a better formal education, but most had neither store or operations experience nor knowledge about operations. By this simple analysis, it became obvious what must be included in a management development program *and* which persons needed what training. This straight forward analysis provides lists of names, the number of persons needing each type of knowledge enhancement, and the recommended source of knowledge.

The next step, after determining who is to be trained and what is to be taught, is to decide upon the methods for the management development. Choices range from sending individuals off to college for a B.S. or M.B.A. to short courses given by seminar organizations. Some of the training could be done "in house" by using existing staff or by contracting for an instructor. And, in other cases, because of the need for operating experience, a job rotation and on-the-job temporary assignments could be used. The selection of methods should be tied to the persons involved, the types of knowledge needing to be imparted, the availability of resources, and the aspirations of those on the management succession list. Many, for example, argue that the persons should just be promoted, and then they will learn what they need to know. This is true for many jobs, but, as one ascends to higher level positions, the discrepencies between the individual knowledge profile and the position knowledge template may forever block advancement. Also, the organization may incur high "tuition" costs if it uses unqualified personnel. The knowledge grids, especially the first, third, and fourth quadrants, specify the worth W of the knowledge. For example, if the knowledge is important to the position, one then works at the first quadrant (the level of knowledge) and the fourth quadrant (the source of the knowledge) to inform a judgment about the development method to be used.

In some industries, such as banking, there are fairly standard task processes that are legally tied to performance. The banking industry has well-organized training and management development programs which are excellent. For a community bank, there is no real need for knowledge grids and procedures described earlier. There are already well-established programs, and what is needed is usually very clear to those in the banking community. For example, loan officers need training in consumer and commercial loans. If they are to expand into real estate loans, there are programs for this. But, for SSI, the supermarket industry is not standardized, and the Food Marketing Institute just cannot match the programs offered by Bank Administration Institute or the American Bankers Association.

PERFORMANCE EVALUATION SYSTEM

There is widespread recognition that companies should be very concerned with peformance evaluation or appraisal. There are useful texts on this subject (cf. Eichel and Bender, 1984; Kirkpatrick, 1982). In most companies I have examined, including universities, performance appraisal is pretty much ad hoc and hit-and-miss. A national food wholesale organization that I worked with had an elaborate MBO system for which there were from 10 to 25 numbers that an incumbent had to satisfy in order to be considered successful. One young M.B.A. was terminated after exceeding every single number. It turned out that he had offended his boss by successfully promoting a new procedure which his boss was on record as opposing. In this case, even the numbers had no effect. In another, the President was terminated after his old family firm was acquired. The new owner fired him because of his *name*, after acknowledging that he was very good. He even offered him the job back as president if he would consent to changing his name! Both organizations had elaborate numbers-based, performance- appraisal systems. But, in my travels, most firms rely on general non-job-specific, preprinted forms. These standard forms are really an insult, but they are probably better than nothing. At least they involve a procedure that can be consistently applied and defended.

A Performance Evaluation System is one of the tools to assist in achieving effective human resources management. The following discussion describes what Mary Bird and I used for Supermarket Systems, Inc. The Performance Evaluation System was designed for at least six purposes:

i. As a tool to guide the supervisor and employee in improving and/or maintaining an employee's performance level.
ii. To maintain a record of salaried employees' performance levels.
iii. As an input to the Salary Review System.
iv. As an input to Placement (Transfer and Promotion) Decisions.
v. As an input to Career Development.
vi. As an input to Training Programs.

There are nine components of SSI's Performance Evaluation System. These are:

i. Performance Evaluation Task Force.
ii. Performance Rating Forms containing the performance evaluation criteria and scales for measuring performance.
iii. A procedure for developing performance evaluation criteria, weighting their importance, and developing scales for measurement purposes.
iv. A procedure for regular review and updating of performance evaluation critera, weights, and scales.
v. Multiple raters may be used for each individual being rated. Normally, up to five (5) raters are used.
vi. A procedure for selecting and weighting the raters.
vii. A system for reducing rating forms to a profile on each individual ratee.
viii. A system for comparing sets of individuals and producing comparative reports and discrepancy reports.
ix. A procedure for administering the performance evaluations.

It should be noted that there are two variations of the Performance Evaluation System. The full system is designed for those positions with a large number of incumbents and where company-wide comparisons are desirable. The modified system is recommended only for those positions with few incumbents, particularly those positions which report to the CEO.

A performance evaluation system involves the participation of many people in the organization. It is important to obtain informed judgments by persons who have direct knowledge of how well a person being rated is doing. Different people, having different relationships to the ratee, will have varying opinions. What one seeks is a fair evaluation, after taking into consideration the specifics of a position, the weights assigned to the various raters, and the weights assigned to different performance dimensions.

It is important to the success of a performance evaluation system that accountability and responsibility be clearly defined. Who is involved and what responsibilities are assigned will vary with each organization. Nevertheless, the CEO must assume responsibility to ensure that the system is implemented and maintained, and is consistent with the objectives for having a performance evaluation system. Usually, the head of the personnel or human resources department is the key player in the development and implementation. This person may set up task forces to ensure interdepartmental coordination, fairness, and consistency. The performance evaluation task force is usually charged with the development of rating forms, including the establishment of criteria, weights, and scales. The task force oversees these developments and ensures approval prior to implementation. It also must ensure that rater and feedback training is provided.

Managers are responsible for getting themselves trained as raters, for completing performance rating forms on each subordinate, and for conducting a performance feedback session with each subordinate. Each person whose position is concerned by the performance evaluation system is responsible for attending a rater training session, for completing a self-rating, and for attending a performance feedback session with the manager or supervisor.

A frequency for use of the performance evaluation system needs to be selected. It must be done at least annually for all selected employees, and should be done as often as pay changes are made. Departments are encouraged to evaluate employees twice annually—once for input into the salary review system, and once for performance review and improvement only. Employees under consideration for promotion, transfer, or demotion should be evaluated unless an evaluation has been performed within the preceding 3 months. Employees should be evaluated prior to termination, except in cases involving theft or violation of pre-agreed policies.

The criteria to be used for rating employees should be based upon the position or job descriptions. Criteria, weights, and scales should be established by consensus of: the personnel officer, the manager who is responsible for the position, one immediate supervisor of the position, and one incumbent. The critera reflect important performance areas as specified by the bundles and modules in a position description. Then the task force should weight the relative value of each performance area. These are the criteria weightings. The sum of these criteria weightings should be 1.0. The next step is to develop a scale for different levels of performance for each criteria. I have found that five levels for the scales usually suffice (100, 75, 50, 25, 0), with 50 being described as "minimally acceptable." These scales must be

1. Approved by the task force

2. Be approved by the Responsible Manager with the concurrence of the Personnel Officer and
3. The raters should attend a rater training session.

It should be noted, however, that this system is linked closely to the Organizational Maintenance System and relies heavily upon the integrity of the position descriptions.

The performance evaluation task force should have a member (the head, if possible) from the Personnel or Human Resources department who is a permanent member. Others are temporary members, such as the manager responsible for a position, one or more immediate supervisors, one or more incumbents, and staff personnel appointed by permanent members. Before a task force is convened, it helps if the position description is reviewed in order to ensure that it is current. If there is an Organizational Maintenance system (stage eight) in operation, this review should not take much time.

The task force then meets to discuss *and reach consensus* on the contents of the Performance Evaluation Development Forms. The following provides an outline agenda:

1. Present the system to new Task Force members.
2. Approve Task Force membership.
3. Agree on raters for the position.
4. Establish weights for each rater (weights must add to 100).
5. Review the Position Descriptions—if changes are needed, these must be passed on to the Personnel Officer for processing.
6. Discuss and agree on the Key Elements of Performance by position incumbents.
7. Discuss and agree on draft questions to be used for evaluating incumbents of the position. There should be sufficient discussion to identify behavior at different performance levels.
8. Discuss and agree on the importance of each bundle.
9. Discuss and agree on the importance of each question.
10. Assign a member of the Task Force (normally a permanent member) to record agreements and to write up questions and behavioral scales following the meeting.
11. Establish a timetable for implementation.
12. Record any special requirements for performance evaluation of this position.

Following the Task Force meeting, the Performance Evaluation Design Forms should be updated to reflect the consensus reached. Questions should be reviewed as needed, and scales written. These should then be circulated to all members of the Task Force for approval prior to implementation. If there are still items on which agreement has not been reached, another Task Force meeting will be required.

After selecting the raters for each position, the next step is to assign relative weights to each of the raters in order that the sum of these weights is 100%. General rules of thumb I have used are to give the immediate supervisor the greatest weight, to give the set of all supervisors doing ratings at least 60% of the weighting, and to assign self-rating a weight from 10-15% of the total raters. Often coworkers, subordinates, and staff personnel who work with the incumbent are included as raters and given weights.

Exhibit B gives a performance evaluation form for a store manager at SSI. Table 11.6 has a tabulation of the question and rater weights for this performance evaluation. The bundle numbers corresponding to each criteria are given on the right-hand column of Table 11.6.

Before applying this performance evaluation system on all store managers, there was a pilot project for 47 stores. The instrument was checked for reliability by using it twice in 2 months for the same raters and ratees. The correlations were 0.91 for store managers and 0.93 for comanagers. There were marked differences between groups of stores, as would be expected, because the stores are grouped by a combination of demographic variables and size. For example, urban wealthy stores are very different from small

Table 11.6. Question and rater weights for store managers

Question	Position: Store Manager Summary	Question weight	Bundle number
1.	Sales volume and gross profit	0.04	206-16
2.	Payroll control	0.04	206-16
3.	Planning	0.08	206-16
4.	Initiative, judgment, decision making	0.17	206-16
5.	Management of employees	0.08	206-17
6.	Personnel selection and management	0.07	206-17
7.	Counselling	0.05	206-17
8.	Paperwork	0.05	206-18
9.	Creative merchandising	0.03	206-19
10.	Product control	0.05	206-19
11.	Supervision and follow through	0.07	206-19
12.	Store cleanliness	0.08	206-20
13.	Store security	0.05	206-21
14.	Customer relations	0.13	206-22
15.	Working relationships	0.04	206-23
Raters	**Title**		
1.	VP and general manager	0.20	
2.	Territory supervisor	0.40	
3.	Store manager (self)	0.10	
4.	Comanager (in same store)	0.15	
5.	Department manager (in same store)	0.15	

POSITION RATED: Store Manager _____ ● _____ INCUMBENT _____ ●

RATER: _____ DATE: _____

Please read the attached instructions **before** completing this rating.

Question 1: Sales Volume and Gross Profit — Does the manager take actions to maximize sales and gross profit as far as factors outside store control allow? How satisfied are you that the manager is getting the most out of the store, taking into consideration competitive conditions and other outside factors?

☐	☐	☐	☐	☐
The manager takes every possible action to maximize sales volume and gross profit. Is imaginative and uses initiative. I am very satisfied that no more could be gotten out of this store no matter what is done.	The manager does not appear to try to maximize either sales volume or gross profit. The manager has no initiative & lacks imagination. Doesn't seem to try to combat competitive conditions or other factors outside control. Just lets things ride.	I believe that the manager's sales volume and gross profit are acceptable given competitive conditions and other factors outside control. With imagination & initiative, however, the manager could get more out of the store.	Most of the time this manager seems to let things ride. Occasionally the manager takes actions designed to maximize sales volume & gross profit. I think both could be improved considerably	I am satisfied that the manager does a good job of maximizing sales volume and gross profit. Store performance is more than acceptable, given competitive conditions and given other uncontrollable factors. The manager could not get much more out of the store

Question 2: Management of Employees — Can the manager get employees to work together productively? Is the manager firm, fair and consistent with employees? Does he/she give positive and negative feedback? Does he/she communicate well with employees? Is he/she building an effective team?

☐	☐	☐	☐	☐
This manager is able to get employees to work very productively. Is firm, fair and consistent with employees and gives positive & negative feedback. Communicates well with employees and builds an effective work team.	Is inconsistent. Communications with employees are poor. Is not able to get employees to work productively.	Is usually firm, fair and consistent with employees. Poor performance may be commented on more often than good. Is usually able to get employees to work productively.	May be inconsistent with employees. Rarely recognizes good performance. Communications with employees may be weak. Is sometimes able to get employees to work productively.	Is firm, fair and consistent with employees & is able to get employees to work productively most of the time. Usually recognizes and comments on good & bad performance

Question 3: Customer Relations — Does he/she communicate well with customers and other consumers in the PTA? Does he/she know regular customers by name and take an interest in their shopping problems? Does he/she encourage employees to be friendly and helpful?

☐	☐	☐	☐	☐
Store is neither friendly nor unfriendly. Tends to treat customers politely - but ignores them when possible. Insists employees be polite, but does not encourage more interest in customers	Store is usually friendly & welcoming. Tries to know customers & to work with them. Encourages employees to do so, and many employees do. Occasionally may be a little curt with a customer.	Atmosphere in store varies, sometimes it is friendly & welcoming, sometimes not. Sometimes, manager & employees treat customers well, sometimes they do not seem interested. May stress efficiency or cleanliness more than friendliness, or may not encourage employees to take time for customers	Store is friendly & welcoming. Knows the customers & enjoys working with them. Generates enthusiasm among the employees for helping customers find products, and for solving other customer problems.	Store & staff tend to be silent. Behaves as if the customer were an intrusion. Tolerates rudeness from employees toward customers. May argue about returns.

Question 4: Creative Merchandising — Does he/she merchandise well? Does he/she check competition, see prices are right? Does he/she have imaginative ideas? Does he/she use rainchecks?

☐	☐	☐	☐	☐
Knows the primary trade area (PTA) thoroughly. Checks competitors frequently & is always imaginative in merchandising. Checks prices. Issues rainchecks properly.	Rarely checks competition, does not know the PTA Is unimaginative in merchandising	Knows the PTA reasonably well & checks competition periodically. Checks prices. Has some imaginative ideas but may lack confidence in implementing them, or may tend to be unimaginative. Issues rainchecks	Only occasionally checks competition Does not know the PTA very well. Rarely has imaginative ideas. Doesn't often bother about checking prices. Often forgets rainchecks	Knows the PTA reasonably well. Checks competition & prices regularly. Is often imaginative in merchandising. Issues rainchecks

Question 5: Store Security — Does the manager take security seriously in the store? Does he/she enforce vendor procedures? Do a store check at night? Check the backdoors are locked? Not leave alone? Does he/she vary bank deposit times & see bank deposits are made properly? Does he/she take proper action on shoplifting, employee theft, and enforce good judgment on check acceptance?

☐	☐	☐	☐
Enforces good security procedures automatically. Always does store check at night, checks back doors are locked, never leaves alone, avoids excess cash in office, makes deposits at varied times, with authorized people & not alone. Takes immediate action on shoplifting & to control employee theft. Is careful accepting checks. Enforces vendor procedures.	Is alert to good security procedures most of the time. Does store check at night, checks back doors are locked, never leaves alone, avoids excess cash in office, makes deposits at varied times, with authorized people or not alone. Takes action on shoplifting & to control employee theft. Is careful on accepting checks. Enforces vendor procedures	Is usually alert to security procedures but may forget them when he is busy on other things. Is fairly consistent about procedures, such as vendor procedures which are currently being stressed, but may be lax about others. May let unauthorized personnel make deposits. May occasionally fail to take action on shoplifting or may be inconsistent about employee theft. Lax on accepting checks. May leave alone.	Treats security procedures as if they were unnecessary. No disciplinary action on employee theft. Lets shoplifters go. Excuses vendor mistakes. May leave alone

Question 6: Initiative, Judgment and Decision Making — Does the manager use initiative and good judgment in decisions affecting the store? Does the manager identify problems? Does the manager use the proper information as the basis for conclusion? Does the manager use imagination in making decisions and have confidence in personal judgment? Does the manager know which decisions to make & which to refer elsewhere? Does the manager involve others properly? Does the manager handle emergencies well?

☐	☐	☐	☐	☐
Is indecisive and/or has poor judgment. Lacks initiative.	Is often indecisive or fails to show good judgment in making decisions. Much of this appears to be caused by insufficient experience and should improve over time.	Most of the time this manager is decisive & uses good judgment in making decisions. Usually acts within the limits of authority. May sometimes lack confidence in judgment. Most of the time shows initiative. Sometimes may appear to lack imagination in decisions. May sometimes react either too fast or too slowly	The manager is decisive and uses good judgment in making decisions. Usually acts within the limits of authority. Usually shows initiative in decision making but may occasionally lack self confidence in judgment. Reacts reasonably promptly and ensures the right information is gathered before acting	The manager is decisive, creative and uses good judgment in making decisions. Knows the limits of authority and uses initiative within those limits. Reacts promptly but takes time to gather needed information.

Question 7: Store Cleanliness and Maintenance — Does he/she make sure the store is properly cleaned and maintained? Are floors, shelves, front end kept clean? Is preventive maintenance program followed? Is compressor checked regularly? Is service person called when necessary? Is backroom clear; product properly stacked, no obstructions; bales made as needed?

☐	☐	☐	☐	☐
Does not enforce cleanliness nor preven a maintenance. The store looks as if nobody cares about it.	May sometimes let the store get dirtier than it should and the preventive maintenance may get behind. Floor, shelves & front end usually left in good condition at night, but backroom may be untidy, obstructive or there may be unbaled materials.	Makes sure the store is usually as clean and properly maintained as business conditions allow. Floors, shelves & front end usually left in good opening condition at night. Preventive maintenance program is usually followed. Backroom conditions are acceptable.	Makes sure the store is almost always clean & properly maintained. Floors, shelves & front end are almost always as clean as business conditions allow & are almost always left in good opening condition at night. The preventive maintenance program is followed. Backroom conditions are good.	Makes sure the store is always clean & properly maintained. Floors, shelves & front end are as clean as business conditions allow & is left in good opening condition at night. The preventive maintenance program is followed. Backroom conditions are excellent.

Question 8: Personnel Selection and Management — Does the manager use good judgment in hiring qualified people? Is he/she able to recognize talent? Does he/she work to develop both potential managers and skilled employees? Does he/she provide on-the-job training? Does he/she encourage team work? Does he/she encourage employees to solve problems?

☐	☐	☐	☐	☐
Sometimes lacks judgment in hiring decisions. Training is sometimes ignored. Employee talent is often not recognized. Teamwork is often not encouraged.	Shows good judgment in hiring decisions. Recognizes potential in employees and develops employee skills. Often takes action to develop management potential. Provides on-the-job training. Most of the time encourages teamwork, encourages & helps employees to solve problems.	Shows acceptable judgment in hiring decisions. Provides on-the-job training and develops employee skills. Occasionally recognizes & develops management potential. Usually encourages teamwork and helps employees solve problems.	Shows excellent judgment in hiring decisions and recognizes talent in employees. Takes action to develop management potential and employee skills. Provides on-the-job training. Encourages teamwork. Encourages employees to solve their problems.	Lacks judgment in hiring decisions. Does not recognize or develop talent. Training is weak. Teamwork and problem-solving are not encouraged.

Exhibit B.   Store manager peformance evaluation system.

Question 9: Product Control – Does he/she work with dept. heads to see the product is there when needed? Is ordering done properly? Is there follow through on out? Are vendors checked in? Are trucks checked in and overages and shortages identified? Are inventory levels appropriate? Are markdowns done properly?

☐ | ☐ | ☐ | ☐ | ☐

Leaves product ordering to dept heads but does make sure they know when & how to do it. Does not follow through on outs & tends to blame shortages on warehouse or some other outside source. Inventory levels are inconsistent. Only occasionally checks trucks in. Markdowns not always handled adequately	Almost always takes action to see the product is on the shelves when needed. Works with dept heads to make sure ordering is almost always done properly, follows through fairly consistently on outs to make sure they are reordered & received. Checks vendors in. Almost always checks trucks & sees overages & shortages are identified. Maintains reasonable inventory levels. Handles markdowns properly	Reasonably consistent actions to see the product is on the shelves when needed. Usually makes sure dept heads submit orders properly. Follow through on outs is acceptable although it may not always be consistent or complete. Checks vendors in. Usually sees trucks are checked in & overages or shortages are identified. Inventory levels are acceptable. Handles markdowns adequately	Takes action to see the product is on the shelves when needed. Works with dept. heads to make sure ordering is done properly. Follows through on outs to make sure they are reordered & received. Checks vendors in. Checks trucks in & identifies overages & shortages. Maintains proper inventory levels. Handles markdowns properly	Leaves product ordering & placement to dept heads. Does not follow through on outs & tends to blame shortages on warehouse or some other outside source. Accepts deliveries without checking for overages or shortages. Doesn't check vendors in. Doesn't use markdowns to sell product. Inventory levels too low or too high

Question 10: How well does the manager plan for daily, weekly and longer-term events? Does he/she have alternative plans? Does the manager involve the co-manager and dept. heads in planning? Does the manager encourage them to hold meetings and communicate plans to all employees? Does the manager work with the co-manager and dept. heads in forecasting? Does the manager take every chance to get involved in planning and budgeting? Does the manager take into account community events?

☐ | ☐ | ☐ | ☐ | ☐

The manager is an excellent planner. Community and competitive events are anticipated. Works with co-manager in dept heads in planning & forecasting for the store. Meetings are held for all store employees to discuss	The manager is a good planner. Community & competitive events are usually taken into account in planning. Works with co-manager and dept heads in planning & forecasting for the store. Meetings are occasionally held for most store employees or plans are communicated through dept heads. Forecasts are realistic	The manager is a reasonable planner. Although community & competitive events are not always taken into account, forecasts are reasonably realistic. May rely too heavily on dept heads or may not involve them regularly	The manager does not plan far enough ahead or sufficiently consistently. Forecasts may appear to be guesswork. Rarely discusses plans with dept heads & employees	The manager does not seem to plan. Forecasts are inaccurate. Competitive & community events are ignored. Tends to act as if planning were useless

Question 11: Counseling — Does the manager listen to employees? Does he/she take the time to counsel on problems, performance, and other job-related matters?

☐ | ☐ | ☐ | ☐ | ☐

Knows the employees well. Listens well to employees and takes the time to counsel them when necessary on problems, performance and other job-related matters	Knows most of the employees well. Listens to employees and most of the time takes the time to counsel them as necessary on problems, performance and other job-related matters	Knows most of the employees. Usually listens to employees and takes time to counsel them as necessary on problems, performance or other job-related matters	May be too busy to listen to employees properly or may not understand what is needed. Sometimes counsels employees but is not consistent or does not know the employees well enough	Does not take time to know employees, to listen to them, or to counsel them

Question 12: Working Relationships — Does he/she maintain effective working relationships with general manager, territory supervisor, field merchandisers and other staff? Does he/she follow their recommendations intelligently? Does he/she initiate and voice own opinion? Does he/she react positively to their suggestions and other company programs?

☐ | ☐ | ☐ | ☐ | ☐

Always works effectively with supervisors & field merchandisers. Follows recommendations intelligently, does not hesitate to express an opinion or question something, reacts positively to suggestion	Does not speak up with supervisors or field merchandisers. Follows recommendations blindly or ignores them completely. Reacts negatively to suggestions	Usually listens to employees supervisors & field merchandisers. Usually follows recommendations reasonably intelligently, usually speaks up & raises questions, usually reacts positively to suggestions	May be hesitant to speak up with supervisors or field merchandisers. May sometimes follow recommendations without thinking, & other times ignore them. May react negatively to suggestions	Almost always works effectively with supervisors & field merchandisers. Usually follows recommendations intelligently, almost always speaks up & raises questions. Reacts positively to suggestions

Question 13: Payroll Control — Does the manager adjust the store work force quickly when sales volume changes? Does the manager increase and decrease both full and part time employees properly? Does the manager balance both immediate and future staffing needs?

☐ | ☐ | ☐ | ☐ | ☐

The manager does not always manage & control payroll sufficiently well. Most of the time budgeted limits are maintained but the manager does not always balance full & part time hours properly	Most of the time the manager does a good job of managing & controlling payroll. Hours are adjusted in response to sales volume & competitive conditions. Full and part time hours are balanced fairly well. Subordinates are encouraged to schedule well	The manager does an acceptable job of payroll control. Budgeted limits are maintained without cutting back too far on full time or over scheduling	The manager does an excellent job on managing & controlling payroll. Hours are adjusted in response to sales volume and competitive conditions. Full and part time hours are balanced so as to maintain a strong and flexible labor force. The manager makes sure subordinates schedule well	The manager does not control payroll acceptably. Hours may be cut too far so as to look good in the short run, or hours may be consistently too high without reason

Question 14: Paperwork — Does the manager make sure all paperwork is accurate & on time? Is mail properly distributed to dept. heads? Is payroll, employment & personnel action paperwork done properly? Are policy & procedure manuals kept up-to-date? Are sales plans maintained? Are financial transactions, sales, DSD documentation and front-end records & balances done properly?

☐ | ☐ | ☐ | ☐ | ☐

Is often late & inaccurate with paperwork	Often has to be reminded to submit paperwork. Records frequently have errors & omissions	Makes sure that critical records & documentation are usually accurate & timely. Makes sure payroll, employment & personnel action paperwork are accurate & timely, & that front-end records & balances are accurate & timely. Weekend paperwork is on time. Other paperwork may be behind but makes sure it is updated when reminded	Makes sure that all records & documentation are usually accurate and timely	Ensures all records and documentation are accurate and timely.

Question 15: Supervision and Follow Through — Does he/she communicate to and follow through with dept. heads on directives, merchandising programs, product preparation procedures, product rotation and dating programs, sales plans, company policies? Does he/she make sure signage and ad items on special are correct? Does he/she make sure depts. use shelf space properly, including blocking and facing, and the collection of strays?

☐ | ☐ | ☐ | ☐ | ☐

Always communicates to & follows through with dept heads on all company directives & group programs. Makes sure correct product preparation procedures are always used, that shelf space is properly used, that signage & ad items on sale are correct	Almost always communicates to & follows through with dept heads on all company directives & group programs. Makes sure correct product preparation procedures are used most of the time, that shelf space is properly used & that signage & ad items on sale are almost always correct	Usually communicates to & follows through with dept heads on all company directives & group programs. Usually makes sure correct product preparation procedures are used most of the time, that shelf space is properly used & that signage & ad items on sale are usually correct	Is inconsistent in communicating & following through with dept heads on company directives & group programs. Does not always enforce correct product preparation procedures. Proper use of shelf space, correct signage or correct ad items	Provides no guidance to dept heads. Does not communicate or follow through regularly. Does not enforce product preparation procedures, proper use of shelf space, correct signage or correct ad items.

Question 16: Please add any extra comments about this person's performance.

_____
_____
_____
_____

Question 17:

Is this manager currently being considered for promotion: _____ If YES. Position

Is this manager ready for promotion   now _____ within a year? _____ If YES. think about the type of position

Comment about promotability _____
_____
_____

Exhibit B.   continued.

212

rural and relatively poor stores. The ratings of store managers and their comanagers were not highly correlated. Store size was not a good predictor of total ratings. There was a lot of enthusiasm for the use of this system by store personnel at all levels (cf. the evaluation at the end of Chapter 12). This enthusiasm may have been due to the fact that it was the first systematic review system that the managers and comanagers had.

During the Organizational Audit (stage two) there were many complaints by store managers and comanagers that they were never sure of how well senior management thought they were doing. They may have been especially interested in a performance evaluation system after the reorganization that took place following the organizational design (stage three). One of the immediate effects in administering this instrument was the quick identification of very weak and very strong store managers and comanagers.

PERFORMANCE INCENTIVE SYSTEM

Ideally, there should be incentives to employees which encourage and reward them for successful performance. A performance evaluation system is very useful for assessing performance but the linkage of performance to incentives needs to be made clear. This follows from the general maxims that: (1) if one rewards A, one is likely to get A, and (2), that it is folly to reward B and then to hope for A (cf. Kerr, 1975).

Companies vary widely in how they link incentives to performance. Some have the philosophy that the reward for doing a good job is to keep one's job. Some hand out bonuses based on overall performance of the company, based on some formula. Some like to have "random" bonuses. One example is the publisher of a weekly advertisement paper who handed out $100 bills to her key people whenever monthly profits were considered good. Some give out trophies and plaques to publicly recognize exceptional performance. Many use the results of performance evaluation to adjust salaries, and for promotions. The immense variety of performance incentive systems reflects managerial inventiveness.

One of the supplementary analyses performed in the OA&A technology is to work with the CEO to develop a performance incentive system that connects the task processes and their interdependencies with the individual and group incentives based upon good performance. I find that most managers (and some owners) are usually enthusiastic about having a performance incentive system developed. This gives each the opportunity for recognition, interpersonal comparisons, and wealth.

One of the more interesting performance incentive systems used in OA&A technology was developed by William Douglas Beynon when he was employed by Organizational Systems, Inc., and Dale A. Arahood of the Chicago office of Deloitte Haskins & Sells, for a community bank in Southeastern U.S.A. This example illustrates a specific solution to a special case which imparts the need for some creativity in the development of performance incentive systems.

Banks have a large number of financial results, and different persons in the bank, because of their position descriptions and interdependencies, have varying effects on different results. These results include average total assets, return on assets, average total loan growth, net interest margins, net charge-offs, noninterest income, noninterest expenses, market share of deposits, and others. These ratios are publicly available for any bank from the FDIC each quarter and year. There were 56 performance measures available for this bank.

One problem is that some banks are in growing areas and some are in depressed areas. Exceptional performance of 3% growth in deposits in a depressed area might be a very poor performance in a rapidly expanding market area. A peer group of banks can be selected in order to establish a base line for judging performance. Another issue is that, because of the volatility of interest rates paid for deposits and earned on loans, an incentive to encourage loan growth might ruin the bank as economic conditions change. One does not want to reward loan growth if the bank decides to cut back on its loan portfolio.

The issue that was interesting to the OA&A technology was to assign relative weights to different officers that reflected their relative impact on each performance factor. The Organizational Logic and the resulting position descriptions could be analyzed to trace (the planning, directing, controlling, coordinating, and execution bundles and modules) these relationships. There is no precise methodology for doing this, but it is not difficult to achieve censensus.

This bank had reorganized from a functional organization to one that was organized about its markets. This market-oriented organization assigned the task processes of the bank to positions in order to better serve the different types of bank customers. This bank had six key officers: President, SVP Marketing, SVP Commercial, VP Retail, VP Bank Services, and the Controller. The performance measurement factors and the relative weights assigned to each of these officers is shown in Table 11.7. Note that this bank included the bank's stock price and a subjective judgment of individual performance. Each of these weights were combined with a measure of performance of each, relative to a standard, to come up with a performance score for each officer. This was then used along with the annual income of each officer to calculate the cash or stock incentive reward.

The expected performance for the financial ratios such as "return on assets" and "loan growth" were defined with respect to peer group banks plus or minus fixed "basis points." For example, analysis of the bank's peformance used Peer − 15 basis points for "return on assets" and Peer +

Table 11.7. Incentive compensation plan participants
and performance measurement factors

Performance Measurement Factor	Officer					
	President	SVP Marketing	SVP Commercial	VP Retail	VP Bank Serv.	Controller
Bank's stock price	15	15	10	10	10	10
Return on assets	25	10				10
Market share (deposits)	25	30	25	25		
Loan growth	10	15	10	10		
Net interest margin	5		15	10		50
Noninterest income	5	10	5	10	30	
Noninterest expense	5	10	10	10	50	20
Net charge offs	5		15	15		
Individual performance	5	10	10	10	10	10
Total	100	100	100	100	100	100

300 basis points for "loan growth." Incentive calculations are made for each measure when the performance exceeds the expected level of performance. The actual incentive increases linearly with the amount the bank exceeded expected levels of performance.

Such a custom-fitted performance incentive plan costs time and money to develop and implement. For the case of this bank, it really helped make the new organizational design work. But a similar solution could not be made for SSI, because peer data is not available in such detail and uniformity and because each store faces a different competitive market. Each organization can expect its specific circumstances to alter how it develops a performance incentive system.

There have recently been some very insightful technologies for peformance appraisal of multi-unit operations. The original mathematical techniques were developed by Charnes, Cooper, and Rhodes (1978). Charnes and Cooper (1980) published a survey of this method, known as Data Envelopment Analysis. Professor Arie Lewin of Duke University has developed a management consulting service applying these techniques to banks and other retail chain operations. Data Envelopment Analysis is an original new approach that, when applied, should enhance management in performing performance appraisals of multi-unit operations, and is, in principle, superior to the method presented in this section.

The objectives of this performance incentive system were to: (1) provide incentive to management for achieving desired performance, (2) provide guidelines for acceptable performance, (3) emphasize the highest priority performance factors which (a) protect the stockholders' interests and (b) follow the Board of Directors' guidelines, and (4) support the bank's goals as defined in the organizational design and financial plans.

The use of the organizational design to help develop both performance evaluation and performance incentive systems makes these analyses a vital part of the OA&A technology. The key is the use of knowledge of the Organizational Logic and the Organizational Responsibility Grouping chart. This is a distinct feature of the OA&A technology, and knowledge of both can generate more accurate and more vital human resources management information.

CHAPTER 12

Design of a supermarket chain

INTRODUCTION

This chapter describes the application of the Organizational Audit and Analysis technology to the design of a complex organization operating in many locations in a fast-moving, highly competitive environment. The engagement began in April, 1981 and ended in February, 1983. The description of the engagement process provides an illustration of the OA&A process and the dynamics of designing an organization.

Chapter 3 described desiderata of an organizational design technology, and Chapters 9, 10, and 11 described the Organizational Audit and Analysis technology. This chapter describes the main features of the application of this technology. The names of individuals, the identity of the firm, its location, and other identifying characteristics are masked in order to preserve confidentiality. The organization is a regional supermarket chain in the U.S.A.

SOME OBSERVATIONS OF THE RETAIL FOOD INDUSTRY

The retail food industry is very competitive, with small profit margins. As a percentage of sales, profits hover about 1% after taxes. This industry is undergoing rapid change because of new technology, such as in-store check out scanners and increasing use of computers to control operations. Economic conditions, changing systems for procurement and distribution, broadening of product mixes, and shifting governmental regulations all affect this industry. Each chain and every store in a chain faces the problems of how to profitably serve its customers in the presence of other local competitors who may be units of other chains or independents.

Typically, employees of supermarket chains face long hours of very hard and unglamourous work. Their education level tends to end with high school, and it is difficult in normal times to attract college graduates, especially women, for managerial positions. The responsibility is very high. For example, a store averaging $100,000/week in sales is a $5,200,000 enterprise. Roughly 40% of these sales involve some form of manufacturing in the meat, produce, and deli-bakery departments. Thus, store managers have responsibility for a wide assortment of task processes. Operations at the stores can easily exceed 100 hours per week, and operations at the distribution centers can go 24 hours per day from midnight Monday morning to noon on Saturday. The need for continuity and coordination at each store and between each store and the rest of the chain never stops.

Despite these conditions, the cadre of full time employees tend to enjoy working in the retail food industry. The work is challenging and change is normal. Employees report that food retailing "gets into one's blood" rather quickly.

In many ways, the food retailing business is analogous to a macro-learning experiment where there are different experimenters and there are many experiments being conducted simultaneously on the same pool of subjects. The subjects have free choice and the purpose of the experimenters is to alter their behavior. The Chief Executive Officer (CEO) of a chain is analogous to one of the experimenters. The CEO runs many mazes in different locations. The management conducts experiments with each maze and across those mazes that the organization controls. The CEO, and all of the other supermarket chain CEOs, continually strive to induce customers to patronize and to increase the percentage of purchases made at their stores. The competition for customers is conducted by continually attempting to reinforce customers to shop and purchase more in one's stores.

The customers, of course, need the retail food stores in order to obtain food-related products and, increasingly, other household-related goods. Advertising attracts customers who have their choice of stores. Store location, parking, and attractiveness entice customers to enter a store. Once a customer enters a store, physical barriers, location of advertised specials, and strategic placement of staples and perishable products encourage the customer to proceed through the store in traffic patterns that stimulate buying. Product merchandising further reinforces buying by artful and strategic display. Speedy and accurate checkouts, courtesy, and other services tend to reward the customer for shopping in a store. The prices and quality of the products provide further reinforcements which encourage customers to patronize a store.

A supermarket is a specific environment in which customers can fulfill their needs for acquiring food products, food-related products, and selected household goods. A supermarket chain is in the business of designing, maintaining, and adapting these environments to serve its customers while earning good returns on its investments.

Consequently, the main problem in running a supermarket chain is to integrate all of the functions in order to provide positive reinforcement to the customer so that he or she buys more and more products from its stores, thus producing sufficient profits to merit investment. These functions include operating the stores, finance and accounting, employee relations, public relations, advertising, warehouse and transportation services, engineering and store design, merchandising and procurement, security, data processing, training and management development, maintenance, real estate, industrial engineering, and special customer sevices. All of these functions must be welded into an efficient, coordinated organization in order to succeed in producing satisfaction for its customers. With small profit margins and with the need to justify investment, it is a very difficult task to operate a supermarket chain well. The customers normally do not realize all of the suport it takes to satisfy them. And they do not really care, because there is almost always another store to choose. Thus, a lot of thought and planning goes into ensuring customer patronage.

A supermarket chain has at least 11 stores and thus operates in a variety of markets. What works in one end of a city may not work in another. The Chief Executive Officer of a supermarket chain cannot perform a pure experiment to determine cause and effect for decisions, because so many variables are changed simultaneously. Consumers are not homogeneous in shopping preferences. Competitors are constantly changing what they do to attract the customers. Suppliers manipulate the chains, and vice versa. Weather conditions and economic changes further complicate assessment of the effectiveness of any policy.

Consequently, despite the availability of lots of data, it is usually difficult to know what works and why. This is why experience, knowledge, and judgment about running supermarkets is so important. Much is learned by direct experience, and seasoned judgment takes time and effort to develop. It takes coordinated teamwork to prevail in this business. The calendar has a strong impact on the task processes because of seasonal changes in the mix of products desired and those available to the chain. For example, at Thanksgiving the pattern of purchases is very different from the pattern at the Fourth of July or Christmas. The uncertainty surrounding the success of any decision, and the complexity of the number and integration of these decisions, make running a chain a never-ending challenge. With up to 15,000 products, choosing a pricing policy and a product mix policy is made under conditions of uncertainty.

Furthermore, the products can deteriorate anywhere in the system. Produce becomes spoiled, meat ages, products are damaged, and new products are introduced and advertised by suppliers. The future in a supermarket is limited to 4-week periods for most decisions. Tomorrow is the near future. On the other hand, the physical plant enjoys an 8-year life. So long term investments must be made in the face of short term operating systems and change. For example, a chain must solve the problems of opening, closing, and remodeling its stores in the midst of uncertainty about how the consumer will react, economic and demographic trends, and how the competition will respond. But, in the final analysis, all decisions are judged against the criteria of whether or not they profitably serve the customers.

One method for coping with the uncertainty is to follow standard operating procedures for most decisions. Traditional institutional habits can dominate decision making. There are always many opinions about what to do. Consequently, rules of thumb and simple heuristics are common and used frequently. Examples include spending 1% of sales revenues in advertising, pricing zone policies, and limiting store labor costs to 8.0% of sales.

The complexity of operations and the rapidity of change create fascinating issues in organizational design. Just how does one design, in an organization, the presence of such rapid and pervasive change? The OA&A technology, when combined with the desiderata for the technology, is one answer.

Supermarket Systems, Inc.

Supermarket Systems, Inc. (SSI) is a regional supermarket chain of less than 100 units. It operates in a market which has the most stores per capita of any region in the USA. Annual sales are less than $800,000,000. SSI is a subsidiary of a holding company traded on a major stock exchange. It is neither family owned nor controlled. The holding company operates in other industries, but SSI is its major company in terms of sales. The directors include several officers of SSI, but power resides in the hands of two of the directors who are related to each other. Generally, the holding company stays out of the operations of SSI except for major investments. During the organizational design process, the author was never introduced to the key directors. The Chief Executive Officer is also an officer of the holding company, but serves at the discretion of the two powerful directors.

Mr. Duncan, the CEO at the time of the study, was formerly Chairman of the Board of SSI. Mr. Willey, the Chairman of the Board, was formerly the CEO. Mr. Duncan traded places with Mr. Willey because he thought that he could do a better job. Mr. Willey was a figurehead with very close ties to the powerful directors, and is a long time, loyal family retainer. The ambiguity of the positions of these two men created exquisitely delicate interpersonal relationships marked by careful and formalized courtesy. Mr. Willey is about 15 years older than Mr. Duncan and served with distinction in World War II and for the powerful directors in a variety of roles. Both are men of high integrity. The situation between the two, while awkward, worked rather well despite the circumstances, because Mr. Duncan was, in fact, given the authority to run SSI. In many ways, Mr. Willey acted as a control for the holding company, but had no real responsibility for SSI during the study. The study ended when Mr. Duncan resigned and Mr. Willey resumed control in February, 1983.

SSI operates dry grocery and perishables warehouses at separate locations. It operates stores in four states. It has a main corporate office in the dry grocery warehouse location, and another set of corporate offices for staff groups at another location. SSI maintains its own fleet of tractors and trailers to support store operations. SSI owns and controls a dairy and has its own bakery. SSI has an Employee Stock Option Program (ESOP) for its employees which provides them with some ownership and retirement income, but no control. SSI is an owner and member of a voluntary wholesale organization serving chains from coast to coast.

Most of the employees of SSI work in the retail stores. Approximately 400 employees are involved in distribution and transportation operations. All of the distribution and transportation employees below the rank of foreman belong to a union with which there is a long history of conflict. One of the goals of SSI is to decertify this union. SSI has won almost all NLRB, OSHA, FEPC, and grievance cases since 1980. SSI has a reputation for quality, friendliness, and fairness, and is embarrassed by the union, which was formed because of some admittedly unsound labor practices of the previous management of SSI. SSI works closely with community groups and charities. SSI is considered an excellent "corporate citizen" almost everywhere it operates.

Up until about 1977, SSI enjoyed a dominant market share in the 100-mile radius surrounding its corporate headquarters. Since then, the economic growth of the region has attracted powerful and well financed new competitors. There was an aggressive national chain which moved in and began building superstores of approximately 43,000 square feet, with the same range of options as SSI's stores. An equally aggressive, foreign-financed, regional chain moved in to capture the "lower end" of the market by constructing stores with 18,000 square feet. This competitor employs a "Japanese" strategy of entering with low prices and limited assortment and then moving up to capture more of the middle income market. There was another chain that moved in with a very different store format developed in Australia. Meanwhile, existing chains upgraded their stores. Consequently, the market share of SSI was dropping. The economic recession and high interest rates were beginning to place strong pressure on SSI's finances. These environmental changes and economic pressures began to create serious organizational problems for SSI by 1980.

In the fall of 1980, SSI hired a new Senior Vice President, Mr. McCale, to head up the functions called Sales and Merchandising. These included all staff product and merchandising departments at Corporate Headquarters, as well as advertising, and customer services. Store operations were headed by Mr. Grey, who was also a Senior Vice President. Mr. Grey was the sixth person in 9 years to head the store organization. Both Mr. McCale and Mr. Grey reported to Mr. Duncan, the CEO. In retail operations, there will always be tensions between the staffs (headed by Mr. McCale) and the stores (headed by Mr. Grey at SSI). They need each other in order to operate, but they have different perspectives and expertise. Conflict over policy is dormant during good times and can become manifest during declines.

The staff product and merchandising departments procure all items sold in the stores. These personnel are expert in various product lines, such as meat, poultry, dairy, frozen food, deli-bakery, grocery, general merchandise, produce, flowers, and plants. Each product line has its own specialized and technical knowledge. These staff employees are genuine experts. They must know what competitors are doing and what is happening nationally to those products for which they bear direct responsibility. They must know how to negotiate purchases, allowances, and advertising promotions. They set the merchandising programs to be followed by the stores. They send field merchandisers out to the stores to train and enforce merchandising policy. For example, in meat operations, they train store meat department personnel on how to prepare meat, how to store it, and how to merchandise it. Small errors in pricing and purchasing can really hurt operations and tie up scarce capital in inventory. But such expert product knowledge is often too general to help the local store manager serve its customers against his competition. Some stores, for example, are in wealthy big city neighborhoods, and some are in factory towns. The customers have different requirements. Consequently, a policy set for all stores will usually not satisfy the needs of every store. Thus, the balance between generalized expertise and specific knowledge of local customers creates conflicts as one side attempts to gain ascendency over the other. The hiring of Mr. McCale signified a shift in power away from the stores. There are parallel problems in advertising. Newspapers and television cut across the markets of the stores. But how does one prepare advertisements that satisfy all of the stores? Differences of opinion and policy are bound to surface, especially when market shares and profits are declining. Tradition helps to mediate conflict. Consequently, any new policy that upsets the status quo can reverberate throughout the entire organization.

There are two standard solutions. The first is to vest all control in the staff departments, who then dictate how the stores are to carry out their policies. The second is to place all control in the store organization, who tell the product staffs what to purchase. Issues often boil down to control of product selection and to how to set gross margins. Both extreme solutions have their strengths and weaknesses. They simplify coordination, but they ignore the interdependency and different bases for expertise. Each seems to work well for a while, and then the inherent problems begin to surface. SSI was earnestly searching for some middle ground between the two polar solutions. However, in a specific context this is easier to propose than to accomplish, because of the complexity and fast pace of retail food chain operations and the uncertainty in assigning cause to effect.

The following sections of this chapter describe how the Organizational Audit and Analysis technology for organizational design was applied at SSI. The description of the application of the OA&A technology covers the highlights of the actual sequences of work for the main stages of the OA&A technology. Details of the study of the Distribution and Transportation area of the firm are mentioned in Chapter 4. A description of some of the supplementary human resources analyses is given in Chapter 11. This chapter is primarily directed to the Strategic Assessment, the Organizational Audit, the organizational design and follow up stages.

APPLICATION OF THE OA&A TECHNOLOGY

Table 9.1 in Chapter 9 outlined 11 stages in the Organizational Audit and Analysis Technology. This study involved the following:

Stage one: Strategic Assessment
Stage two: Organizational Audit
Stage three: Organizational Design
   Supplementary Services
     3.1 Strategic Planning
     3.3 Market Analysis and Planning
Stage four: Implementation Planning
   Supplementary Services
     4.4 Performance Standards System
     4.5 Manpower Planning System
     4.6 Management Succession Analysis and Planning
     4.8 Career Planning System Design
Stage five: Monitoring the Implementation
Stage eight: Organizational Maintenance
   Supplementary Services
     8.1 In-house Organizational Maintenance System
     8.3 Custom Client Software
     8.4 Install Micro-computer Software for Client
     8.6 Crisis Intervention
     8.7 Executive Counselling
Stage nine: Systems Review

Stages one, two, three, and four, and supplementary service 3.1, are described in this chapter. Other stages and supplementary services involved new technology, described in Chapters 10 and 11. It is hoped, however, that the discussion of the key stages will provide the reader with an understanding of the OA&A technology for organizational design.

Stage one: strategic assessment

The description of Stage one provided in Chapter 9 was followed in this study. The project began in March, 1981 with Mr. McCale, SVP of Sales and Merchandising, to develop a 75-page questionnaire. On April 2, 1981, these questions were reviewed by Mr. Duncan, Mr. McCale, Mr. Grey, and Mr. Well, the Vice President of Finance. After adjusting the questions for SSI and industry language usage, the questionnaire was administered on April 3, 1981 to these four, plus four other Vice Presidents reporting directly to Mr. Duncan. The others were Mr. Boulware, VP of Employee Relations, Mr. Chips, VP of Data Processing, Mr. Seaman, VP of Store Development, and Mr. Scott, VP of Warehouse and Transportation. The organizational chart for senior management at SSI at the time of the Strategic Assessment is given in Figure 12.1

The questionnaire inquired about all elements of the ABCE Model (cf. Chapters 1 and 6), and was designed to examine the organizational congruency conditions. Each officer independently completed the questionnaire and then mailed it to the author for analysis. The report on the findings was delivered on April 30, 1981. The full report was first presented to Mr. Duncan, and then, later the same day, to all eight for review and discussion.

The results of the Strategic Assessment can be easily tabulated in Table 12.1 by the 11 organizational congruency conditions (cf. Chapter 6). SSI was judged congruent for 6 of the 11 organizational congruency conditions. The pattern was very clear. Regarding goals, strategies, and environments, there was high degree of consensus and consistency. On these congruency conditions regarding design premises (cf. Chapter 6), and on the Organizational Technology, the congruency was very low. Basically, SSI was organized around its internal functions rather than its markets. Increasing the return on investment was the prime financial goal. It was important for the health of the organization and because year-end bonuses depended upon it. Failure to achieve bonus was an important reason for concluding that the results were incongruent with the goals. There was unanimity that financial results should be much better. The Organizational Logic As Seen At The Time of the Strategic Assessment is given in Figure 12.1.

One of the most interesting findings was that, despite the desire and recognized need for planning, most of these eight officers spent the majority of their time putting out brush fires. The inherent lack of organizational congruity of the Organizational Technology within itself, and in comparison to the design premises, indicated a need to rethink the basic Organizational Technology. The agreement on goals and strategies, coupled with the inability to produce desired results that matched the goals, suggested that the *organizational means for achieving results* was the problem. Figure 12.3 depicts the actual organizational chart at the time of the Strategic Assessment.

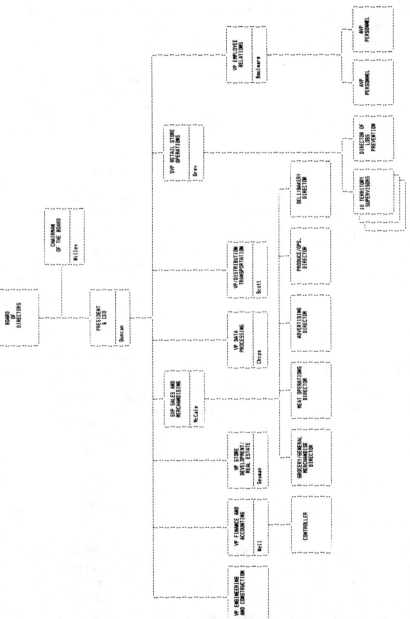

Figure 12.1. Stage one organizational chart for senior management at SSI.

Table 12.1.   Results of organizational congruency tests for SSI after Strategic Assessment

Organizational congruency condition	Result	Comments
1. Goals and environment	Yes	Strong consensus for current, short term and long term. Increased return on investment
2. Strategies and environment	Yes*	Strong consensus on aggressively seeking opportunities to increase ROI, build adaptive management teams and improve efficiency
3. Goals and strategies	Yes*	Strong consensus that goals can be met by the strategies
4. Agreement by senior management	Yes	High concordance on goals, strategies, and environment
5. Design premises and environment	No	Assumed more control over market than what would be realistic
6. Strategies and design premises	No	Strategies for marketing were inconsistent with reality of competition and store formats
7. Design premises and Organizational Logic	No	Functional Organizational Logic was inconsistent for controlling vulnerabilities facing SSI
8. Organizational Logic and Organizational Architecture	Yes*	Assessments of the macro features of the Organizational Logic matched the macro features of the Organization Architecture
9. Organizational Logic and actual organization	No	Very many major processes bypassed the organization. Too many meetings and committees
10. Results and Organizational Technology	Yes	Less than satisfactory financial results highly consistent with existence of inappropriate Organizational Logic and Architecture
11. Results and goals	No	Results do not meet goals for ROI, for teamwork, and development of a management team

*The results of the Organizational Audit reversed these conclusions

After discussion of the findings of the Strategic Assessment, it was decided that the analysis and conclusions were fundamentally correct and that steps should be taken to improve the Organizational Technology. But because of the magnitude and complexity of SSI, the decision to conduct an Organizational Audit on only part of the organization was seen to be cost effective and met other desiderata. The decision was made by Mr. Duncan to have an Organizational Audit performed for the Sales and Merchandising

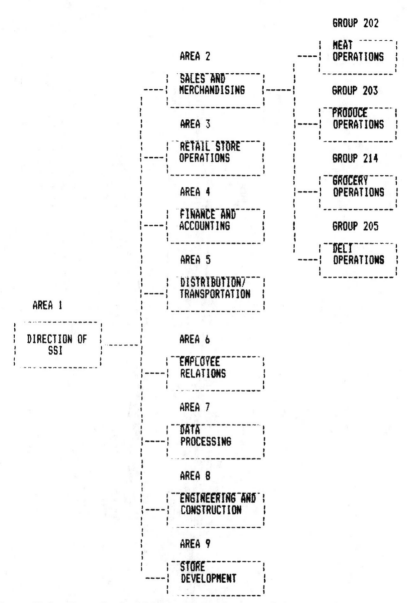

Figure 12.2.   Organizational logic as seen at time of the strategic assessment.

departments and the retail store organization. Arrangements were made for conducting the study and it began immediately. The actual Organizational Audit began on May 11, 1981, and the "State of the Organization" report was delivered on July 6, 1981.

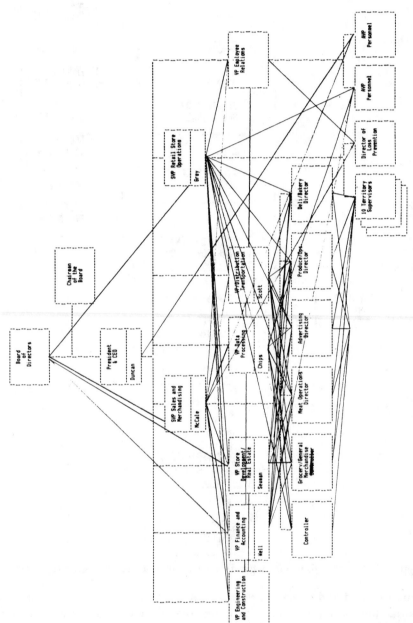

Figure 12.3.   Stage one actual organizational chart for senior management at SSI.

Stage two: the Organizational Audit of sales and mechandising and retail store organizations

The decision to restrict the scope of the Organizational Audit initially left only three of the eight executives participating in the Strategic Assessment involved in this next step. Because research, experience, and the Strategic Assessment indicated that the problems existing between the Sales and Merchandising departments and the store organization were paramount, the Organizational Audit was initially limited to the President, both SVPs, 16 middle managers, and a visit to three stores.

As the 8-week study unfolded, 45 persons were intensively interviewed and 35 stores were visited. In addition, 16 other people helped provide information. The additional work was necessary for three reasons: (a) the lack of documentation about the jobs, (b) the necessity for validating the assumptions, and (c) the extensive overlapping of responsibilities. In addition to the personal interviews, the other five types described earlier in Chapter 9 were also completed. A Store Manager Questionnaire was developed and administrated to all store managers, in order to document and verify field impressions.

The main conclusion was that SSI was an organization of organizations, each of which was organized functionally to suit its own interests. These organizations were inconsistent with each other. This created many extra organizational interdependencies that inhibited responsiveness, reduced flexibility, made planning difficult, and complicated the direction, coordination, and control of SSI. The current logic for the task processes, the Organizational Logic, was inconsistent with the Organizational Architecture.

This finding of incongruity between the Organizational Logic and the Organizational Architecture reversed the conclusion from the Strategic Assessment on this organizational congruency condition. The Organizational Logic for the Sales and Merchandising and Retail Store Operations as shown in Figure 12.4 is not consistent with the Organizational Architecture as represented in Figure 12.1.

The organizational chart described after the Strategic Assessment remains basically unchanged. The organizational charts for each unit of SSI covered in the Organizational Audit were prepared. The process and structural maladaptations indicated in the Strategic Assessment were verified and amplified in detail. The actual organization was a maze of process and structural maladaptions. However, the inconsistency between the Organizational Architecture and the actual Organizational Logic allows one to pinpoint the main structural problem at SSI.

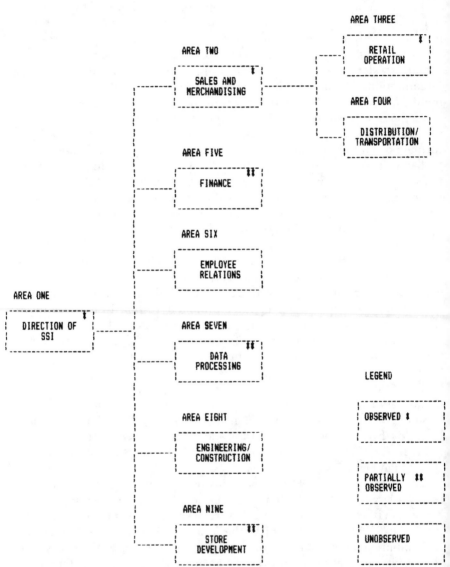

Figure 12.4. Organizational logic as seen after the Organizational Audit of sales and mechandising and retail store operation.

230

The main structural problem

The longer the chain of command, the longer it takes to have a flow of information among each pair of levels. One-way flows are relatively efficient, but two-way flows create complex combinations that can take a lot of time to work through the levels. For example, if there are six levels in a chain of command, it takes only five messages to transmit one way. Once two-way flows begin, assuming no transmission errors, it could take up to 30, with the minimum being 10. For this reason, centralized organizations with long chains of command are often slow in responding to change. They also slow down because intermediate level persons can act in their own interests by restricting the flow. There are two classic solutions. The first is simply to bypass the long chain of command, to go directly. This is often accompanied by a lack of keeping other levels informed. One can expect many "turf" disputes and controls being imposed in order to protect the integrity of the organization and to protect one's interests. The second is to alter what type, what amounts, and the frequency of information flows by delegating selected blocks of decisions to lower levels. The main problem in decentralizing is reducing the time taken for all of the interactions while maintaining effective power. Decentralizing requires careful analysis of exactly what can be delegated to whom.

Two parallel chains of commands complicate the problems of a single chain of command when the two chains are interdependent. Osculating task processes become common (cf. Chapter 8). Hence the combinations rise geometrically. The confusions increase with the increase in the combinations of who is working with whom on what. Establishing one-way communications cuts down the communications and speeds up the system. However, with one-way flows, information that could be provided and which may be needed does not get into the decision making. The result is increasing demands for control, increasing emphasis on "numbers" management, and decreasing responsiveness to the information generated at the lowest level in both parallel chains of command.

The interdependencies among members of a group can be described in terms of the task processes, task process resources characteristics, and interpositional relationships. Normally, it works well to place dependent task processes into contiguous organizational units. This, however, is easier said than done because of a host of organizational realities. One of the relevant realities is to consider the time period which is allowable for a set of given transactions to occur. Those whose interdependencies require very rapid response should definitely be grouped together organizationally. Contiguous task processes allowing longer responses can be organizationally separated. This distinction is recognized by how authority is delegated as well as by the type and nature of contact with those persons outside the organization.

At SSI, the chain of command for Retail Operations had at least six levels between the President and an employee in a store: President, Senior Vice President of Retail Operations, Territory Supervisor, Store Manager, Department Manager, and Employee. There were other possible gradations, such as Comanager and full-time vs. part-time employees. The store personnel worked directly with the customers and had needs for frequent and rapid communications. Parallel to Retail Operations was another chain of command for Sales and Merchandising, which had at least four levels: President, Senior Vice President for Sales and Mechandising, VP of Product Group, and buyers and merchandisers who report to the product Vice Presidents. In some product departments, there was a head buyer and a head of field merchandisers plus secretaries. The Sales and Mechandising organization was complicated, because it had to work with both outside vendors and with the stores. Its functional division of work mirrored its environmental interdependencies with the vendors rather than the store organizations.

Each of these parallel organizations was organized functionally. The organization of Retail Operations was straightforward, with territories, stores, store departments, and loss prevention. Sales and Merchandising was organized by type of product and by special staff units, such as advertising, retail services, and price checking. These two organizations operated in parallel but were not in parallel by function. The product group and service group divisions in Sales and Mechandising did not match those in the stores. For example, Meat Operations included meat, dairy, frozen food, and bakery operations. The meat part was parallel with the market manager in a store, but the rest overlapped with grocery, and deli-bakery. Produce operations included produce, deli-bakery, and wine and beer. These overlapped with deli-bakery and groceries in a store. The grocery and general merchandise product department roughly paralleled the corresponding departments in a store. However, items such as orange juice can be in produce, frozen food, dairy, or grocery, which creates additional complications. So SSI had those two parallel organizations which were not parallel in function. The result was excessive organizational interdependencies.

There were other parallel organizations at SSI, such as Distribution/Transportation, Finance and Accounting, Data Processing, Employee Relations, Real Estate, and Engineering. Each of these orgnizations was also functionally organized. But the distribution of functions in each was not parallel. This situation further exacerbated the problem of direction, coordination, and control. Thus there were eight organizations at SSI, each functionally organized for its own convenience, attempting to interact where the allowable response time lag was often very short.

The result was an incredibly complex organization with self-imposed interorganizational complications. The forebearance, courtesy, and good will among the officers was extraordinary. However, despite the best of intentions, the entire set of organizations was too complicated to be able to provide rapid adaptiveness and good two-way consultation. Meetings and committees had been extensively employed to overcome the basic design problems. Diminishing returns had set in on having more meetings and committees. SSI needed to reorganize itself after recognizing the normal interdependence.

The main structural problem was that the current formal organization was needlessly complex. It needed to be simplified and streamlined in order to be both more responsive and more professional, by eliminating excessive organizational interdependencies.

The problem of organizational logic

During the Strategic Assessment, there was widespread agreement on the principle features of the main Organizational Logic at SSI. This Organizational Logic is given in Figure 12.2. The formal organizational chart of SSI was consistent with the Organizational Logic. The main conclusion of the Organizational Audit was that this earlier representation of the Organizational Logic was not correct.

Because this study was primarily concerned with Retail Store Operations and Sales and Merchandising, special emphasis was given to understanding the actual Organizational Logic. The earlier Organizational Logic had Sales and Merchandising and Retail Operations in parallel. In fact, the decisions and activities of Sales and Mechandising drove Retail Store Operations. They set the programs, did the buying, selected the ads, set up merchandising, did price checking, and they selectively attempted to enforce these decisions and programs by their field merchandisers. These decisions also governed the activities of the distribution and transportation: what is received at the warehouse, how it is stored at the warehouse, and what is shipped from the warehouse to the store. Consequently, the actual Organizational Logic is as shown in Figure 12.4.

When the Organizational Logic and the Organizational Architecture are congruent, the organizational problems of direction, control, and coordination are simpler. Because the actual Organizational Logic for Sales and Merchandising and Retail Store Operations was inconsistent with the formal architecture of SSI, there were many excessive organizational interdependencies. These showed up in endless rounds of meetings and rapid conferences, a loss of two-way flow of communications, and strong pressures to overstaff and to centralize all decisions. However, each of these organizational effects tended to inhibit market responsiveness, which ought to be a primary competitive advantage of SSI over other larger chains. Overly centralized decision making creates strong incentives to have one program for all stores.

The solution to these problems lay in decentralization of selected decisions to a lower level than senior management in the corporate headquarters, and reorganizing the two interdependent parallel organizations of Retail Operations and Sales and Merchandising in order to better balance the requirements for control and the requirements for rapid coordination. There was no "magic wand" which could be waved for achieving a solution. It required a step-by-step, detailed analysis of each separate activity. The documentation of the existing organization provided a basis for this analysis. And, as the solution unfolded, the solution changed. The keystone was the meshing of Retail Operations and Sales and Merchandising. The rest of the organizational design was built around this integration.

The incongruity between the Organizational Logic and the Organizational Architecture had a source higher in the ranking of organizational congruency tests. Starting from the first, C_1, there was still strong congruency between the environment and the goal of increasing return on investment, although the target ROI had been set too high for the circumstances. The prime goal of increasing ROI was confirmed. The means for achieving this were conspicuous by their absence.

Normally, if an organization has a clearly structured goal there will be performance planning, performance review, and performance incentives in place to reach the goal. SSI had communicated this goal, but only four of those interviewed knew what ROI meant. There was no mention of ROI in any of the many reports that were generated anywhere in the system, with the exception of the financial accounting system. It was not used as a criterion for decisions. The incentives to obtain increased ROI were absent, except for poorly understood bonuses calculated at the end of each fiscal year. (Later in the study, it became clear that the formula for calculating ROI understated it by ignoring interest payments). This had the effect of reducing the probability of obtaining bonuses. There were no reports on inventory turns, which, for retailers, is a useful surrogate for improving ROI of inventory. Consequently, the goal of improving ROI, while accepted in principle, was not operational at SSI.

Futhermore, decisions to open new stores, close old stores, and remodel existing stores were not strongly guided by the goal of increasing ROI. The analysis of how decisions were made to close a poorly performing store showed that ROI was not a major factor. Sitting in on a task force to review each store for this purpose led to a succession of analyses which led to this conclusion.

The Real Estate department had data on "business position," "market attractiveness," relative market share (RMS), and the growth rate of the Primary Trading Area (PTA) of every store. The relative market share and the growth rate were used to classify a store according to whether it was a "star," a "cash cow," a "questionable" store, or a "dog." A star has a growing market share in a growing market. A "dog" has a shrinking market share in a shrinking market. A "cash cow" has a growing market share in a slow growing maket, and a "questionable" has a shrinking market share in a growing market. At one store-closing meeting held on May 28, 1981, it was decided to close a "cash cow," a "questionable," and two "dogs." Several other "dogs" were left open. The store closing decisions were not based solely on RMS or growth rate of the PTA.

There was no useful measure of ROI for the stores, so I worked with Mr. Well, the Treasurer, to develop a measure called Return on Working Capital Employed at each store. This measure, called ROWCE, was the ratio of store contribution to cash on hand, plus inventory, with an allowance for outstanding accounting payables multiplied by 100. ROWCE provided a simple measure of how well each store deployed the assets it controlled. Values of ROWCE varied from -3.0 to $+5.8$. The relative values of ROWCE were understandable.

The next step was to conduct a statistical analysis of ROWCE in terms of 22 store variables, such as square feet of selling area, storage, sales per square foot, dollar unit of sales by product groups, "business position," "market attractiveness," size of city, territory, number of PTA competition, and pricing zones. The best predictor of ROWCE was sales per square feet of selling area. The correlation was 0.80. Weekly sales correlated 0.54 with ROWCE. Customer count correlated with ROWCE at 0.68. These data support conventional wisdom that "good sales can cover up a lot of problems." However, they also suggested that, given the wide variation in peformance, the strategy of using the same merchandising policy at every store, regardless of local conditions, was a mistake.

The ROWCE measure was used to try to explain the decisions to close or not close a store. ROWCE had only a weak correlation to the variables (business position and market attractiveness) provided by the Real Estate department. Because ROWCE was a good predictor of ROI at the store level, it became clear that the data provided by Real Estate were not very useful in making store closing decisions based on ROI.

An analysis of the stores selected for closing also showed that stores were not closed which had worse values for both business position and market attractiveness. Consequently, it was concluded that neither a variable by itself nor in combination was a good predictor of store closings.

The next step was to examine the details of the two variables to understand (1) how they were calculated, and (2) how each variable was relevant to the decision for a store closing. Tables 12.2 and 12.3 explain business position and market attractiveness variables, respectively.

Table 12.2. Business position

Component	Weight	Relevance to: Opening	Relevance to: Closing	Relevance to: Operations
Merchandising philosophy fitting the market	15			X
Store management quality	15			X
Location	25	X		
Site	5	X		
Experience in market	5	X		X
Size of store	5	X		
Condition of facility	5			X
Price of product	15			X
Total	100	4	0	5

Table 12.3. Market attractiveness

Component	Weight	Relevance to: Opening	Relevance to: Closing	Relevance to: Operations
Average family income	5	X		
Per capital income	10	X		
PTA population	15	X		
Single family units	2	X		
White-collar work force	8	X		
Grocery purchases/capita	2	X		
Growth	15	X	Change is relevant	
Competition	20	X		
Sales/sq. foot	20	X		
Total	100	10	1	0

The main conclusion about the business position variable was that it can be very useful for decisions for opening a store, remodelling a store, and operating a store. However, it was not useful for store-closing decisions. The main conclusion is that market attractiveness is very useful for decisions involving opening a store, but not very helpful in decisions to close a store.

During the process of interviewing many executives of SSI, and having observed a store-closing meeting, it became apparent that SSI had a more subtle decision process for reaching a decision to close a store. First, there was great concern for the welfare of the employees at a store and commitments made to maintain a store. Second, there was a concern for the strategic consequences of possible SSI decisions. Third, there was concern about the financial aspects. These considerations made the decision more difficult than a mechanical calculation. They also weighed the decision against store closings.

An attempt was made to model the use of information in arriving at a decision. To this observer, there were seven main considerations, which are listed in Table 12.4. Each consideration is treated as a binary (yes, no) variable. Figure 12.5 represents how the variables are combined to arrive at one of three decisions about a store:

Close it
Postpone or table the decision to a later date
Keep it open

Given this diagram (called a mapping function), there are 3 paths leading to the conclusion to close a store, 15 paths leading to a postponement of the decision, and 7 paths leading to the conclusion to keep a store open.

This mapping function was an attempt to describe the decision process leading to the observed outcome to close, postpone closing, or to keep a store open. There are probably other considerations that would lead to a revision of this mapping function. However, this model did fit the pattern of decisions observed, and had other strategic uses.

Table 12.4. Mapping function variables for store closing decisions

Explanation of variables in the mapping function to keep a store open or closed.

X_1	Does at least one of the following indicate a healthy outlook for the store?	$X_1 \begin{cases} 0 \text{ if no} \\ 1 \text{ if yes} \end{cases}$
	Store contribution Store net profit Store return on capital employed	
X_2	Is the trend of the store health improving?	$X_2 \begin{cases} 0 \text{ if no} \\ 1 \text{ if yes} \end{cases}$
X_3	Can management turn store health & trend around?	$X_3 \begin{cases} 0 \text{ if no} \\ 1 \text{ if yes} \end{cases}$
X_4	Will there be a change in competition?	$X_4 \begin{cases} 0 \text{ if no or not much} \\ 1 \text{ if yes, very strong} \end{cases}$
X_5	Is there a feasible change we can make to neutralize competition?	$X_5 \begin{cases} 0 \text{ if no} \\ 1 \text{ if yes} \end{cases}$
X_6	Can we get out of lease without losing too much?	$X_6 \begin{cases} 0 \text{ if no} \\ 1 \text{ if yes} \end{cases}$
X_7	Has a commitment been made to keep the store open?	$X_7 \begin{cases} 0 \text{ if no} \\ 1 \text{ if yes} \end{cases}$
Y	Decision to open, close, or postpone store closing.	$Y \begin{cases} 2 \text{ if close} \\ 1 \text{ if postpone} \\ 0 \text{ if open} \end{cases}$

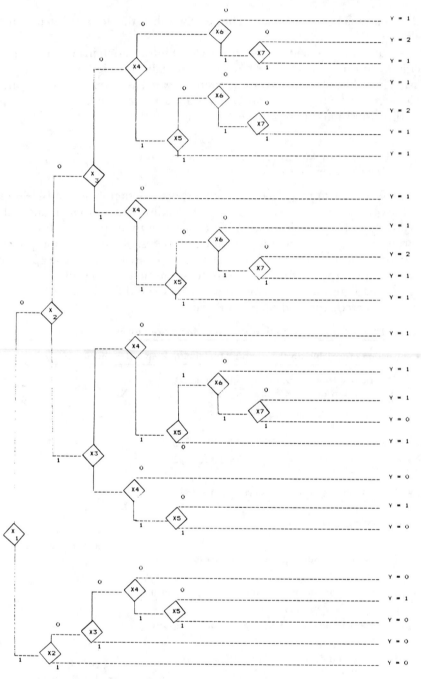

Figure 12.5. Mapping function for store closing decision.

238

This exercise of running down an assumption during an Organizational Audit often results in a successive unfolding of corporate problems that had not been anticipated before the study but which arose during a study. The unsatisfactory ROI results led to the simple question, "Does anyone understand ROI?" The fact that only the President, the two SVPs, and the VP Treasurer understood ROI raised flags. This led to the questions of if and how ROI was used. The absence of performance information, performance evaluation, and performance incentives based directly on ROI raised the next question. Did SSI even have ROI measures for its stores? A new measure, ROWCE, was developed and then used to understand the determinants of ROWCE at each store. This eventually led to the analysis of store-closing decisions which showed that, even for major investment decisions, ROI was not very important.

These analyses about the ROI goal of SSI led, step by step, to questioning the basic strategy of SSI. What is congruent with the environment of SSI? Was it congruent with the ROI goal of SSI? The earlier Strategic Assessment had concluded that these two congruency tests were met. Reassessing these during the Organizational Audit reversed these conclusions.

The statistical analysis of the determinants of ROWCE, plus the impressions gained from interviewed persons involved with Retail Store Operations, plus visits to a few stores, created much doubt about the strategy of SSI. The main strategy for SSI was to cater operations to middle- and upper-income families. This strategy was pursued by clean, brightly lit stores with wide aisles and attractive merchandising. It meant many customer services. It meant broad product assortments and high-quality products. It meant more emphasis on perishables than on grocery and general merchandise. It meant a lot of upscale options, such as deli/bakery units, special programs for aging beef, specialty departments to cater to the needs of more affluent, wider assortments of produce, and a policy of quick markdowns of not-so-fresh products. For example, at 7:00 p.m. each day, bakery goods in the deli departments were marked down 50%. In short, an SSI store was designed to appeal to the more affluent and to build their patronage. SSI meant high-quality products, services, and facilities. Even their advertising followed this high-quality theme. To ensure that this strategy was followed, the product staff group under the SVP of Sales and Merchandising controlled how each store was to operate. This basic strategy was enforced at every single location in every state, regardless of the local conditions. Strenuous efforts were made to ensure uniformity and consistency. For example, field merchandisers were set out to inspect the stores and to ensure compliance. Even store openings and remodelling had to follow this strategy. The idea was that an SSI customer should be able to stop at any SSI store and feel at home.

There is an old adage that a retailer should provide the goods and services at the prices the customers want. What happens if a retailing strategy seems more devoted to providing the goals and services that SSI believes they should want at the prices SSI thinks they should pay? Well, the strategy should work to the extent to which it satisfies customers' needs.

The analysis of store data in the analysis of the determinants of ROWCE demonstrated that, for *some stores,* the strategy was right on target. But for the majority of the stores it seemed inappropriate. After a lot of work with these data and after many discussions with Mr. Duncan, it became clear that SSI served four different types of customer-store combinations. The existing strategy was very good for one of these four: the larger stores in wealthy neighborhoods in larger metropolitan areas. However, it was inappropriate for factory towns of mostly blue-collar families and for rural and not wealthy areas. It was not far off for wealthy small towns.

However, classifying the stores by their consumer-store combinations indicated that the geographical division of the market area contained mixtures of each combination of customer-store. For example, one territory had all four types of stores. Another territory had mostly the wealthy, urban customers, etc. The data suggested that the strategy was not appropriate to all stores and that the store organization was also inconsistent, because sales territories contained, in most cases, combinations of different types of customer-stores.

The possibility that SSI's strategy was inconsistent with some of its environments led to more analysis. This meant visiting 35 stores in different territories and talking with store personnel in order to gain an intuitive grasp of the realities behind the numbers produced at the corporate headquarters. The store personnel were often very critical of the basic SSI strategy as it applied to their stores. Impressions from these visits and interviews tended to confirm the findings of the statistical analysis. In order to document these impressions, a Store Manager Questionnaire was developed and administrated to every store manager. The store managers were relatively satisfied with their jobs and working conditions. They were unhappy about the bonus program, personnel policies, and performance evaluation. They tended to view field merchandisers negatively. Whenever the strategy did not seem to be working, most wanted to have more discretion in adapting to their specific markets. There were territorial and regional differences that mirrored the results of the supplementary analysis of goals and strategies. The store managers outside the wealthy, urban stores were very critical of the television ads and the policy of dropping the early-week newspaper ads in order to pay for the television spots.

A separate study was made on the backgrounds of the store managers. The typical manager was a 36-year-old white male high school graduate with a grocery background. He was not like the customers at whom the strategy was aimed, and he did not have the expertise in perishables needed by the strategy. In short, the strategy was ill-fitted to most of the store managers.

The strategy of treating every store as if it was serving a middle-upper income group in a large metropolitan area did not make sense in the majority of the stores. This led to the conclusion that SSI's strategy was incongruent with the environments. It also led to the inescapable conclusions that SSI's goal for increasing ROI was incongruent with this strategy.

The State of the Organization report consisted of two volumes. The first was the text of the report, and the second was the Organizational Logic, with details about the many activities performed by Sales and Mechandising and Retail Store Operations. The details of the Organizational Logic were verified by directly checking the description with those interviewed. Organizational charts were printed out on the computer showing the official organizational chart (which had never existed in one piece prior to the report). The numerous maladaptations were superimposed onto the official organizational chart to give visual representation to the text of the State of the Organization report.

There were four areas, 29 groups, 135 bundles, 548 modules, and 3737 lines of text for the activities in the Organizational Audit's report on the Organizational Logic. These data are summarized in Table 12.5. Please note that data were obtained for Area One-Corporate Direction and for Area Four (then called Finance and Data Processing) as a by-product of the Organizational Audit of Sales and Merchandising and Retail Store Operations. Note that while Area Three had, by far, the most employees, Area Two had the greater variety of task processes.

The report was presented to the steering committee of the President, the two SVPs, and the VP for Finance and Accounting. After serious discussion of the report, it was agreed to extend the Organizational Audit to include Real Estate, Employee Relations, Engineering and Construction, and Finance and Accounting. At this point, the author was joined by Dr. Mary E. Bird to assist in the study. The time taken for the interviews was beginning to slow down the work of thinking through the organizational design issues. The data processing problems of continually updating the Organizational Logic began to divert the author's time from the main issues. And while the

Table 12.5.   Number of entries in the Organizational Logic after the Organizational Audit of sales and merchandising and retail store operations?

Area	Number			
	Group	Bundles	Modules	Lines of activities
1. Corporate direction of SSI	3	21	119	573
2. Sales and mechandising	18	76	270	2022
3. Retail store operation	6	32	139	1002
4. Finance and data processing (preliminary)	2	6	20	141

work was being done, many changes were being made by the officers. We were in danger of violating the desideratum of speed (D_5).

The careful reader will note that two major parts of SSI were still excluded from the study. Distribution/Transportation was left out because of the sensitivity of the problems SSI was having with the union. Data Processing, a world and power unto itself which was physically sealed off from the rest of the corporation, commissioned another consulting firm to review its operations. The result of this review was an unwarranted "clean bill of health" and a bill for approximately twice what my services would have cost. This special case is discussed in Mackenzie (1984a).

Stage three: organizational design

The organizational design stage was concurrent with the supplementary unit Organizational Audits. During the organizational design, the author worked primarily with the President to develop the Organizational Blueprint. As the organization design emerged, it became clear that the President and the consultant were working jointly. It is unclear, in retrospect, who was the architect for the resulting design. Probably the author played more of a catalytic role and the main idea for the new organizational design was mostly that of the President.

The main idea of the organizational design was to minimize extra organizational interdependencies by organizing the structures around the Organizational Logic. A key concept here involved the *timing* of the interdependencies. We decided first to combine the many task processes by functional interdependencies, and then to break them apart according to whether they required fast or slow interdependencies. The result was a new Sales and Merchandising area of the firm and a Store Support Area. Sales and Merchandising now included the Product VPs, a VP for Marketing, four Store Group Directors (one for each category of store), and an Administrative Manager to do projects for the SVP of Sales and Merchandising. After the design was completed, the title of SVP of Sales and Merchandising finally made sense. The Store Support Area included various staff units to support store operations, such as real estate, training, engineering and construction, front end systems, productivity analysis, etc. It was headed by the former SVP of Store Operations. He now became SVP of Store Support.

The four store groups were each headed by a Store Group Director who was responsible for the gross profit of the stores under his direction. The store groups were named after the Store Group Directors. For example, if Jones was named the Store Group Director, his Store Group was named Store Group Jones. The naming of the store group directors still left the explosive issue of the relationships between the product staff and the store personnel. At least now they all reported to the same person, the Senior Vice President of Sales and Merchandising.

It was decided to have the product VPs act more like *wholesalers* in that they purchased the products and gave technical advice but had to *sell* the Store Group Managers on their merchandising and advertising programs. Before, they just would have issued edicts. Now they had to sell their ideas. They were more involved with inventory and less involved in determining the gross margins and advertising selections. Each of the Store Group Directors was essentially given a small retail store chain of relatively homogeneous units and told to run them profitably with the aid of others. In a real sense, the product VPs lost some power and the store personnel gained some.

The new strategy of marketing led to a new Organizational Logic and thus to a new Organizational Architecture. It also implied the need for a new kind of manager—a general manager. Heretofore, the only general manager in the old functional organization was the President. After the Store Group Directors were named, a program of rapid management development was begun to train them to carry out the new duties. Thus the design had the dual purpose of implementing a new market strategy *and* developing a cadre of general managers about whom SSI could expand in the future. General managers would permit a future strategy of acquisition and merger, and allowed greater flexibility in meeting existing and new competition.

The system of committees was redesigned to provide forums in which to meet, exchange ideas, conduct training and development, test one's mettle, and debate issues. These now followed the new chain of command. The charges to the committees were worked out and built into the Organizational Logic. The committees provided "expansion joints" to relieve stresses in adjusting to the new organization and adjusting the new organization to changes.

The new organizational design was completed in late August, and the new organization began to function as of September 29, 1981. The exact date that the new organizational design was completed is difficult to pin down, because there were many little changes being made all during the process and especially during the implementation planning stage. There were the usual problems due to employee turnover and adjusting the details as implementation planning came up with new problems. For example, three new Vice Presidents (one for Produce Operations, one for Marketing and Communications, and one for Grocery Operations) were added from the time the Organizational Audit was almost over until the time of the "cut over" ceremony. Each of these changes forced alterations in the Organizational Logic, because each involved new directing, controlling, coordinating, and planning task processes which had to be stitched into the whole design. Table 12.6 summarizes the number of task processes by area for the new organizational design. There were 19 groups, 244 bundles, and 1101 modules in the five areas of task processes studied. There were approximately 8,000 lines of activities.

A comparison of Areas One to Three at the time of the Organizational Audit and with the data in Table 12.7 at the time of "cut-over" shows the shifting that takes place upon reorganization. There are two main patterns. First, because of decentralization, there is one less group, 15 fewer bundles, and 16 fewer modules in Area One. Second, the decentralization decreased the number of groups in Sales and Mechandising from 26 to 7. However, the number of bundles increased by 22 and the number of modules increased by 129. These data are marked by growing specificity about the task processes and the downward shifting of the task processes.

The new design initially changed less than 1% of all of the jobs. Thus, it met the test of parsimony (D_6). It was considerably simpler than the previous one, and simpler than the alternatives that were developed during the design process. Thus, the desideratum of simplicity was met (D_7), with the possible exception of the field merchandising staff assignment procedures. Great care was made to be very exact about the precise duties of positions in the company. Design premises and other assumptions were written down for the purpose of explication and analysis. The resulting Organizational

Table 12.6. Number of entries in the Organizational Logic of the new organizational design

Area	Number: Group	Bundles	Modules	Lines of activities
1. Corporate direction	2	16	103	
2. Sales and mechandising	7	130	538	
3. Store support	4	43	219	
4. Distribution/transportation	Not included in stage 3			
5. Employee relations	1	9	40	
6. Finance and accounting	5	46	201	
7. Data processing	Not included in stage 3			

Table 12.7. Comparison of task processes between the organizational design and the Organizational Audit

Area	Groups: After Audit	Groups: After Design	Groups: Changes	Bundles: After Audit	Bundles: After Design	Bundles: Changes	Modules: After Audit	Modules: After Design	Modules: Changes
Corporate direction	3	2	−1	21	16	−5	119	103	−16
Sales and merchandising (including retail store operations)	26	7	−19	108	130	+22	409	538	+129

Logic contained approximately 9,000 activities, modules, bundles, groups, and areas within it. Thus the desideratum of specificity was met (D_8). The solution appears robust because it increased the core but preserved the strategic flexibility of SSI to change if conditions warranted it. Thus, the desideratum (D_9) of robustness was apparently met. The new design for Sales and Mechandising was certainly implementable. It worked the day it was cut over (September 29, 1981). The Store Support was cut over at the end of October, as were Employee Relations (little change) and Finance and Accounting.

Some of the details of the new Organizational Design reflected existing power and influence relationships. For example, every effort was made not to fire anyone, to recognize experience, and to leave dormant some long-standing issues. During the latter stage of the organizational design process, there were literally hundreds of adjustments, title changes, and altered reporting relationships. Between the time when the final blueprint became clear, the general meeting to present the new design, and the cut over, many little changes were negotiated within the guidelines of the blueprint.

The new macro-organizational chart is shown in Figure 12.6. Note that the number of officers reporting directly to the CEO dropped from 9 in Figure 12.1 to 6 in Figure 12.6.

The organizational chart for Area Two is presented in Figure 12.7. Note the four new General Managers of the Store Group, and that the previous director of Store Development and Real Estate has become the General Manager of Store Group Seaman. The product staff group directors have been promoted to Vice Presidents. The new VP of Marketing and Communication is shown on the left. To help the SVP of Sales and Merchandising on special projects, an administrative manager has been added. It should be noted that the new VPs were appointed to their new status against my advice, because (a) I thought that first they should prove themselves, and (b) title inflation reduces future flexibility for the organization. The former deli/bakery director was given a Store Group. Two former territory supervisors were given Store Groups. The position of Deli Manager was given to the son of one of the powerful Directors of the holding company and assigned to the Produce Operations Group, as a side payment to the new VP of Produce. Thus, some politics were involved in moving from the Organizational Blueprint to the organizational design.

The organizational chart for Meat Operations is given in Figure 12.8. This was not a very good design. This department remained overstaffed and was later changed by Mr. McCale. This department was often referred to as the Meat Kingdom.

This gave the VP of Meat Operations a more powerful base, which he tried to work to maintain the dominance of the product staff groups over the general manager.

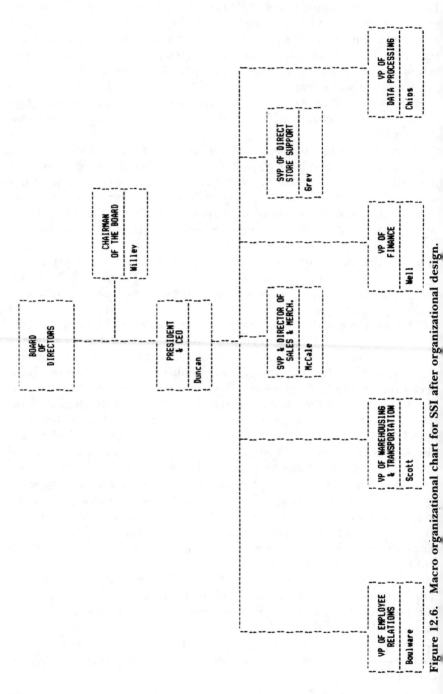

Figure 12.6. Macro organizational chart for SSI after organizational design.

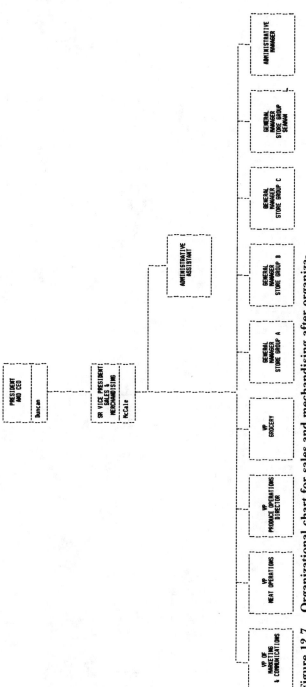

Figure 12.7. Organizational chart for sales and mechandising after organizational design.

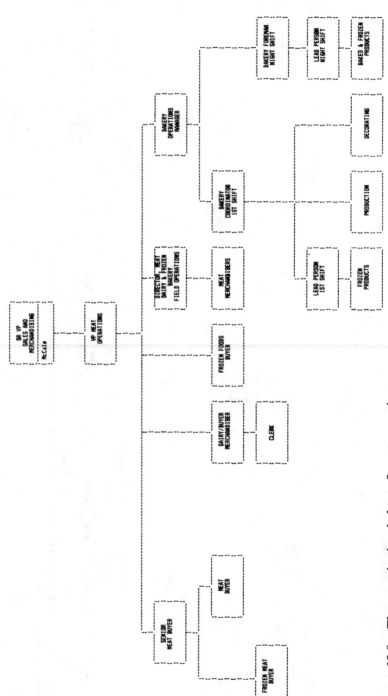

Figure 12.8. The organizational chart of meat operations.

Figure 12.9 shows the organizational chart of one of the Store Groups with the attached field merchandiser for the product staff group.

Figure 12.10 shows the organizational chart for the Store Support under the SVP, Mr. Grey. This was a hodge-podge of support staff departments whose purpose was to support Store Operations in Area Two. Mr. Grey, having lost considerable power and influence after the organizational design, was not very excited about his new position. However, his wide experience in both finance and store operations placed him in a very good position to use his knowledge and experience to bring these staff departments under close supervision. His physical appearance improved after the relief from the stress of running Retail Store Operations in the previous confused organizational design. The transfer of Mr. Seaman to be a General Manager of a Store Group depleted the expertise of both market analysis and real estate. This was approved because SSI wanted to cut back on its losing stores, and regroup before again launching into a store-building program. The Front End Manager was eventually shifted to Finance and Accounting. The Store Human Resources Manager was later shifted to the expanded Employee Relations department. Thus, the change occurring in the organizational design set in motion numerous subsequent changes. Throughout these changes, the work itself remained remarkably stable. Eventually, Store Support was shifted to support Sales and Merchandising directly, and Mr. McCable, the SVP, was promoted to Executive Vice President and Chief Operating Officer.

The Employee Relations department was relatively unchanged and remained the least overstaffed staff group at SSI. Mr. Boulware neither gained nor lost as an immediate result of the organizational design. The OA&A technology's human resources services gave him the base to improve this area of the company.

Finance and Acounting was a powerful bastion at SSI, because the functions performed by it are critical to the success of any retail chain operation. It was also important because the VP, Mr. Well, saw himself as a manager rather than as an accountant. The President, Mr. Duncan, and the SVP of Store Support, Mr. Grey, were both former financial managers and understood the challenges and limitations of these functions. Mr. Well had a longstanding complaint with Mr. Chips of Data Processing. This conflict was eventually resolved by shifting the functions of both Finance and Accounting and Data Processing. Mr. Well was promoted to SVP. The new Management Information Systems department under Mr. Chips now reported directly to Mr. Well. Thus, eventually, the end run by Mr. Chips to have his own independent organizational study did not work for him. Mr. Well triumphed in the end.

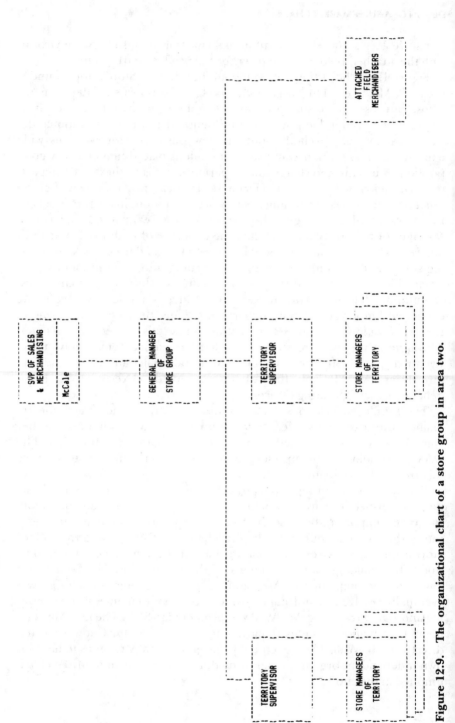

Figure 12.9. The organizational chart of a store group in area two.

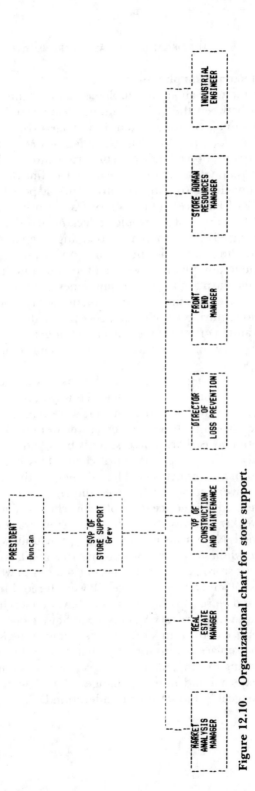

Figure 12.10. Organizational chart for store support.

251

Stage four: implementation planning

I need to explain more about the Implementation Planning stage. About a month existed between the general announcement and the official cut over. During this time, care was taken to arrange offices, make business cards, learn the new jobs, provide cross training, solve secretarial issues, etc. The complete Organizational Logic was converted into detailed position descriptions. The position descriptions were used to define the changes and to determine the immediate training requirements. Especially vital was the work with the VP of Finance and the VP of Data Processing to ensure the management information systems would reflect the new demands for information flow. During all of this, there were ongoing negotiations to purchase another office building, and other problems whose bearing on the new design and implementation planning were all too apparent. Thus the design changed even while the planning for the implementation was begun. One issue that had to be solved was the level of compensation for the new positions. This had to be done during the change process in order to advise the new position holders and in order to arrive at a new budget. About this time, the President became very concerned that the new organization not cost more than the old to operate.

The "cut over" went smoothly and, in the first 4-week sales period, increases in profit were double our total fees. However, numerous problems began to emerge. Many of the store managers were found to be inadequate by the new Store Group Directors. Seven stores were sold to the regional store chain mentioned earlier. These seven stores had low ROWCE and competed directly with the national store chain. This improved SSI and weakened its two main competitors. The sale helped the smaller regional chain continue to over extend itself, forced the bigger store chain into further losses, and helped SSI reduce some of its overheads. The procedure for determing the weekly ads was changed. A new store was opened. Several more were planned. Numerous new business opportunities surfaced, such as using another wholesaler for slow-moving dry goods and becoming a wholesaler for a 10-store group in an adjacent state. A new Marketing and Communications VP and a new Produce VP were hired during the organizational design and were learning their jobs. Several merchandising functions were shifted. A new Grocery VP was brought in to beef up the staff, to provide better service to the four store groups, Some of the Real Estate staff left and had to be replaced. This list goes on and on. The point is that the process of monitoring the implementation is very active and must be done in the context of external and internal changes. The organizational design proved to be manageable and satisfied desideratum D_{11}.

Supplementary service 3.2: strategic planning

Following the operations of SSI under the new organizational design, the author and Mr. Duncan began a 5-month project to define the corporate objectives, strategies to achieve each objective, and charges to each senior officer for planning. Basic principles behind the objectives were developed. One of the most interesting strategies involved the very nature of a supermarket and a definition of options which allowed each type of store in all four store groups to establish its own merchandising strategies. This new orientation ameliorated many of the conflicts between the product vice presidents in the staff departments and the general managers of the store groups.

After carefully developing the text of the corporate objectives and strategies, meetings were held to obtain reaction and responses. Slowly, the final version evolved. During the time for strategic planning, other analyses (cf. Chapter 11) were set into motion. And, of course, new changes were incorporated in both the Organizational Logic and Organizational Architecture.

RESULTS

Two of the main differences between the real-world intervention and a laboratory experiement are the loss of control and the confusion of the cause—effect linkages. Ongoing processes and environment changes do not stop just because one wishes to study the linkage between cause and effect. There are so many reasons for explaining any result or outcome that the issue of cause-effect is moot. Consequently, the reader should not attribute results directly to the work on organizational design.

For many reasons, profits and return on investment improved. Sales were up per store about 20% on the average. Managers made bonuses for the first time in 3 years. SSI had definitely turned around. It stopped losing and began to regain market share. It stopped closing and selling stores and began to remodel and build stores.

Some officers at SSI praised the organizational design. Some claimed that it made little difference, because improved results were attributed to what they, as officers, were now doing, and some, especially Mr. Willey, were skeptical. The pattern of praise and blame seemed to follow along the lines of who benefitted and who lost as a result of the organizational changes.

One of the direct benefits to SSI was the increased professionalism of its officers. Another was the development of backup personnel who were qualified for greater responsibility. The organization is now certainly more aggressive and responsive. SSI has stopped being the "playground fat boy" who gets tormented by competitors and is ineffective in retaliating. Prior to the new organization, rival chains acted as if they could attack SSI with relative impunity. SSI has moved from a defensive posture and has become an opportunistic and agile competitor capable of holding its own. The "playground fat boy" has become trim and more aggressive. This shift is partly a result of the organizational design and of the new opportunities for more of its officers to exert leadership and take risks. It is also a result of the leadership of Mr. Duncan, his successor, Mr. Willey, and the energetic Mr. McCale.

But, in the supermarket business, events change, and it will be the continual growth of SSI and its profits, independent of interventions by outside consultants, that are the true test of any organizational design. It is still too early for such an assessment, but there is some evidence that this desideratum (D_{13}) is being met. The holding company controlling SSI recently acquired a chain with about half as many stores which operates in contiguous markets. This should allow SSI to spread its fixed costs over more units, improve the efficiency of its distribution and transportation system, create more impact for its advertising dollars, provide new opportunities for its personnel, and give it more leverage for procurement. SSI continues to plan and build new stores and to remodel older ones. Thus, SSI seems to be able to compete effectively in its markets and adapt its organization to meet its challenges. As of April, 1984, the number of stores went up 67%, the sales estimated for 1984 fiscal year compared to its 1981 fiscal year is up approximately 84%, and ROI has improved despite large expected outlays for expansion. There appear to be healthy and significant results. I don't think that they could have happened without the application of the OA&A technology. But, on the other hand, they reflect mainly on the ability of the management to seize the initiative. Organizational design can create conditions for allowing results to improve, but it is the courage, determination, and efforts of those in the organization to make them happen.

EVALUATIONS FROM SSI

The Chief Operating Officer, Mr. McCale, and one of the General Managers, Mr. Seaman, each wrote an evaluation of the work that was done for SSI. Both evaluations are printed verbatim except for identifying information. The work was done under the auspices of Organizational Systems, Inc., of Lawrence Kansas. The old OSI has been replaced by a new firm called Mackenzie And Company, Inc. Both evaluations were written for public distribution, which is why they are addressed To Whom It May Concern. However, I feel that SSI's interests would be best served by masking its identity.

Evaluation by the chief operating officer, Mr. McCale

October, 1983

TO WHOM IT MAY CONCERN:

Thoughout 1980 and early 1981, the top management of Supermarket Systems, Inc. began to come to grips with several serious problems:

1. It was experiencing compound negative growth in existing stores.
2. The company was centrally driven, yet the Board of Directors wanted more freedom given to store management.
3. Several men had attempted to run retail operations, but none lasted longer than 2½ years.
4. The incumbent President was going to leave the company in 1983 to pursue another career.
5. It did not have an effective performance evaluation system.
6. It did not have a wage/salary administration program. In particular, the staff salary system was "whatever the traffic will bear." Merit increase at all levels throughout the company were non-existent.
7. Entry into several cities had been disastrous.
8. Management was by committee, upon committee, upon committee. Incredible hunks of time were chewed up in meetings.

Organizational Systems, Inc. (OSI) initially performed a Strategic Assessment of SSI's top management in April, 1981. This assessment helped the company to understand the fact that the company served a number of communities with enormous differences in demographics and psychographics. OSI recommended that retail operations be organized around these demographic clusters. They further recommended that the responsibility for sales and profit be clearly that of Store Operations. Five months after the Strategic Assessment, a major reorganization of Retail Operations and the centralized Sales/Merchandising operation ensued and was in place October 1, 1981. Within 60 days real growth in existing stores emerged which has existed each and every month since and shows no sign of abating. The real growth has occured in spite of fierce competition, including numerous direct competitive openings.

OSI also conducted Organizational Effectiveness studies in Data Processing, Finance, Real Estate/Construction and Employee Relations and then fit them to the new design described above.

OSI was heavily involved in planning for the implementation of the new design. They developed detailed Position Descriptions which made the implementation quite smooth and provided the foundation for Performance Evaluations.

Ken Mackenzie and Mary Bird provided 95% of the direct contact between OSI and SSI. Both are thoroughly professional, extremely cooperative and very competent professionals who always placed their client's interests before their own.

OSI did not propose or promise personnel reductions as a result of the reorganization. In fact, they allayed fears within the organization by informing everyone that in the several years they have been designing organizations, not one individual had lost his job. OSI believes that organizations designed with a high degree of congruency between *goals, strategies, environment, organizational technology* and *results* will become more productive.

We believed that the talent inherent in a centralized operation, left in place although stripped of power, would enhance our ability to create an excellent gross profit rate while maintaining satsifactory real sales growth. That didn't happen. Further, we began to realize that our overhead expense was substantially higher than our competitors and other retail food chains whose results we follow closely.

During the second calendar quarter, 1983, we eliminated 20 jobs including five Vice Presidents. The top layer of merchandising staff was removed. This reduction in expense is over one million dollars annually. The transition was incredibly smooth, due to a great degree of the detailed task driven position descriptions provided by OSI. Further reductions have been achieved in the third calendar quarter.

OSI was vulnerable to two situations at Supermarket Systems, Inc. One, SSI's President chose not to inform the parent company of OSI's involvement. I believe it is absolutely critical that the highest level be sold on the consultant. (The flip side is that we might not have been able to use their services if the senior officers of the parent company had been informed.) Two, we have been conditioned to *expect* reductions in expense as a product of "reorganization." Although the cost of OSI's services were less than the cost of a major remodel of a store, senior management of the parent company were more than disappointed that reductions in overhead expense did not ensue, although shortly after OSI left, the million dollar reduction took place. SSI's management did not come to grips with the problem of high overhead expense through '80 & '81. Witness our Organizational Assessment midrange scores when ranked in importance of such a goal as "Efficiency of Operations" or of a midrange score for "Low Productivity as a Roadblock to Achieving Goals." Upon reflection the Organizational Assessment conducted in May, 1981, mirrors the lack of concern within the organization of the need to be extremely cost conscious and of the need to communicate that effectively.

Record profits were achieved in Fiscal Year 1982, helped considerably by a 53rd week. Profits declined in Fiscal Year 1983 in spite of real sales growth; largely due to high overhead and store operating expenses. But even the period profits were unsatisfactory for SSI, which seeks to operate at a level consistent with the results of food retailers who achieve pretax returns on equity of 30% and more. Fiscal Year 83-84 holds great promise for approaching that goal. OSI's contribution to making the promise possible is enormous . . .

* Real growth is a fact
* Increasing responsibility & freedom is given to store managers

* Retail operations' Senior Management has been in place two years, is solid and in harness for the long pull
* Top management changes are orderly, planned with succession foremost
* A performance evaluation system has been installed
* A merit based wage/salary program will be installed within 6 months
* Stores and markets have been selectively pruned
* Committee management has been abandoned.

Respectfully,
Mr. R.S. McCale
Chief Operating Officer

Evaluation by the V.P. and General Manager, Mr. Seaman

May 25, 1983

TO WHOM IT MAY CONCERN:

Organizational Systems, Incorporated (OSI) has recently performed consulting services for Supermarket Systems, Inc. I have carefully reviewed the services OSI delivered, how they affected SSI (the Company), and how I was personally affected by the plans. Following is my assessment of the services rendered.

SSI is a retail grocer with less than $800,000,000 in annual sales. The Company has many outlets mainly in three states. The roots of the Company reflect two organizations started in the 1930's. One of these entrepreneurs started his business in the largest metropolitan area in two states, the other began doing business in small rural areas. The two companies merged in the early '60s and later sold the interests to a holding company.

SSI continued a growth pattern in the 70's. New stores were developed in both metropolitan areas and rural settings. The Company experienced growth pangs, although it remained profitable and successful.

In April, 1981, the Company elected to retain OSI in order to assess its strategic position in the market place. The Company was additionally interested in an evaluation of its internal design, primarily to determine if its structure could meet the demands of its business position.

OSI revelations elucidated a number of areas which could be re-designed and make the Company a far more effective retailer. The studies clearly indicated SSI was attempting to service distinct and separate demographic areas with identical marketing programs.

OSI recommendations, which the Company implemented, re-designed SSI's organizational structure. Distinct groups of stores were organized on a demographic basis as opposed to the geographic areas previously established.

OSI further recommended each grouping of retail stores be responsible to a General Manager. Merchandising support would be specifically tailored to each particular group's consumer requirements as requested by that group's general manager.

In order to clarify the responsibilities and authorities of the personnel in Sales and Merchandising, OSI was requested to develop job descriptions. OSI carefully evaluated the positions and the requirements for each position. OSI conducted interviews and reviews with the majority of the personnel in Sales and Merchandising and subsequently drafted appropriate position descriptions for the various functions required to effectively operate and support the operations of the Company.

The Company further requested that OSI develop an organizational design which would support the sales and merchandising arm of the Company. Store support functions such as engineering, real estate, employee relations, training, industrial engineering, and loss prevention, were consolidated under a Senior Vice President. The organizational advantage to the Company became apparent at once. Store support functions were immediate in the response to service requests. Sales personnel were immediate in seeking advice and help from the various functions which had always been in place, but were cloudy to the sales arm.

OSI was also charged with assisting in the development of achievable goal statements and strategic planning models designed to assist us in reaching our goals. SSI personnel were able to develop workable strategies as a result of guidelines and direction provided.

Of preferred interest to SSI was a workable, understandable, and communicable personnel evaluation system and its natural follower, a career planning and development program. Our employees had expressed a continuing desire to be evaluated on a fair and equitable basis. Numbers of talented people were unsure of their future as promotions in the past had been more or less a personality contest, or worse yet, a promotion from an area where they had failed. The results of OSI's work in this area has caused excitement, and an unequaled demand for attention to talent on the part of vast numbers of our people.

My personal involvement with OSI was with Ken Mackenzie and Mary Bird. Both, it became immediately apparent, were vitally interested in our success. They shared information and findings, continually solicited input from all SSI management people, including all of our store managers. Their approach and communication was so open that never once did I hear any expression of concern from any SSI personnel. No one lived in fear of their job. Everyone looked forward to their opportunity to contribute. Some very major organizational changes were effected with absolutely no negative response on the part of a single employee.

Mackenzie and Bird were outstanding problem solvers. They listed numbers of alternate solutions to each problem statement, requested input as to positive and negative effects of each alternate, and creatively disposed of the problem area. The work was extremely professional and our personnel were excited to be a part of the problem solving.

The end result of the many and varied assignments performed by OSI is an entirely new management structure at SSI, an entirely new set of corporate objectives and strategies, and clear, concise evaluations and career path planning. Our employees are more excited about our business than they have ever been. And down on the line where the stockholders look, SSI completed its biggest profit year in its history. We continue to produce at a record rate this year also. It was a privilege and a great personal learning experience for me to work with OSI, and most particularly with Ken Mackenzie and Mary Bird.

Mr. Seaman
Vice President-General Manager

POSTSCRIPT

Throughout the discussion concerning my work with SSI, I refrained from making too many evaluative comments on the personnel involved. I wanted the reader to have a description of the problems and the OA&A organizational design process without these distractions. I should like to express my gratitude to SSI for allowing me to work with such a fine group of decent and intelligent men and women.

Mr. Duncan, the former CEO, is one of the few men that I really admire. His Herculean task of redirecting SSI, his work in modernizing his organization, and his support and intelligence in the conduct of the Organizational Audit and Analysis merit the highest praise. I admire his forebearance and his dignity. He was instrumental in helping me formulate the idea of organizational congruence. He had the vision to take the steps necessary to convert SSI from a faltering chain into a winner. His lovely wife stood by him through all of his trials. She even fed a certain hungry consultant on numerous occasions. I respected the manner in which he shouldered the burdens of his office and the way in which he fought to protect employees at SSI. Mr. Duncan is a leader who has a keen and original mind. The Clan Duncan can be very proud of his strength and virtue.

Mr. McCale, the current Chief Operating Officer, is legendary here in Lawrence. His physical energy seems boundless. He has a quick and lively mind. He can make hard decisions with courage and determination. He is the sparkplug at SSI. I am honored to call him a good friend. He even taught me how to ski. It is his nature to ski the dangerous black slopes and ridges, and yet take time to encourage a middle-aged professor to point his skis downhill for the first time. Mr. McCale is the type who is a downhill rather than a cross country skier. When I was working with SSI, he never once deviated from doing what was best for SSI. I cannot recall an instance when he replaced the question of "What is right?" with "Who is right?" I do not want to give the impression that he is impulsive. He's not, although he did remove his office door in order to communicate his open-door policy. He is just a

fast thinker who is able to exert great self control in being patient. If someone could attract 10 McCales into a company, it would quickly become one of
the Fortune 500. His attractive wife is very forgiving, tolerant, and in love
with her dashing husband. His staff called him the "white tornado" because
of his white hair and energy. Some referred to him as the "cookie monster"
because of the way he used to chain chew cookies. It's very hard to keep slim
at the corporate headquarters of a supermarket chain, because of all of the
wonderful samples from its vendors.

I never really got to know Mr. Willey. I would have liked to have known
him better. He is a courteous, private, and thoughtful man. He is a war hero
and an accomplished photographer. Both he and Mr. Duncan symbolize
that rare group of men one thinks of when the word "gentlemen" is taken seriously. Mr. Seaman is a big lovable rogue. He has a quick wit, a lot of energy,
and is very smart. I wish him all the best. Mr. Well is a perceptive manager
who happens to also be a treasurer. He stays on top of the details of SSI's operations and was unfailing in his enthusiasm and good advice throughout
the whole study. He also saw to it that we were paid on time, which was *really*
appreciated. Mr. Chips is an extraordinary manager of data processing. He
genuinely strives to serve SSI. Unlike most others I have met in this field, he
has a good feel for the business of which he is a vital part. Mr. Grey is a
winner. He is always willing to jump in where he is needed and, once there,
perform well. I both like and respect all of these men.

Mr. Scott is special. He ran the distribution/transportation organization as
a benevolent despot. He has one of the most demanding, thankless, and exhaustive jobs at SSI. It was because of Mr. Scott that I began to understand
the task processes resources characteristic of "continuity of DCC task processes." He has to run an organization which supports SSI's operations for
132 hours nonstop every week of the year. I think he does this with elan,
guile and competence. Mr. Boulware of Employee Relations is a professional who persistently worked to make SSI more effective in the management of
its human resources.

There were so many other fine people at SSI who helped in this study.
Special mention should be made of Emily Watkins. As Administrative Assistant to both Mr. Duncan and Mr. McCale, she worked closely with me in setting up appointments and handling many administrative details. What a
diplomat! She is a credit to the secretarial profession.

The atmosphere at SSI made it a consultant's dream come true. SSI has
fine people and a great future. I cannot thank them enough for their many
kindnesses and unstinting support.

CHAPTER 13

Summary and conclusions

PRODUCING USEFUL KNOWLEDGE FOR ORGANIZATIONS

This is a book about an 8-year adventure by a laboratory scientist to convert a theory of group structures into relevant knowledge. In 1976, after approximately 13 years of research, I had reached a state of knowledge about group structures that was usable, useful, used, and relevant for the study of little laboratory organizations. I had assumed that it was also usable, useful, and relevant for the study of real world organizations. I was wrong. The carefully crafted laboratory knowledge about group structures was potentially useful but not yet in a fit condition for use in real world organizations. In fact, in 1976, I could not see why the 1976 knowledge about group structures was not relevant to the organizational design of real organizations. Despite this blindness, I had the good sense to realize that it was up to me to find out if the potentially useful knowledge from the laboratory was relevant to organizational design.

I have a lot of faith in the basic theory and in my belief that a good theory should be usable and relevant. Add to this the facts that this professor was not wealthy, had a modest income, and immodest expenses in supporting four daughters in the colleges of their choices, is a Scot, and you will conclude that I had a vested interest in converting my scientific theory into a usable, useful, used, and relevant organizational design technology.

There is almost no section of this book that could have been written with the scientific knowledge I possessed in 1976. The main goal of this research has always been the pursuit of improvements in a theory of group and organizational structures. This work is a step towards developing a process-based theory of the firm. I believe that diminishing marginal returns have begun to set in on the knowledge gained from organizational design, and that more effort should be directed toward codifying and extending the theory and less toward charging in the direction of cannons described in the Preface.

In October of 1982, Ralph Kilmann and his associates at the University of Pittsburgh organized and held a conference entitled Producing Useful Knowledge for Organizations. This was a fascinating conference. The book consisting of the main papers presented at that conference (Kilmann et al.,

1983) is a milestone in the recognition that academic researchers have a long way to go in converting their theories into knowledge that is useful to organizations. I wrote a paper entitled "Some Real World Adventures of a Bench Scientist" (Mackenzie, 1983) which summarized what I have learned as a result of the efforts to develop a technology for organizational design.

One lesson is that all knowledge involves both recognized and unrecognized assumptions. Assumptions represent unsolved problems, and unrecognized assumptions involve unrecognized problems. The shift from the laboratory to real organizations has forced me to recognize and deal with many heretofore unrecognized assumptions. To me, knowledge is useful to organizations only when it is used to solve real problems. The usefulness of knowledge is directly proportional to the net benefit of using it. The desiderata of Chapter 3 are guidelines to improving the usefulness of knowledge of a theory of group structures to the design of organizations. Most of the knowledge in the 1976 volumes (Mackenzie, 1976a,b) is *strange* in that it was not recognized as solving a real problem. The research strategy described in Chapter 2 is one means of removing strangeness. The application of this strategy to organizational design has had the real benefit of forcing me to confront many unrecognized assumptions and to improve the theory.

ORGANIZATIONAL DESIGN AND THE DEVELOPMENT OF A TECHNOLOGY

Development of organizationally useful knowledge is a research process to make knowledge less strange to those in the organization. There are four ways in which a researcher appears strange to such managers. First, scientists and managers typically do not speak the same dialect of English. This leads to all sorts of communication problems. These are best resolved by first changing ourselves so that we desire to help the managers. Managers tend to lack sympathy for researchers who intend to use their organizations as a means to increase the internal validity of theories. Second, academic knowledge about organizations is strange. For example, there is very little published research about organizations as a whole, and lots of published research on selected aspects or properties of individuals or processes within organizations. At best, most of the published research is relevant to a piece of an organizational problem. It also tends to be so general as to have little direct significance to a busy CEO. Our collective obsession with internal validity has hindered the external validity of our theories. Third, our techniques for producing knowledge are strange to managers. Desk top research on others' research, research on research methods, research on speculative theories, and research to invent syllogisms meant to inspire others to do the work appear very strange to a manager. After all, a manager is successful when he produces good *results*. In essence, we expect the manager to do this research in removing strangeness for us when we are not sure how we could do it ourselves. Our methods tend to be too rigid to fit a manager's circumstances, and they tend to be too slow with their focus on explaining the past. Managers are expected to be more fluid, opportunistic, and contingent in how they apply our theories than the theorists. It is unrealistic to expect a busy manager to do this work for us. Fourth, we have different ideas of what we mean by an application of knowledge. To a typical bench scientist, applications refer to the capability of application in principle or to the likelihood that a theory would not be disconfirmed. The manager is more interested in doing something that benefits himself and his organization than in confirming another's hypothesis. He must be concerned with implementation and side effects that may not have even been considered by the theorist. We can say, "Whoops! That's very interesting!" Our surprises may mean the end of his career in the organization.

The strategy for developing a theory and a technology for organizational design presented in Chapter 2 has five elements:

1. Development of the conceptual framework
2. Development of methods for applications to real organizations
3. Applications of these methods to designing organizations
4. Analyses of the results and the processes of each application
5. Identification of needs for improvements of the conceptual framework and methods.

The interdependencies among these five parts was shown in Figure 2.1.

The application of this strategy from 1976 to the present has had many tangible results in the conceptual framework, the methods, and the identification of needs for improvements. Let us consider each in turn.

Impact on the conceptual framework

The way to see the magnitude and scope of the impact on the theoretical framework is to compare Volume One of *A Theory of Group Structures* (Mackenzie, 1976a) with what is presented in Chapters 4 through 8, and the issues of structure and structural change. The emphasis here is on task processes and task process resources characteristics. The understanding of task processes for the laboratory world has been totally inadequate for analyzing the task processes of an organization. This has led to the invention of Organizational Logics and the recognition of task process resources characteristics (which were not even recognized in 1976). The discussion of task processes interdependencies, task processes resources characteristics interdependencies, and environmental interdepedencies in Chapter 8 are topics that were only faintly recognized in 1976. In fact, in 1976 there was really no mention of organizational goals, strategies and environments.

Knowledge about group and organizational structures and their dependency on task processes in 1976 have fared well in application. The views of organizational structures in Table 5.1 have remained intact from 1976 to the present. However, the carefully developed theories of structural change in the earlier work have remained useful as a background but not usable in application. I believe that this would be a fruitful area of research. Some work has been done by Mary E. Bird (1981). The basic theory of structural change appears robust.

Knowledge about the dynamics of organizational change has, of course, broadened to consider the environments, virtual positions, design premises, stable and regular task processes, and data base organizations and organizational congruency. Authority-task gaps and authority-task problems were recognized by 1975 but were not part of the 1976 books. Chapter 6 could not have been written in 1976. The recognition of virtual positions came about as a result of both additional laboratory studies (Mackenzie and Bello, 1981), reading the work by Jeffrey Pfeffer (1978, 1982), and from puzzle solving in actual organizational design work. The recognition of design premises grew out of the application and the need to have a link between strategic options and the Organizational Technology. Some of these ideas flowed out of reading Chandler (1962, 1977), some literature on strategic planning, and the questions raised by CEOs who wanted a simple way of explaining the organizational design. The idea of organizational congruency grew directly out of conversations with Mr. Duncan, CEO of Supermarket Systems, Inc. Later I read about earlier work by others such as J. Galbraith (1977) on this topic. It turns out that the collective literature became salient when my mind was prepared to listen. The ABCE Model was a result of trying to construct a general doodle to describe the emerging framework for the means-ends linkages involved in organizational design. Writing for publications has always proven very helpful in formulating ideas.

Chapter 7 is concerned with organizational boundaries, an issue that never crossed my mind while working with little laboratory experiments. This issue was recognized in 1980 (Mackenzie, 1981a), and this chapter is the first effort at publishing the new framework for analyzing organizational boundaries. This is an area crying out for more systematic research.

Some of the concepts in Chapter 8 concerning organizational interdependence have already been mentioned. The new class of organizational forms based upon the stability and regularity of task processes rather than properties of the macro organizational charts was recognized in working with start up, high-tech firms. The idea of a data base organization simply never occurred to me in 1976, and was only recognized as a phenomenon in 1983. It is, however, a logical outgrowth for the research of organizational interdependencies.

The development of the idea of an organizational play, and the invention of the techniques of Organizational Playbooks and Organizational Game Plans, were a direct result of running a rapidly changing management consulting organization. These were developed to design my own little organization. I think that these are promising technologies that deserve more development.

The range of human resources analyses described in Chapter 11 grew directly out of applications. The clients demanded them and we had to respond by developing these methods. Laboratory research with Andy Luzi (Luzi and Mackenzie, 1982) led to investigations on performance incentive systems that has proven catalytic in the concern for, and my interest in, such systems for client organizations (cf. Chapter 11). The analyses of qualifications grew out of trying to develop a technology for task processes resources characteristics, and to answer a real need in a client organization for a better career-planning system and for designing its management development programs. There is a separate academic subfield for each of the human resources analyses used in this book. The recognition that all flow directly out of the organizational design helps to provide a consistent logical framework for these techniques. There was no concern for such problems in the earlier laboratory studies.

Thus, the application of the strategy for development has had major impact on the theory of group structures and its extensions to organizational design technology.

Impact on the organizational design technology

The best way to see the growth and maturation of the OA&A technology is to compare the listing of stage and supplementary analyses in Table 9.1 with the first publication mentioning this technology (Mackenzie, 1978d). In the 1978 article, the emphasis was on exploiting the very strong and positive correlation between a process-based measure for the degree of hierarchy and various performance measures. This measure, developed for laboratory groups, was the foundation of the earliest field technologies and the object of a large amount of investment in computer programming. The measure has very nice properties. First, it is always greater than or equal to the measure of efficiency. Second, it correlates about 0.94 with efficiency. Third, it allows tracking the combinatorial relationships created by process and structural maladaptions. Fourth, it fosters simulation of structural changes in order to test the robustness of design and to examine effects of different alternatives. Fifth, it allows reports to be generated for the effects of changes on process maladaptions. Overall, it is a very useful measure for laboratory groups, having great promise in application. But it has practical drawbacks. It was programmed for a given set of fixed task processes. But, as we have learned, the task processes change as the design process evolves through its stages. In 1978, I had only the suggestion of task process laws and their levels. Developments in the understanding of task processes made the old programs obsolete. I decided not to invest heavily in reprogramming to calculate this measure until more theoretical progress had been made on the structures of task processes. While I believe that this should be done, I have had neither the resources nor the time to do so. Besides, with experience, I have learned that I can beat the computer in diagnosing structural problems.

The 1978 paper describes the OA&A technology as consisting primarily of an Organizational Audit and Organization Analysis. Organizational Analysis was essentially organizational design. There was a beginning of an organizational maintenance process. The concern for implementation was very strong in this early publication.

Table 13.1 summarizes the growth in the number of services from 1976 to 1983. Note that there was little growth from 1976 to 1979. The applications of organizational design work did not really get started until 1978. The earlier period was one of converting a laboratory theory into the beginning of a field technology. The number of services in 1982 includes 10 that have been either consolidated or dropped from the OA&A technology. The number for 1983 is the number listed in Table 9.1. Figure 13.1 illustrates the services in Table 9.1 and their interdependencies.

Clearly, the Organizational Audit and Analysis technology has evolved since 1976. The strategy for development of a theory and a technology for organizational design works quite well. The theory, the methods, and the applications have developed together. Each seems to help improve the other two. The strategy for development has served its purposes.

Another aspect for the examination of the OA&A technology is to compare it against its own desiderata. It has demonstrated fidelity with achieving these 13 desiderata. While the methods of this technology have improved markedly since 1976, there is much more progress needed. The use of the OA&A for data base organizations is going to require productivity improvements in developing Organizational Logics and strategic planning. In the case of Supermarket Systems, Inc., most of the desiderata of Chapter 2 were met. In the case of banks, there has been a tenfold improvement in speed of developing an Organizational Logic and performing the Organizational Audit. I expect that, with better data bases on task processes, that I should be able to jump productivity at least another 100%.

Table 13.1. Growth of services in the OA&A Technology

	1976	1977	1978	1979	1980	1981	1982	1983
Number of services	4	6	6	7	16	26	42	32

The Organizational Audit and Analysis technology represents a major advance over other known methods for organizational design. Mackenzie (1981a) compared it to five other approaches. These were markets and hierarchies, Tavistock (Herbst, 1974), ICA Audit (Goldhaber and Rogers 1979), MAPS (Kilmann, 1977), and Organizational Development (French and Bell, 1978). The paper contained three tables comparing and contrasting these five and the OA&A technology (pp. 278-280).

The first comparison was with respect to the desideratum of completeness in terms of the full ABCE Model. Only the OA&A technology is complete. The OA&A technology actively and systematically involves every part of the ABCE Model in Stages 1, 2, 3, 4, 5, 8 and 9.

The second comparison is with respect to how the organizational design problem is viewed. Here one must acknowledge that the definition of organizational design given in Chapter 1 serves as the basis for any comparison. In terms of task processes, the OA&A technology examines task processes, task process interdependencies, task process resources, task process resources characteristics, interpositional interdependencies, and environmental interdependencies. Its focus is on the entire organization, as well as on any subunit covered by the analysis. Its goals are to improve organizational effectiveness and interpersonal relationships, and to allow the organization to be better able to maintain its own organizational design.

The third comparison concerns the methods for data acquistion and analysis. The OA&A technology involves six types of interviews and many negotiations to improve accuracy and validity with the members of the organization. It relies on intuititive judgment followed up by theory-based computer analyses of information. The OA&A technology is essentially statistics-free, except for special subanalyses. Its focus is always upon how the organization actually works. It does not assume behavior is either random or linear. The emphasis is on the logical algebra of task processes and structures.

A fourth comparison is with respect to the 13 desiderata presented in Chapter 3. Table 9.2 summarizes the desiderata addressed at each of the main stages of the OA&A technology. Consideration of design desiderata were not included in the 1981 survey paper.

The major emphasis in the OA&A technology lives in the strategy for developing the science and technology for organizational design presented in Figure 2.1. The OA&A technology is intentionally linked to developing an improved theory of group and organizational structures. As noted in Table 13.1, the OA&A technology has been under continual development since its inception. The goal has always been the improvement of the theory, the technology, and the effectiveness in application.

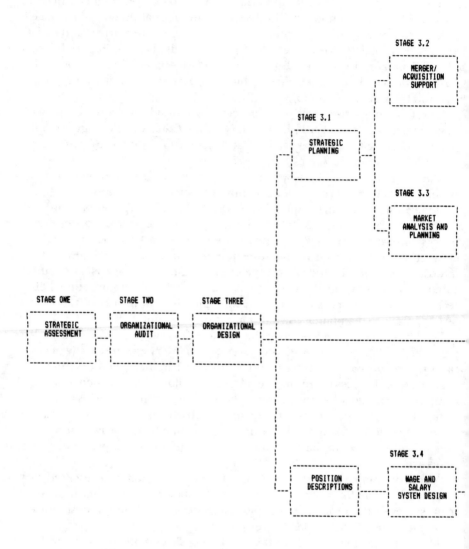

Figure 13.1. The Organizational Audit and Analysis Technology for organizational design.

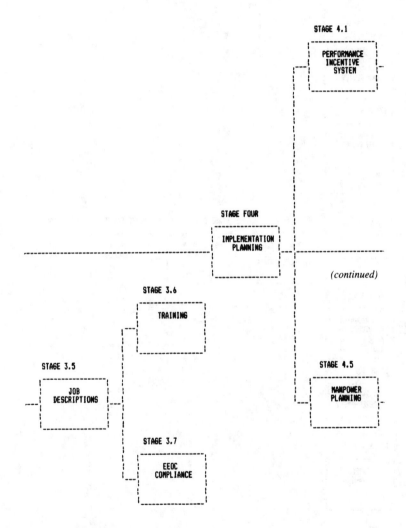

STAGE 4.1
PERFORMANCE
INCENTIVE
SYSTEM

STAGE FOUR
IMPLEMENTATION
PLANNING

(continued)

STAGE 3.6
TRAINING

STAGE 3.5
JOB
DESCRIPTIONS

STAGE 4.5
MANPOWER
PLANNING

STAGE 3.7
EEOC
COMPLIANCE

Figure 13.1.   continued.

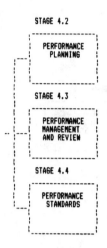

STAGE 4.2

```
+--------------------+
| PERFORMANCE        |
| PLANNING           |
+--------------------+
```

STAGE 4.3

```
+--------------------+
| PERFORMANCE        |
| MANAGEMENT         |
| AND REVIEW         |
+--------------------+
```

STAGE 4.4

```
+--------------------+
| PERFORMANCE        |
| STANDARDS          |
+--------------------+
```

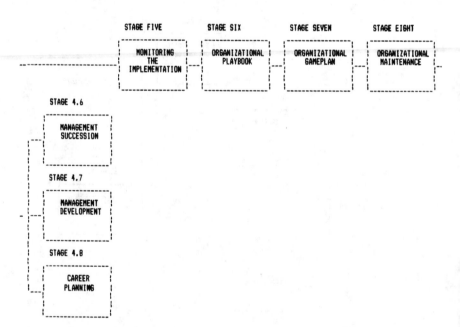

STAGE FIVE	STAGE SIX	STAGE SEVEN	STAGE EIGHT
MONITORING THE IMPLEMENTATION	ORGANIZATIONAL PLAYBOOK	ORGANIZATIONAL GAMEPLAN	ORGANIZATIONAL MAINTENANCE

STAGE 4.6

```
+--------------------+
| MANAGEMENT         |
| SUCCESSION         |
+--------------------+
```

STAGE 4.7

```
+--------------------+
| MANAGEMENT         |
| DEVELOPMENT        |
+--------------------+
```

STAGE 4.8

```
+--------------------+
| CAREER             |
| PLANNING           |
+--------------------+
```

Figure 13.1.   continued.

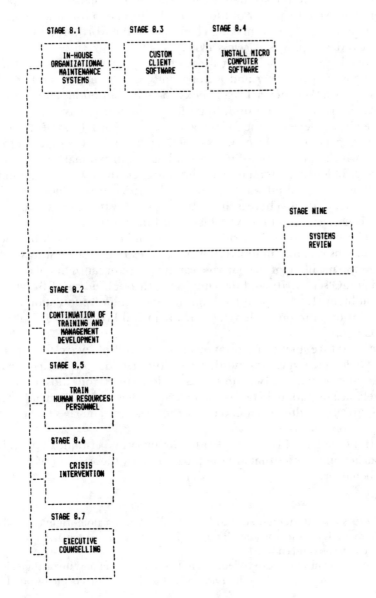

STAGE 8.1

IN-HOUSE
ORGANIZATIONAL
MAINTENANCE
SYSTEMS

STAGE 8.3

CUSTOM
CLIENT
SOFTWARE

STAGE 8.4

INSTALL MICRO
COMPUTER
SOFTWARE

STAGE NINE

SYSTEMS
REVIEW

STAGE 8.2

CONTINUATION OF
TRAINING AND
MANAGEMENT
DEVELOPMENT

STAGE 8.5

TRAIN
HUMAN RESOURCES
PERSONNEL

STAGE 8.6

CRISIS
INTERVENTION

STAGE 8.7

EXECUTIVE
COUNSELLING

Figure 13.1. continued.

271

THE THEORY UNDERLYING THE ORGANIZATIONAL DESIGN TECHNOLOGY

It is well to remember that the fate of all theory is to either be ignored or improved. It is unreasonable to expect that the theory described in this book will remain unchanged. The fact that it has changed so much since 1976 suggests that it will continue to change in the future. This realization is especially poignant given the power of the earlier 1976 version for little laboratory organizations. Thus, even making claims about the worth of a theory that one is busy developing is a useless activity.

About all I can say that has not already been said in the book is that the existing theory is promising and is apparently usable, useful, and relevent when I apply it. Whenever I read books about organizations and articles in scholarly journals, I keep wondering why the authors persist in using ideas that are obsolete even by the 1976 book level of theory. I have come to believe that the theoretical framework contained in this book is superior to any other of which I am aware for understanding organizational structures and processes. This belief is tempered by the awareness that, when it is examined in 1992, it will be found wanting, just as the 1976 version looks primitive when viewed in 1984. There is the distinct possibility that some theory that I believe is not very good today will later become central to future development. There are a lot of very smart theorists and practitioners whose ideas and intuitions remain untapped. It would, for example, be exciting to think through the meaning of the garbage can model of organizational choice by March and Olsen (1976) and the "muddling through" ideas of Braybrooke and Lindblom (1963). I wonder about the meaning of population ecology models for organizational design (cf. Hannan and Freeman, 1977; Pfeffer, 1982, Ch. 5).

The literature about organizations is chock full of interesting speculations, typologies, and viewpoints that constitute a gold mine and a mine field of ideas and methods. My main points of departure from most of it is the over-reliance on rational and psychological models which are mainly teleological. I prefer deductive, nomological theories based on laws that describe *how* a phenomena occurs.

Pfeffer (1982, p. 79) contains a pithy summary and critique of microlevel rational action theories that are the focus of many theories about organizational behavior.

There is no consideration of how (or why) collective action originates and whether it is the sum (or something else, including independent) of individual cognitions and choices.

But, organizations are collective entities, embodying and involving collective action. One might well wonder whether theories that begin by build-

SUMMARY AND CONCLUSIONS   273

ing up from the level of individual rational cognitions can ever really hope to explain the aggregation of behavior that occurs in larger social systems. It is at least a question worth posing.

These six issues—(1) the presumption of purpose or intent occurring in advance of the action—that behavior is foresightful rather than retrospectively rational; (2) the reliance on information processing (as contrasted, for instance, with sentiment-based) explanations of attitudes and behavior; (3) the neglect of the effects of context and the possibility that the perspective is structurally incapable of incorporating context very well; (4) the tautological nature of the explanations; (5) the reliance on hypothetical constructs that reside largely in people's heads, with consequent problems for observation and measurement; and (6) the use of individual-level constructs to try to explain collective or macrolevel behavior—pose a set of fundamental challenges for the theories of behavior reviewed here and the many similar types of theories that we have not even covered. The perspective being critiqued has come to dominate not only the field of organizational behavior but many other social sciences as well. This dominance does not seem to be warranted either by the data or by the fundamental problems confronting such an approach.

At the level of theory for deriving developments of an organizational design technology, I agree with him.

I also believe that these types of models have led to the inability to see the forest for the twigs on the trees. The absence of serious work on Organizational Logics and multiple organizational structures is one direct result, because such variables are not considered "theoretically relevent." That's a silly position when one tries to develop a theory and a technology for organizational design. This also leads to a trivialization of the perception and analysis of change as a mere setting for intrapersonal conflict. There are massive environmental changes taking place whose structural effects must be incorporated in any new theoretical improvements.

Whichever theory is "best," I think that the attempts to try to make it useful by applying it to the development of a technology for organizational design is an effective means of bumping into the theory's hidden assumptions. John Miner, an astute observer of theoretical science in the organizational sciences, recently wrote a book (Miner, 1982) filled with trenchant assessments of existing theory, and a delightfully irreverent article in *The Academy of Management Review* (Miner, 1984). He asked various experts to nominate theories that were considered important according to three criteria: (a) usefulness in understanding, explaining, or predicting the functions of organizations, (b) having clear implications for practice and applications, and (c) having generated significant research. His conclusions were:

1. There is no evidence of any relationship between frequency of nomination and estimated scientific validity.

2. There is no evidence of any relationship between frequency of nomination and estimated usefulness in application.
3. Miner was circumspect but I think he would conclude that there seemed to be a negative relationship between internal validity and usefulness for studying organizations.

My view is that useful ideas for organizational design are not going to emerge from psychological or sociological research traditions, but rather from adventures such as the ones described here. We need to begin *studying whole organizations.* Surprisingly, little of the literature about organizations involves the actual study of an organization. Organizational design is one line of attack in the development of theory.

FUTURE RESEARCH

The theme of this book has been that of change and the need to adapt. Chapter 2 describes a strategy for the development of a science and a technology for organizational design. There would be no need for such a strategy if changes were not deemed necessary. The desiderata for organizational design in Chapter 3 emphasize the need for such a technology to incorporate change. The theory presented in Chapters 4–8 were centered on change processes and structural change. The OA&A technology described in Chapters 9–11 stressed the capacity to track and handle changes to an organization. The description of an organization is dynamic rather than static. Thus, it is fitting that this book end with a discussion of future research. The basic strategy as it continues to be applied is surely going to spark further changes in the theory and in the OA&A technology.

There are many lines of future research that I have come to believe important for improving the theory and the technology for organizational design. Let me list a few of the more important ones of which I am aware.

1. The statements of theory and technology here do not do justice to values, commitment, and whatever we mean by "corporate culture" (cf. Davis, 1971; Deal and Kennedy, 1982). Those literatures tap what may be essential ideas but their theory and technology remain mostly fuzzy.

2. Environmental descriptions, boundaries, environmental design premises, and environmental interpedenedencies are still too vague and general in the current state of the art in the OA&A technology. Much research is needed to integrate these ideas into a more comprehensive and consistent theory.

3. There needs to be a better conceptualization and operationalization of organizational congruency. Are there other conditions such as viewing an organizational culture as means for ensuring organizational congruency?

The ordering of the 11 organizational congruency conditions in Chapter 6 needs to be more carefully studied.

4. The description of task processes in Chapter 4 and organizational interdependence in Chapter 8 are the tip of a mountain of fascinating research questions. For example, I have extended the concept of an Organizational Play into an exhaustive taxonomy based on the structure of the task processes and the positions involved. These can be converted into 24 primitive play sheets. These in turn are reducible to 14 patterns of compacted play sheets. These elemental patterns are content-free but constitute building blocks, which, when augmented by algebraic rules, can be used to construct Organizational Logics out of elementary modules. Future research will address how to construct DCC and planning process laws from combinations of the integrable task processes. These developments will speed up the construction of an Organizational Logic and should improve the ability of the OA&A technology to integrate its stages.

The analyses of task processes and structures has led to an algebra for determining the relative importance of any two positions within an organization. To date, this has only been employed to verify and analyze wage and salary comparisons. This research then led to the development of what I call *organizational positioning charts*. An organizational positioning chart combines the ideas of an Organizational Logic, organizational chart, and the relative importance of any two positions. This development allows one to rethink career paths as well as compensation. More research will be necessary, however, to convert those ideas into practical organizational design tools.

5. Improvements need to be made in the development of the concept of data base organizations. We need to understand how organizations alter their structures and task processes to fit their informational, cognitive, and computational capacities.

6. The possibility of parallel Organizational Logics needs to be explored as a method of achieving integration in the face of uncertainty of change. For example, do ideas concerning corporate cultures employ a different type of Organizational Logic? Or do the existing planning and DCC task law level processes contain the seeds of a technology for organizational culture?

7. The biggest question in my mind is how to link the language and tools of economic theory to the selection, adaptation, and distribution of task processes in an organization. Answering this will do a lot for improving the theory of the firm. My hunch is that the development of an algebra (cf. point 4 above) is the key to developing a process theory of the firm.

8. Another looming question is how to develop a methodology for tracing cause and effects in a dynamic open process. I think it will require process theories of causal linkages to analyze processes. Our current statistical techniques are hopelessly outclassed in their capacity to articulate linkages and any causes and effects. The recent book edited by Cameron and Whetten

(1983) points out the many problems one is likely to encounter in tying design to results.

9. There is a practical need to understand more about the ability of an organization to implement organzational design changes. At this time, I do not have a good feel for how to even formulate the issues involved. For example, what determines the limits by which an organization can adapt to change? My hunch is that the idea of a data base organization will prove useful here.

10. There is a need to know more about the dynamics by which authority-task gaps generate authority-task problems. For example, in periods of excessive organizational slack, there seems to be more tolerance for ATGs than in periods of cutbacks.

11. Despite the paper by Mackenzie, Martel, and Price (1982), the linkages to human resources modelling are yet unclear. For example, different types of growth create needs for different organizational interdependencies, and hence on the formulation of human resource management problems. Filley and Aldag (1980) speak of metamorphic as well as mitotic growth models. Do different types of growth imply fundamentally different change processes?

12. One major bottleneck is the resistance of information systems to change. A recent paper of mine (Mackenzie, 1984a) argued that the technologically augmenting information systems of most organizations create numerous process and structural maladaptations. The problem seems to be the incorporation of task processes into the design of management information systems. George Huber has an interesting paper on the issues of organizational design in the post-industrial age (Huber, 1984).

13. A special case of the above involves accounting information systems. Can the chart of accounts be tied to task processes? Is it possible to link the planning and DCC task processes to the allocation of overheads? Do accounting-task gaps exist which are analogous to authority-task gaps? I am sure this is the case, but there is yet no theory for such problems in the OA&A technology.

14. Up to now, I have avoided all contact between the OA&A technology and governmental organizations. There may be fascinating theoretical problems in developing a theory of control systems built upon a system of checks and balances which create parallel Organizational Logics. Is it possible to improve the theory and the technology of organizational design by incorporating such nonhierarchical constraints? My hunch is that these involve parallel Organizational Logics and a hierarchy of osculating task processes activated by events outside the organization.

15. There seems to be a need to extend the ideas of task processes and organizational interdependencies to cover the special case of what might be described as *ricochetting organizational processes*. In such an organizational process, the logic of the task process bounces in and out of different organ-

izational positions and, as it does, it triggers a round of unanticipated events setting off other, often far-separated, task processes. Ricochetting task processes are currently handled as exceptional cases in the OA&A technology. Extension to governmental organizations may bring this assumption into doubt. If so, is there a theory and a technology needed for managing such processes?

16. The research by Roger Hall (cf. Hall, 1984) on building causal maps of assumptions in the area of policy making is very promising. The analysis of strategic options in the OA&A technology could be improved by employing some of Hall's methods. This line of research by Hall should also be helpful in relating design premises (which are assumptions) to the selection of Organizational Logics.

17. At a whole different level of aggregation, there is the solid, systemic work by Fleishman and his colleagues (cf. Fleishman and Quaintance, 1984) on how to describe tasks. His research suggests the importance and the value of basing psychological and ergonomic analyses of human tasks on a sound and consistent footing. If we are ever capable of understanding and predicting human performance, the pioneering work by Fleishman and his associates will be important. This work is too micro for organizational design. One line of future research is to attempt an integration of a taxonomic description of human tasks to the analyses of task processes (cf. Chapter 4) and organizational interdependence (cf. Chapter 8).

In addition to this short list of theoretical and methodological research questions, there are many improvements needed to build a better organizational design technology. My hunch is that most of the OA&A technology could be developed into an integrated, computer-based technology which would free the designer to examine the less technical side of organizational design problems. I try to use space age technologies for handling the routine, and stone age technologies for working the novel and the important.

The Organizational Audit and Analysis technology is a research based technology for designing organizations to be more productive. It is a result of over 20 years of sustained research into a theory of group structures, and approximately 8 years of application. It has been used in a wide variety of organizations of different sizes and industries. It has been instrumental in sparking many more theoretical developments which, in turn, have improved the OA&A technology. It represents another research path in the development of an emerging science of organizations. It is the harbinger of the future of organizational research.

References

Aldrich, H.E. and Herker, D., "Boundary Spanning Roles and Organizational Structure," *Academy of Management Review*, Vol. 2, 1977, pp. 217-230.

Baligh, H.H. and Burton, R.M., "The Movable Boundaries Between Organizations and Markets," *International Journal of Policy Analysis and Information Systems*, Vol. 6, No. 4, 1982, pp. 435-449.

Baligh, H.H. and Damon, W.W., "Foundations For a Systematic Process of Organization Structure Design," *Journal of Information and Optimization Sciences*, Vol. 1, No. 2, 1980, pp. 133-165.

Bernhardt, I. and Mackenzie, K.D., "Acceptance of Change: A Theory Models," *Management Science in Planning and Control* (J. Blood Jr., ed.), New York: TAPPI STAP No. 5, 1969, pp. 321-350.

Bernhardt, I. and Mackenzie, K.D., "Some Problems in Using Diffusion Models for New Products," *Management Science*, 1972, *19* No. 2, pp. 187-200.

Bird, M.E., *Development of a Theory of Work: Application in a Community Bank*. Unpublished doctoral dissertation, University of Kansas, Lawrence, KS, 1981.

Bowey, A. and Lupton, T., *Job and Pay Comparisons: How to Identify Similar Jobs in Different Companies and Compare Their Rates of Pay*. Epping, Essex, UK: Gower Press Ltd., 1973.

Braybrooke, D. and Lindblom, C.E., *A Strategy of Decision*, New York: The Free Press, 1963.

Burack, E.H. and Negandhi, A.R., *Organizational Design: Theoretical Perspectives and Empirical Findings*. Kent, OH: Kent State University Press, 1977.

Cameron, K.S. and Whetton, D.A., Eds., *Organizational Effectiveness: A Comparison of Multiple Models*. New York: Academic Press, 1983.

Chandler, A.D., *Strategy and Structure: Chapters in the History of the American Industrial Enterprise*. Cambridge, MA: MIT Press, 1962.

Chandler, A.D., *The Visible Hand: The Managerial Revolution in American Business*. Cambridge MA: Harvard University Press, 1977.

Charnes, A. and Cooper, W.W., "Management Science Relations for Evaluation and Management Accountability: A Comment," *Journal of Enterprise Management*, Vol. 2, No. 2, 1980, pp. 143-167.

Charnes, A., Cooper, W.W., and Rhoades, E., "Measuring the Efficiency of Decision Making Units, *European Journal of Operational Research*, Vol. 2, No. 2, 1978, pp. 429-444.

Child, J. *Organization: A Guide To Problems and Practice*, New York, Harper and Row, 1977.

Davis, L.E. and Taylor, J.C., Eds., *Design of Jobs* (2nd Ed.). Santa Monica, CA: Goodyear Publishing Co., Inc., 1979.

Davis, S.M., *Comparative Management: Organizational and Cultural Perspectives*, Englewood, NJ: Prentice-Hall, 1971.

Deal, T.E. and Kennedy, A.A., *Corporate Cultures: The Rites and Rituals of Corporate Life*. Reading, MA: Addison-Wesley, 1982.

Eichel, E. and Bender, H.E., *Performance Appraisal: A Study of Current Techniques*. New York: AMA Research and Information Service, 1984.

Ellis, R.J., *The Process of Response: An Empirically Derived Approach for Managing in Turbulance*. New York: Praeger, 1984.

Emery, F.E. and Trist, E.L., "The Causal Texture of Organizational Environments," *Human Relations*, 1965, Vol. 18, pp. 21-32.

Filley, A.C. and Aldag, R.J., "Organizational Growth and Types: Lessons from Small Institutions," *Research in Organizational Behavior*, Vol. 2. (B.M. Staw and L.L. Cummings, Eds.). Washington, DC: JAI Press, Inc., 1980, pp. 279-320.

Fleishman, E.A. and Quaintance, M.K., *Taxonomies of Human Performance: The Description of Human Tasks*. New York: Academic Press, 1984.

French, W.L. and Bell, C.H., Jr., *Organizational Development: Behavioral Science Interventions for Organizational Improvement*. (2nd Ed.), Englewood Cliffs, NJ: Prentice-Hall, 1978.

Galbraith, J.R. *Organizational Design*. Reading, MA: Addison-Wesley, 1977.

Gerlach, L.P. and Palmer, G.B., "Adaptation Through Evolving Interdependence," in *Handbook of Organizational Design, Vol. 1: Adapting Organizations To Their Environments* (Nystrom, P.C. and W.H. Starbuck, Eds.). Oxford, UK: Oxford University Press, 1981, pp. 323-381.

Goldhaber, G.A. and Rogers, D., *Auditing Organizational Communication Systems: The ICA Communications Audit*. Dubuque, IA: Kendall/Hunt, 1979.

Greiner, L.E. and Metzger, R.O., *Consulting To Management*. Englewood Cliffs, NJ: Prentice-Hall, 1983.

Hall, R.I., "The Natural Logic of Management Policy Making: Its Implications For the Survival of an Organization," *Management Science*, Vol. 30, No. 8, 1984, pp. 905-927.

Hannan, M.T. and Freeman, J., "The Population Ecology of Organizations," *American Journal of Sociology*, 1977, Vol. 82, pp. 929-964.

Harrison, A.J., "Science, Engineering and Technology," *Science*, Vol. 223, No. 4636, 10 February 1984.

Hart, B.H.L., *Strategy*. New York: Praeger, 1954.

Herbst, P.G., *Socio-Technical Design: Strategies in Mutli-disciplinary Research*. London, UK: Tavistock Pubs., 1974.

Hirshhorn, L. and Associates, *Cutting Back: Retrenchment and Redevelopment in Human and Community Services*. San Francisco, CA: Jossey-Bass Inc., Rubs., 1983.

Huber, G.P., "The Nature and Design of Post Industrial Organizations," *Management Science*, Vol. 30, No. 8, 1984, pp. 928-951.

Kerr, S., "On the Folly of Rewarding A, While Hoping for B," *Academy of Management Journal*, 1975, pp. 769-783.

Khandekar, R.P., *Development of a Theory of Interorganizational Structure: Exploration in a Field Setting*. Unpublished doctoral dissertation, University of Kansas, Lawrence, Kansas, 1983.

Khandwalla, P.N., *The Design of Organizations*. New York: Harcourt Brace Jovanovich, 1977.

Kilmann, R.H., Pondy, L.R., and Slevin, D.P., Eds., *The Management of Organization Design: Strategies and Implementation.* (Vol. I). New York: North-Holland, 1976.

Kilmann, R.H., Pondy, L.R. and Slevin, D.P., Eds., *The Management of Organization Design: Research and Methodology* (Vol II). New York: North-Holland, 1976.

Kilmann, R.H., *Social Systems Design: Normative Theory and the MAPS Design Technology.* New York: North-Holland, 1977.

Kilmann, R.H., "The Costs of Organization Structure: Dispelling the Myths of Independent Divisions and Organization-Wide Decision Making," *Accounting, Organization, and Society,* Vol. 8, No. 4, 1983, pp. 341-357.

Kilmann, R.H., Thomas, K.W., Slevin, D.P., Rath, R. and Jerrell, S.L., Eds., *Producing Useful Knowledge for Organizations,* New York: Praeger, 1983.

Kirkpatrick, D.L., *How to Improve Performance Through Appraisal and Coaching.* New York: AMACOM, 1982.

Kubr, M. (Ed.), *Management Consulting: A Guide to the Profession.* Geneva, Switzerland: ILG, 1978.

Lippitt, M.E., *Development of a Theory of Committee Formation.* Ph.D. Dissertion, University of Kansas, 1975.

Lippitt, M.E., and Mackenzie, K.D., "Authority-Task Problems," *Administrative Science Quarterly,* 1976, 21, No. 4, pp. 643-660.

Lippitt, M.E. and Mackenzie, K.D., "A Theory of Committee Formation," *Communication and Control in Social Processes* (K. Krippendorff, Ed.), New York: Gordon and Breach Science Publishers, 1979, pp. 389-405.

Luzi, A. and Mackenzie, K.D., "An Experimental Study of Performance Information Systems," *Management Science,* 1982, *28,* No. 3, pp. 243-259.

Mackenzie, K.D., *A Mathematical Theory of Organizational Structure.* An unpublished Ph.D. dissertation, University of California, Berkeley, CA, 1964.

Mackenzie, K.D., "Decomposition of Communication Networks," *Journal of Mathematical Psychology,"* 1967, *4,* pp. 162-172.

Mackenzie, K.D., "The Structure of a Market," *Management Science in Planning and Control* (J. Blood, Jr., Ed.), New York: TAPPI STAP No. 5, 1969, pp. 167-216.

Mackenzie, K.D., "Organization Theories: State of the Art for the Problem of Bureaucracy," *Manpower Planning Models* (D.J. Clough, C.C. Lewis, and A.L. Oliver, Eds.), London, UK: The English Universities Press, Ltd., 1974, pp. 3-24.

Mackenzie, K.D., *A Theory of Group Structures, Volume I: Basic Theory,* New York: Gordon and Breach Science Publishers, Inc., 1976 (a).

Mackenzie, K.D., *A Theory of Group Structures, Volume II: Empirical Tests,* New York: Gordon and Breach Science Publishers, Inc., 1976 (b).

Mackenzie, K.D., *Organizational Structures.* Arlington Heights, IL: AHM Publishing Company, 1978 (a)

Mackenzie, K.D., "A Process Based Measure for the Degree of Hierarchy in a Group, I: The Measure," *Journal of Enterprise Management,* 1978, *1,* pp. 153-162 (b).

Mackenzie, K.D., "A Process Based Measure for the Degree of Hierarchy in A Group, II: Some Empirical Experiences with Small Group Data," *Journal of Enterprise Management*, 1978, *1*, pp. 163-173. (c)

Mackenzie, K.D., "A Process Based Measure for the Degree of Hierarchy in A Group, III: Applications to Organizational Design," *Journal of Enterprise Management*, 1978, *1*, pp. 175-184. (d)

Mackenzie, K.D., "Where is Mr. Structure?" *Communications and Control in Social Processes* (K. Krippendorff, Ed.), New York: Gordon and Breach Science Publishers, 1979, pp. 73-88.

Mackenzie, K.D., "Concepts and Measurement in Organizational Development," *Dimensions of Productivity Research, Vol. I* (John D. Hogan and A. Craig, Eds), Houston, TX: American Productivity Center, 1981, pp. 233-304. (a)

Mackenzie, K.D. "Organizational Congruency Tests," *Journal of Enterprise Management*, 3, No. 3, 1981 pp. 265-276. (b)

Mackenzie, K.D. "Manpower Waste," *Human Systems Management*, 3, 1982, pp. 136-142.

Mackenzie, K.D. "Some Real World Adventures of a Bench Scientists," in *Producing Useful Knowledge for Organizations*, (R.H. Kilmann, K.W. Thomas, D.P. Slevin, R. Nath, and S.L. Jerrell, Eds.). New York: Praeger Publishers, 1983, pp. 100-118.

Mackenzie, K.D. "Organizational Structures as the Primal Information System: An Interpretation," *Management of Office Information Systems* (S.K. Chang, Ed.), New York: Plenum, 1984, pp. 27-46. (a)

Mackenzie, K.D. "An Essay Concerning Organizational Boundaries," Unpublished manuscript, Lawrence, KS: Mackenzie And Company, Inc. 1984. (b)

Mackenzie, K.D., "A Strategy and Desiderata for Organizational Design," *Human Systems Management* 1984, *4*, No. 3, pp. 201-213. (c)

Mackenzie, K.D., "The Organizational Audit and Analysis Technology for Organizaional Design," *Human Systems Management* 1985, *5*, No. 1 (in press).

Mackenzie, K.D., "Design of a Supermarket Chain," *Human Systems Management*, 1985, *5*, No. 1 (in press).

Mackenzie, K.D. and Bello, J.A. "Leadership as a Task Process Uncertainty Control Process," *Human Systems Management*, 1981, *2*, No. 3, pp. 199-213.

Mackenzie, K.D. and Barron, F.H., "An Analysis of a Decision Making Investigation," *Management Science*, 1970, *17*, No. 4, pp. B224-B241.

Mackenzie, K.D. and Frazier, G.D., "Applying a Model of Organizational Structure to the Analysis of a Wood Products Market," *Management Science*, 1966, *12*, pp. 340-352.

Mackenzie, K.D. and House, R.J., "Paradigm Development in the Social Sciences: A Proposed Research Strategy," *Academy of Management Review*, 1978, *3*, No. 1, 7-23.

Mackenzie, K.D., Martel, A., and Price, W.L., "Human Resource Planning and Organizational Design," in *Work, Organization and Technological Change* (G. Mensch and R.J. Niehaus, Eds.) New York: Plenum, 1982, pp. 213-228.

Magnusen, K.O. *Organizational Design, Development, and Behavior*, Glenview, IL: Scott, Foresman and Co., 1977.

March, J.G., "Footnotes to Organizational Change," Unpublished manuscript., p. 70, cited in *In Search of Excellence* by T.J. Peters and R.H. Waterman, Jr., New York: Harper and Row, 1983, p. 107.

March, J.G. and Olsen, J.P., *Ambiguity and Choice in Organizations*. New York: Columbia University Press, 1976.

McCormick, E.J., *Job Analysis: Methods And Applications*, New York: AMACOM, 1979.

Metcalf, L., "Designing Precarious Partnerships," in *Handbook of Organizational Design, Vol. 1: Adapting Organizations To Other Environments* (P.C. Nystrom and N.H. Starbuck, Eds.). Oxford, UK: Oxford Universities Press, 1981, pp. 503-530.

Miller, E.J. and Rice, A.K., *Systems of Organizations*. London, UK: Tavistock Pubs, 1967.

Miner, J.B., *Theories of Organizational Structure and Process*. Hinsdale, IL: Dryden Press, 1982.

Miner, J.B., "The Validity and Usefulness of Theories in an Emerging Organizational Science," *The Academy of Management Review*, 1984, Vol. 9, No. 2, pp. 296-306.

Mintzberg, H., *The Structures of Organizations*. Englewood Cliffs, NJ: Prentice-Hall, 1979.

Moore, G.L., *The Politics of Management Consulting*. New York: Praeger, 1984.

Monge, P.R., Farace, R.V., Eisenberg, E.M., Miller, K.I., and White, L.L., "The Process of Studying Process in Organizational Communication," *Journal of Communication*, Vol. 34, No. 1, 1984, pp. 22-43.

Nystrom, P.C. and Starbuck, W.H., Eds., *Handbook of Organizational Design, Vol. I: Adapting Organizations To Their Environments*. New York: Oxford University Press, 1981.

Nystrom, P.C. and Starbuck, W.H., Eds., *Handbook of Organizational Design, Vol. II, Remodelling Organizations And Their Environments*. New York: Oxford University Press, 1981.

Ouchi, W. *Theory Z: How American Business Can Meet the Japanese Challenge*. Reading, MA: Addision-Wesley, 1981.

Pennings, J.M., "Strategically Interdependent Organizations," in *Handbook of Organizational Design, Vol. 1: Adapting Organizations To Their Environments* (P.C. Nystrom and W.H. Starbuck, Eds.). Oxford, UK: Oxford Universities Press, 1981, pp. 433-455.

Peters, T.J. and Waterman, R.H., *In Search of Excellence: Lessons From America's Best-run Companies*. New York: Harper and Row, 1983.

Peterson, R.A., "Entrepreneurship and Organization," in *Handbook of Organizational Design, Vol. 1: Adapting Organizations to Their Environments* (P.C. Nystrom and W.H. Starbuck, Eds.), Oxford, UK: Oxford Universities Press, 1981, pp. 65-83.

Pfeffer, J., *Organizational Design*. Arlington Heights, MI: AHM Publishing, 1978.

Pfeffer, J. and Salancik, G.R., *The External Control of Organizations: A Resource Dependence Perspective*. New York: Harper and Row, 1978.

Pfeffer, J., *Power In Organizations*. Marshfield, MA: Pitman, 1981.

Pfeffer, J., *Organizations and Organization Theory*. Marshfield, MA: Pitman, 1982.

Rice, A.K., *The Enterprise and Its Environment*, London, UK: Tavistock Pubs., 1958.

Starbuck, W.H., "Organizations and Their Environments," in *Handbook of Industrial and Organizational Psychology* (M.D. Dunnett, Ed.). Chicago, IL: Rand McNally, 1976, pp. 1069-1123.

Thompson, J.D. *Organizations In Action*, New York: McGraw-Hill, 1967.

Thucydides. *The History of the Peloponnesian War* (trans. by R. Crawley). Chicago, IL: Encyclopaedia Britannica, Inc., 1952.

Weick, K.E., *The Social Psychology of Organizing*. Reading, MA: Addison-Wesley, 1979.

Williamson, O.E., *Markets and Hierarchies: Analysis and Antitrust Implications*, New York: The Free Press, 1975.

Yu, P.L. "Behavior Bases And Habitual Domains of Human Decision/Behavior-An Integration of Psychology, Optionization Theory and Common Wisdom," *International Journal of Systems, Measurement and Decisions*, Vol. 1, No. 1, 1981, pp. 39-62.

NAME INDEX

A

Aldag, R.J., 276
Aldrich, H.E., 105
Allen, A., ix
Arahood, D.A., 213
Archibong, C.B.A., x
Arneson, G., x

B

Baker, W., x
Balderston, F., xii
Baligh, H.H., 105, 106
Barron, F.H., 21
Bell, C.H., 267
Bello, J.A., 264
Bender, H.E., 206
Bernhardt, I., 37
Beynon, W.D., x, xi, 213
Bird, M., x, xii, 241, 255, 258, 264
Boulware, 224, 249
Bowey, A., 183
Braybrooke, D., 272
Brooks, J., x
Burack, E.H., 26
Burch, J.L., viii, ix
Burton, R.M., 105, 106

C

Cameron, K.S., 275
Chandler, A.D., 264
Charnes, A., 215
Child, J., 26
Chips, 224, 249, 260
Christoffersen, R., x
Churchman, C.W., xii
Clough, D., x
Cooper, W.W., x, 215
Cyert, R.M., xii

D

Damon, W.W., 105
Davis, L.E., 182, 278
Davis, S.M., 274, 279
Deal, T.E., 274
Downs, C., x, xi
Duncan, 220, 224, 253, 254, 259, 264

E

Eichel, E., 206
Eisenberg, E.M., 282
Ellis, R.J., 127
Emery, F.E., 44

F

Farace, R.V., 282
Filley, A., x, 276
Fleishman, E.A., 277
Frazier, G.D., 21
Freeman, J., 272
French, W.L., 267
Friedman, L., x

G

Galbraith, J.R., 26, 264
Gallup, A., x
Gerlach, L.P., 113
Goldhaber, G.A., 267
Goodale, R.S., viii, ix
Gordon, L., x
Greenwood, J., ix
Greiner, L.E., 25
Grey, 221, 222, 224, 249, 260

H

Hall, R.I., x, 277
Hannon, M.T., 272
Harrison, A.J., 22
Hart, B.H.L., 9
Herbst, P.G., 267
Herker, D., 105
Hirschorn, L., 19, 115
House, R., x
Howes, M.E., x
Huber, G.P., 276

J

Jerrell, S.L., 280, 281
Joyce, J., ix

K

Kennedy, A.A., 274
Kerr, S., x, 213
Khandekar, R., x, 105, 107, 113
Khandwalla, P.N., 26
Kilmann, R.H., x, 8, 21, 26, 261, 267

Kirkpatrick, D.L., 206
Krippendorf, K., 280, 281
Krogh, H., x
Kubr, M., 25

L
Lashuutka, S., ix
Lewin, A., x, 215
Lindblom, C.E., 272
Lippitt, M.E., 85, 87
Lupton, T., 184
Luzi, A., x, 265

M
Mackenzie, C.B., x
Mackenzie, K.D., ix, xi, xii, 21, 22, 26, 27,
37, 69, 73, 80, 81, 85, 87, 101, 111, 121,
181, 242, 255, 258, 262–265, 267, 276
Mackenzie, N.D., x
Mackenzie, S.G., x
Mackenzie, S.M., x
McCale, 221, 222, 224, 245, 254, 255, 257,
259
McCormick, E.J., 182
McMillan, J.A., viii, ix
Magnusen, 26
March, J.G., xii, 10, 272
Martel, A., 276
Metcalf, L., 282
Metzger, R.O., 25
Miller, E.J., 44, 282
Miller, K.I., 44
Miner, J.B., 273
Mintzberg, H., 3, 26
Mitchell, W., x
Mitroff, I, x
Monge, P.R., 44
Moore, G.L., 17

N
Negandhi, A.R., 26
Nichols, M.L., x
Nicosia, F., x, xii
Nystrom, P.C., 26

O
Olsen, J.P., 272
Ouchi, W., 26

P
Palmer, G.B., 113

Pennings, J.M., 105
Perrin, A.L., x
Peters, T.J., 3, 10, 113
Peterson, R.A., 113
Pfeffer, J., x, 26, 105, 264, 272
Plato, 3
Pondy, L.R., 26
Posey, J., ix
Price, W.L., x, 276

Q
Quaintance, M.K., 277

R
Rath, R., 280
Reed, R., x
Rhoades, E., 215
Rice, A.K., 44
Rogers, D., 267
Rothwell, K., x

S
Salancik, G.R., 105
Scott, 224, 260
Scott, B., ix
Seaman, 224, 249, 254, 257, 259
Simon, H.A., xii
Slevin, D.P., 26
Smissman, C.F., x
Staples, C., ix
Starbuck, W.H., 26, 105

T
Taylor, J., x
Taylor, J.C., 278
Thomas, A.L., 280
Thompson, J.D., 44, 117
Thucydides, 9
Tollefson, J., x
Toole, D., x
Treanor, B., ix
Trist, E.L., 44
Tuggle, D., x

V
Voigt, M.J., xi

W
Waterman, R.H., 4, 10, 113
Weick, K.E., 9
Weigel, C.K., x

SUBJECT INDEX

A

ABCE Model, 10, 12, 29, 31, 36, 85, 95, 99, 100, 103, 125, 126, 134, 138, 140, 144, 147, 154, 165, 224, 264, 267

Activity, 12, 48, 49, 52, 53, 56, 59, 61, 62, 64, 152, 157, 163, 164, 168, 171, 174, 192, 193, 197, 233, 234, 241, 144, 245, 272

Activity List, 152, 153

Actual organization, 6, 98, 100, 126, 133, 147, 153, 229

Actual Organizational charts, 224

Area (of processes), 56, 59, 62, 63, 130, 131, 168

Authority, 17, 88, 159, 170, 220, 258

Authority-role system, 86, 95, 140

Authority-task gap, 85, 87, 88, 91, 102, 125, 126, 134, 140, 182, 264, 276

Authority-task problems, 85, 87–89, 151, 264, 276

B

Boundary, 104–115, 125, 134, 159, 274

Boundary play, 106, 108

Boundary spanning member, 108

Bundles, 53–64, 97, 119, 130, 132, 140, 152, 157, 168, 171, 192, 198, 209, 210, 214, 241, 244, 245

C

Calendar plays, 168, 171, 174, 176, 179

Calendar task process, 168

Career planning, 39, 181, 188, 201, 204, 205, 223, 265

Catalytic task processes, 61, 62

Census of committees, 149, 151

Centralization, 44

Chain, 6, 9, 47, 51, 52, 56, 57, 62, 77, 78, 83, 90, 118, 122, 151, 171, 189, 215, 217–221, 223, 231, 232, 234, 243, 249, 252, 254, 259, 260

Change, 3, 5, 6, 9–12, 14, 16, 17–20, 28, 29, 33–39, 43, 45, 47, 50, 51, 60–62, 64, 67, 69, 70, 73, 75–77, 79, 80, 83, 84–89, 91, 94–98, 101, 102, 104–106, 114, 115, 124–132, 134, 141–143, 145, 147, 151, 156–159, 161–165, 167, 168, 170, 172, 174, 182–184, 186–189, 200, 208, 209, 214, 217–221, 231, 234, 242–245, 249, 252–254, 262, 263, 272–276

Closed compound processes, 51

Committees, 49, 79, 87–89, 91, 96, 145, 148, 151, 156, 188, 233, 241, 243, 255, 257

Compatible task processes, 124

Components of a play, 171

Composite Positions, 79

Compound task processes, 51

Conflict, 9, 17, 19, 21, 27, 29–31, 35, 38, 86, 115, 147, 148, 150, 179, 221, 222, 249, 253, 273

Control, 5, 12, 13, 17, 18, 20, 22, 24, 28, 30, 31, 36, 27, 39, 63, 73, 76, 82, 84, 85, 87, 95, 97, 100, 102, 103, 105, 107, 112, 114, 126–128, 132, 148, 150, 155, 160, 165, 170, 186, 189, 204, 217, 218, 220–222, 229, 232, 234, 253, 260, 276

Core logic, 155

Cousin relationships, 80, 152

Culture, 150, 161

D

Data base organizations, xiv, 51, 117, 126, 128, 129, 132, 264, 266, 275, 276

Data envelopment analysis, 215

Decentralization, 155, 234, 244

Delegation, 17, 30, 184

Deregulation, 5, 97, 102, 129, 146, 186

Desiderata of organizational design process, 29–40

Design premises, 36, 95, 96, 98–102, 125, 140, 142, 152, 155, 164, 187, 224, 244, 264, 277

Diffusion of Innovation, 73

Directing, controlling, and coordinating play, 169

Directing, controlling, and coordinating task processes, 16, 48, 49, 56, 61, 65, 67, 98, 119, 122, 123, 132, 167, 168, 172, 260, 275, 276

Directly integrable task processes, 124

Directly task process interdependent, 119

Disjoint positions, 83

Downsizing, 115

E

EEOC, 181, 188

Effectiveness, 8, 18, 20, 33, 66, 114, 142, 143, 184, 219, 257, 258, 267

Efficiency, 82, 254, 256, 265

Environment, 3, 5, 9–11, 17, 27–29, 31, 36, 51, 74, 84–88, 91, 94, 95, 99–103, 104, 106, 108, 116, 125, 126, 129, 133, 140, 145, 147, 155,